Cinecepts, Deleuze, and Godard-Miéville

Cinecepts, Deleuze, and Godard-Miéville

Developing Philosophy through Audiovisual Media

Jakob A. Nilsson

EDINBURGH
University Press

Edinburgh University Press is one of the leading university presses in the UK. We publish academic books and journals in our selected subject areas across the humanities and social sciences, combining cutting-edge scholarship with high editorial and production values to produce academic works of lasting importance. For more information visit our website: edinburghuniversitypress.com

© Jakob A. Nilsson, 2023, 2025

Grateful acknowledgement is made to the sources listed in the List of Illustrations for permission to reproduce material previously published elsewhere. Every effort has been made to trace the copyright holders, but if any have been inadvertently overlooked, the publisher will be pleased to make the necessary arrangements at the first opportunity.

Edinburgh University Press Ltd
13 Infirmary Street,
Edinburgh, EH1 1LT

First published in hardback by Edinburgh University Press 2023

Typeset in 10/14 Ehrhardt by,
Cheshire Typesetting Ltd, Cuddington, Cheshire

A CIP record for this book is available from the British Library

ISBN 978 1 4744 9998 9 (hardback)
ISBN 978 1 3995 0020 3 (paperback)
ISBN 978 1 3995 0021 0 (webready PDF)
ISBN 978 1 4744 9999 6 (epub)

The right of Jakob A. Nilsson to be identified as the author of this work has been asserted in accordance with the Copyright, Designs and Patents Act 1988, and the Copyright and Related Rights Regulations 2003 (SI No. 2498).

EU Authorised Representative:
Easy Access System Europe
Mustamäe tee 50, 10621 Tallinn, Estonia
gpsr.requests@easproject.com

Contents

List of Figures   vii
Acknowledgments   viii
Preface   x

Introduction   1

1. Towards a Theory of Cinecepts: A Reorganization of Deleuze's Categories   23

2. Setting the Stage: *2 or 3 Things*, *Le gai savoir*, and *Ici et ailleurs*   53

3. The Problem of the New: Ideas, Cinema, Concepts   84

4. Sonimage: A Problem Space and Six Embryonic Cinecepts   112

5. *Rapprochement*, Concepts, and Cineceptual Form   161

6. Scholarly Video Essays: A Critical Examination and a Cineceptual Alternative   169

7. Notes on Cinecepts as Multimedia Practice   189

Abbreviations of Works by Gilles Deleuze   196
References   199
Index   212

For Sally, Anna, Arega.

List of Figures

I.1a–c	*France tour détour*, movement 1	2
2.1	*Le gai savoir*	59
2.2a–c	*Le gai savoir*	61
2.3a–b	*2 or 3 Things I Know About Her*	64
2.4a–b	*Ici et ailleurs*	75
4.1a–d	*Numéro deux*	114
4.2a–b	*Six fois deux*, ep. 2A	126
4.3a–b	*Six fois deux*, ep. 4A	133
4.4a–b	*Six fois deux*, ep. 4A	134
4.5	*Six fois deux*, ep. 4A	136
4.6a–c	*France tour détour*, movement 5	147

Acknowledgments

I am grateful to my editor Gillian Leslie for her generous openness to this project and for her and assistant editor Sam Johnson's patience and gentle guidance during its completion. Thanks also to their skilled and accommodating colleagues on the production side.

Many thanks to the readers of the manuscript in its various stages: the two anonymous reviewers of the proposal and the reviewer of the whole text for their strongly favorable and encouraging evaluations, to Kristoffer Noheden for strengthening comments on parts of a late draft, and to Anna Widestam and Marius Dybwad Brandrud for perceptive and reaffirming readings of the whole manuscript. Thanks also to Marius for inviting me to lecture on Deleuze and film-philosophy at Stockholm University of the Arts in 2020, and to Petra Bauer for inviting me to hold a seminar on this topic at the Royal Institute of Art in 2018. Thanks to Jacob von Heland for inviting me to join as subject editor for *Annals of Crosscut*, and to its participants for the conversations, especially William Brown. Thanks to the Deleuze and film community, David-Martin Jones, Dennis Rothermel, Susana Viegas, and many others, for the exchanges over the years.

Continuing to look back, I take the opportunity to thank three key early teachers in filmic thinking and philosophy respectively: Trond Lundemo, Fredrika Spindler, and Sven-Olov Wallenstein. Credit also to Lundemo and Spindler for reading early drafts of what eventually became a journal article, which Chapter 1 below takes as point of departure.

Thanks to Daniel W. Smith for feedback on the (tricky) subject of Guattari's role in the writing of *What is Philosophy?* And thanks to Nicole Brenez, Michael Temple, and Michael Witt for advice on a Godard-Miéville copyright issue (although the copyright holders, Institut national de l'audiovisuel, persisted in being a little less than helpful). Thanks also to Danial Brännström for information and Antoine Gaudin for moral support on this issue.

Credit to the students that took my scholarly video essay course 2020–2022, in relation to which some of the material for Chapter 6 was worked out and during which we screened works by Godard and Godard-Miéville. A special thanks to former student Simon Carlsson, not least for kindly reading the manuscript. Thanks also to Patrik Sjöberg for recurring guest lectures on the jurisprudence of videography. And to Dagmar Brunow and Anna Sofia Rossholm for inviting me to participate in workshops on video essays.

Cheers, Niklas Gustafsson, for an enduring and important friendship. And thanks to those involved in our late "film circle", to Timo Menke for the "letter" conversions on video art, Doron Galili for the ongoing chats on film studies "here and elsewhere", and to Noah Roderick for the theory talks in the department corridor at Örebro University.

Thanks to the Swedish Research Council for generously funding part of the research that led up to this book: the individual project "Modern Essay Films as Thought-Maps of Globalization" (2015–18), which included concerns with "filmic conceptualization" from reimagined Deleuzian perspectives. Thanks also to Magn. Bergvalls stiftelse for a grant for research material.

Chapter 1 is partly based on the following previously published article, with kind permission from the editors: Jakob Nilsson (2018), "Deleuze, Concepts, and Ideas about Film as Philosophy: A Critical and Speculative Re-Examination", in *Journal of French and Francophone Philosophy* 26(2): 127–49. Chapter 3 partly takes as points of departure elements from the following two previously published texts, both with kind permission from the respective editors: Jakob Nilsson (2014), "Thought-Images and the New as a Rarity: A Reevaluation of the Philosophical Implications of Deleuze's Cinema Books", in *Cinema: Journal of Philosophy and the Moving Image* 6, ed. Susana Viegas, "Gilles Deleuze and Moving Images", 94–121; Jakob Nilsson (2020), "Notes on Three Phases in Deleuze's Thinking on Novelty", in *Material: Filosofi, Estetik, Arkitektur: Festskrift till Sven-Olov Wallenstein*, ed. Marcia Sá Cavalcante Schuback, Helena Mattsson, Kristina Riegert, and Hans Ruin, Stockholm: Södertörn Philosophical Studies 24, pp. 155–64.

Finally and most importantly thanks to my beloved family, Anna and Sally, for your patience during this project and for being wonderful people.

Preface

On the widest level, this study deals with the following problem: As reading declines, especially among the young, and distribution of knowledge and even theory becomes an increasingly audiovisual matter (most broadly on YouTube), how can original philosophy adapt in ways that develop—instead of dilute—philosophical rigor and specificity? How can philosophy exploit the potential in audiovisual media—which are more formally multidimensional than text-only—for conceptualizing more registers of reality with more precision and depth? In this book I present a theory of such a formal development of philosophy through audiovisual media: a theory of cinecepts. While addressing the wider problem just described, this theory is also highly specific: it regards Gilles Deleuze's definition of philosophy as the art of creating concepts and a reconfiguration of this definition that allows for concept formation advancing *directly* in and through the audiovisual. This entails a careful synthesis of what Deleuze himself kept apart:

> [P]hilosophy is the art of forming, inventing, and fabricating concepts. (WP 2)[1]

> [T]hose of you who do cinema [...] do not invent concepts—that is not your concern. (TRM 314)

The synthesizing of these positions is premised on a view largely shared with Alexandre Astruc:

> [T]he cinema [can] [...] become a means of writing [at least] as flexible and subtle as written language. [...] The most philosophical meditations [...] lie well within

its province. [...] [Cinema] is not so much a particular art as a language which can express any sphere of thought. (Astruc 2014 [1948]: 604f)

I proceed, however, through close reexaminations of Deleuze's work, his conceptions of philosophy, cinema, art, politics, and novelty, but also through a close study of philosophical problems and cineceptual tendencies in Jean-Luc Godard and Anne-Marie Miéville's 1970s Sonimage period, as well as logics of montage developed in Godard before and after this period, and lastly through connecting the theory of cinecepts to a contemporary world of video essays and multimedia. I also build on and critically engage with a variety of scholarly works on Deleuze and on Godard primarily, as well as from within Film-Philosophy, Film and Media Theory, Philosophy, Critical Theory, and Videographic Film Studies.

A key question for late Deleuze: what distinguishes philosophy, as a mode of thinking, from art and cinema with philosophical dimensions? His main answer, as seen in the quotations above, is concept creation. Philosophy produces concepts—defined as a particular kind of determination of problems and condensed constellations of potential[2]—and art and cinema do not produce concepts. Are media forms entailed in this distinction? Are philosophical concepts necessarily tied to speaking and writing? Or could film / video / audiovisual media—if regarded as concrete forms instead of specific conducts generalized as art or cinema—be used to formulate philosophical concepts? And could this be a way to advance Deleuze's (Nietzsche-inspired) concern with the formal renewal of philosophy? Deleuze did not himself raise these questions, which is curious given his life-long concern precisely with the formal renewal of philosophy, his focus on art and cinema as sources of inspiration for such renewal, and his interest in advanced thought in and through moving images with sound. These questions have remained unexamined, moreover, despite Deleuze being central for the increased focus in recent decades on the film/philosophy relation, and for the by now extensive literature on film *as* philosophy.[3]

The theory of cinecepts is an answer to these questions, which is essentially one question with three sides: How could film / video / audiovisual media[4] function as direct means for concept formation in a Deleuzian sense of concepts? How can Deleuze's thought itself be reexamined and partly reconfigured in this regard? Given his ongoing concern with renewing philosophy on the level of form, what happens if we keep to Deleuze's abstract definition of philosophy, but expand the concrete parameters of its formal renewal to film / video / audiovisual media?

Cineceptual theory builds on Deleuze but is also a critical response to his (complex but categorical) separation between filmic thinking and philosophical conceptualization, and his tendency to implicitly restrict the latter to the actual form of words-only.[5] The cinecept is also a response to film-philosophical engagements with these aspects of Deleuze's thought, which tend to assume that Deleuze equated cinematic thinking with philosophy, which he did not.[6] For Deleuze, cinematic figures of thought are preconceptual (however much they can suggest or give rise to concepts), and philosophy has the "exclusive right" to concept creation (WP 8). The theory of cinecepts results from an immanent critique and reorganization of parts of Deleuze's philosophy which takes us beyond this restriction.

Similar restrictions abound in the literature on film as philosophy (whether analytic or continental, "bold" or "moderate"). The meaning attributed to the idea of film as philosophy varies, not least because different definitions of philosophy are at play. Still, most—including those connected to or even based on Deleuze—tend to agree that philosophical thinking in and through film is necessarily *nonconceptual*[7]—albeit in a much broader sense than Deleuze's concept of concepts.[8] Film as philosophy or philosophically inclined cinematic thinking—beyond the mere illustration of pre-existing philosophy—is commonly understood instead as either affective or poetic thinking; thought experiments; (something in line with the classical idea of art and cinema containing) advanced themes; making or evaluating arguments; expressing the unrepresentable; cuing philosophical thought in spectators; or reflecting on the conditions of film itself. Such understandings are often attached to claims or assumptions about medium specificity that determine what is possible to express philosophically: what can be done through film (more or less) beyond the capacity of written(/spoken) philosophy and vice versa. And again, concepts (however defined) tend to find themselves outside the realm of film as philosophy.

Can film / video / audiovisual media serve as means for original philosophical concept creation in a Deleuzian sense of concepts? As said, this is a question Deleuze himself avoided, concerned as he was with more abstract differences between art and philosophy and with "secur[ing] a function for philosophy" through concept creation, and implicitly delimiting his notion of philosophical concepts to the *actual form* of words, and words only (WP 8). Yet, he leaves openings to go beyond this implicit delimitation, and in this study I identify and exploit these openings. *What is Philosophy?* allows for and even invites us to think the possibility of philosophical concept creation "proceeding by" formal means other than (only) linguistic sentences, while also offering a framework for defining philosophy as concept creation on more abstract levels, regardless of the actual form.

Given Deleuze's own concern with actual form, how does the cinecept differ from his ideas about taking inspiration from art and cinema for the formal renewal of philosophy? "The search for new means of philosophical expression was begun by Nietzsche", Deleuze writes in *Difference and Repetition*, "and must be pursued today [1968] in relation to the renewal of certain other arts, such as the theatre or the cinema" (DR xx; see also DI [1968]: 141). This means two things: 1) taking inspiration from formal developments within the arts (such as painting going from graphic representation to abstraction) and 2) letting advanced ideas within art or cinema provoke philosophy into new lines of thinking. The present study investigates a third option: treating film / video / audiovisual media as not just a non-philosophical material that philosophy can be formally inspired by or provoked to conceptualize in writing, but as direct formal means for philosophical conceptualization itself.

The theory of cinecepts, then, extends the Deleuzian/Nietzschean problem of the formal renewal of philosophy to different media. The point, therefore, is not merely to examine if philosophy can be conducted also through film / video / audiovisual media—and not at all to indicate a hierarchy with philosophy as a lofty goal that producers of such media should aspire to[9]—so much as how philosophy can be formally developed through these means. Why would philosophy need to be formally developed? If there is such a need, it is philosophical and social, rather than cosmetic, artistic, or pedagogical (i.e. making philosophy more rousing or approachable). Philosophical: audiovisual form could be used to conceptualize political, material, and ideational realities with more direct nuance. Social: our societies are currently changing from being text-based to being increasingly audiovisual and screen-based. We need ideas for adaptation to these changes that advance instead of water down philosophy. This book provides a theoretical framework for such an adaptation.

Six preparatory clarifications about cinecepts

- In this book film / video / audiovisual media are seen as media form. As such they differ from each other and from other media, but they do not imply a particular conduct or use—documentation, narrative, art, philosophy, and so on—any more than the category "the written word" implies a particular conduct or use.
- The cinecept is not a merger of philosophy and art, but philosophical conceptualization through expanded formal means.
- The cinecept entails conceptualization according to a specific idea about philosophical conceptualization. It is derived from Deleuze's concept of concepts and developed primarily as regarding concrete form. The cinecept is therefore not to be conflated with
   - more general notions of conceptual art (whether tied to 1960s discourses with roots going back to Duchamp, or to broader contemporary usages of the term)
   - with ideas about film or art having a concept in the loose sense of a guiding idea (most if not all works could be boiled down to concepts in that sense)
   - with theories of how films or images can signify abstract ideas.

Philosophical concepts, Deleuze writes, "must not be confused with general or abstract ideas" (WP 24). "An idea is not a concept, it is not philosophy. Even if one may be able to draw a concept from every idea" (TRM 318).

- Relatedly, it has been common throughout world history for *images* to function as carriers of what can be called "concepts", but concepts then generally tend to mean pre-existing conceptions, ideas, conventions, myths, or wisdoms. This would include what Deleuze calls Figures, as exemplified by "Chinese hexagrams, Hindu mandalas, Jewish sephiroth, Islamic 'imaginals,' and Christian icons" (WP 89). Or just various kinds of symbols—visual signs representing abstract ideas (however dynamic in their aesthetic expression or manner of signification, as in hieroglyphs, Renaissance or Baroque painting, or, as discussed in Chapter 1, Eisensteinian intellectual montage). While they share with cinecepts an irreducibility to words, they do not share an underlying concept *of* concepts. (It would be interesting to compare the cinecept as developed in this book with visual concepts in neglected, especially non-Western, traditions that may come close also in their concept of concepts, to the extent they exist, but this is outside the scope of this study.)
- Cinecepts expand the formal parameters of philosophical conceptualization but are in no way about supplanting or excluding written or spoken language. Not only are cinecepts meant as a *complement* to philosophical words-only textual or verbal presentations, they are themselves audiovisual compounds that *include* (or are combined with) verbal and/or written language.
- Cinecepts are philosophical determinations in themselves *first*. That is, cinecepts are not dependent on spectators/readers to provide them with a philosophical determination. Since cinecepts, as we will see, have a certain kind of open and modifiable rather than static determination, they can certainly vary and change (perhaps necessarily so) through spectators/readers. But reinterpretations, redeterminations, creative misunderstandings, unexpected applications, personal takes, and so on, come *after* philosophical determinations already existing in and through the cinecepts.[10]

Clarification about notes

For straight references to external texts I use parentheses in the main text. The notes, in contrast, contain additional arguments, explanations, critical readings, interpretations, definitions, quotes, and/or dispositional orientation. I therefore advise the reader to at least glance at each note and read those of interest more carefully.

Notes

1 I credit both Deleuze and Guattari as co-authors of *What is Philosophy?*, as in the list of References, but in large parts of this study I refer only to Deleuze as the author. I explain this choice in a note on the Abbreviations page below.
2 Deleuze's definition of concepts is explored most directly in Chapter 1. The meaning of concepts as potentials is further explained in Chapter 3.
3 For a critical examination of three semi-exceptions in Bernd Herzogenrath (2017), John E. Drabinski (2008), and D. N. Rodowick (2015), where some of these questions are at least briefly present if not examined, see the Introduction, note 3, and Nilsson (2018).
4 These terms are defined in the Introduction.
5 Yes, he *does* keep cinematic thought figures and philosophical concepts separated *also* at the end of *Cinema 2*. These points are developed in Chapter 1 below.
6 This assumption is crystalized in explicit claims by David Sorfa (2016) in an editorial for the journal *Film-Philosophy* that overviews the film-philosophy field.
7 As Siegfried Kracauer already said (with Hegelian resonances): "conceptual thinking is an alien element on the screen" (1960: 264). Or Pasolini: "The linguistic or grammatical world of the filmmaker is composed of images, and images are always concrete, never abstract [...] [T]herefore, cinema is an artistic and not a philosophic language. It may be a parable, but never a directly conceptual expression" (2005 [1965]: 171f).
8 One exception outside a Deleuzian frame of inspiration or concern: Stephen Mulhall mentions at one point, and from a more analytic-philosophical perspective, that films can "do" philosophy also by engaging with what seems to be a partly Nietzschean sense of concepts. However, this is about "interrogation" and "analysis" of existing concepts, not film as means for concept formation (Mulhall 2008: 4–6, 87, 94).
9 To further clarify what is said about hierarchies here: A cinecept is distinguished from other figures of thought by its modal and formal nature. A non-cineceptual filmic thought figure may be more brilliant and insightful than a cinecept. And there can be mediocre cinecepts, just as there can be mediocre words-only concepts.
10 Here I am keeping to Deleuze's general view of inherent determination in philosophy, art, and cinema (which is underacknowledged in film-philosophy and in the film-theoretical reception of Deleuze in which spectator activity is generally seen as a more central and primary factor). For more on this, see the following notes below: Introduction, notes 2A, 6, 8; Chapter 3, note 20; Chapter 5, note 9.

Introduction

LET US START with ekphrastic notes on a cineceptual *tendency* (more closely analyzed later): Towards the end of movement 1 of Jean-Luc Godard and Anne-Marie Miéville's *France / tour / détour / deux / enfants* (1977/8), following words about hi/story [*histoire*], beginnings, and the existence of the future, a curious audiovisual arrangement appears. We see a naked pregnant woman—from chin to knees—standing in a bathroom combing her hair. The word TOI [*you*] is electronically positioned over her belly, a second later swapped to MOI [*me*]. Handel's aria *Lascia ch'io pianga* enters the soundtrack. The word MOI disappears as a man starts talking in voice-over. The camera then zooms in towards the woman's belly, directly followed by a round separate shot of a baby that seems, through video montage, to emanate from the womb. This separate image rapidly expands and approaches the borders of the main frame nearly covering the image of the woman. It contracts and then expands again a few times before taking over the whole screen. The shot of the woman's belly then comes in from the middle as a round separate shot growing in a similar way as the shot of the baby. This is followed by similar movements also involving a black image, both as round form and as background. During these movements the male voice-over reads pointed philosophical statements—not as a dictation of the meaning of the images but as an integral part of an audiovisual composition—about memory, visibility, and obscurity in conception in a broad sense of what we may call the conception of the new.

Philosophically—bracketing the purely poetic or essayistic—much goes on here in both content and form. In content there are connections to earlier and later themes in Godard, concerning memory, projection, and conditions of re/production. Is this sequence philosophical expression also in *form*? Some of its formal aspects seem to point beyond current notions of "film as philosophy"—certainly beyond

2 | CINECEPTS, DELEUZE, AND GODARD-MIÉVILLE

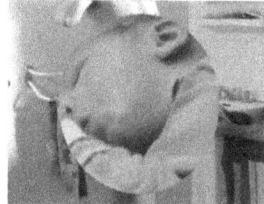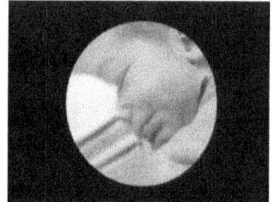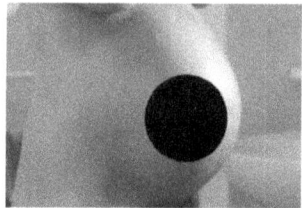

Figures I.1a–c *France tour détour*, movement 1

illustration, thought experiments, or (however independent) explorations of a philosophical theme in a narrative. To an extent the sequence exemplifies "cinematic thinking" in the sense of advanced thought in filmic form that is *comparable* to philosophy. That is, the notion we find in Deleuze, and many others, of cinematic thinking as *preconceptual* and as formally occurring outside of philosophy proper (even when dealing with similar problems). This is an apt way of understanding most advanced thinking films, certainly those that are narrative. This *France tour détour* sequence, however—which is more closely examined in Chapter 4, along with similar sequences—also points beyond such notions of cinematic thinking and *towards* what this book calls cinecepts.

The term cinecept crystalizes the following idea: philosophical concepts formed as *compounds of moving images / sounds / voice / texts / graphics / montage*. Not all these parameters are necessary for all cinecepts, but as *cine*-cepts they must contain movement—although they could just as well come as part of multimedia compositions containing non-moving parts, such as digital multimedia texts, as long as the cinecepts themselves are partly made up of moving images (more on this multimedia aspect in Chapter 7). As a neologism the term accentuates the transmedia part of such a general formal expansion of concepts and signals a break with tradition in this particular regard.[1] The term also helps distinguish things from plainly different notions of concepts in film, ranging from Eisenstein's discussion of concepts in intellectual montage (as addressed in Chapters 1 and 2) to conceptual art.[2] As abstract content, however, cinecepts are philosophical concepts, as defined by Deleuze (this definition is explored at length in Chapter 1 and partly in Chapter 3). The cinecept, moreover, is itself a philosophical concept.

In this study I develop a concept and a larger theory of cinecepts as an answer to the three-sided question posed in the Preface: How could film / video / audiovisual media function as direct means for concept formation in a Deleuzian sense of concepts? How can Deleuze's thought itself be reexamined and partly reconfigured in this regard? And, given his ongoing concern with renewing philosophy on the level of form, what happens if we keep to Deleuze's abstract definition of philosophy, but expand the concrete parameters of its formal renewal to film / video / audiovisual media? One would expect to find such questions at the heart of much of the literature on "film as philosophy" for which Deleuze is a central impetus. Yet, they have barely been raised and much less substantially examined, whether in the field of film-philosophy, Deleuze studies, critical theory, artistic research, or related areas.[3]

The theory of cinecepts, as an answer to these questions, is developed through a set of movements in three main areas:

1. *Deleuze*. Chapter 1 begins with his definitions of philosophy. I examine how he distinguishes philosophy from other genres of thought (primarily art and cinema), as well as how the logic of multiplicity undergirding his notion of philosophical concepts differs from logics that can appear close, such as Hegel's. This leads to a critical reexamination of parts of Deleuze's thought as implicitly offering ways to conceive of philosophical concept formation proceeding through media other than words-only, and the chapter ends with reflections on how audiovisual forms can serve this function. Chapter 1 also analyzes a set of unacknowledged similarities—with a focus on classification, reorganization, and recutting—between what Deleuze says about concept formation and about Godard's method of filmic thought (and this comparison is continued at the end of Chapter 2).

   Developing the cinecept also entails a novel reading of Deleuze's conception of the new. Part of his—complex and partly technical—definition of concepts is the idea that they make up structures of potential. A "concept speaks the event", Deleuze writes in *What is Philosophy?*, in the sense of "the contour, the configuration, the constellation of an event to come" (WP 32f). Chapter 3 explores what this means as part of a broader reconsideration of how Deleuze conceives of the production of the new, and a critique of dominant understandings in the literature on Deleuze. The chapter begins by reconsidering *Difference and Repetition* from this perspective, then looks at how Deleuze's thinking on novelty partly shifts in *Cinema 2*—or rather, how it develops an aspect already found in *Difference and Repetition* (although there somewhat overshadowed by the concern with a being of becoming)—towards conceiving of the new as rare, mostly blocked, and concerning social and political struggle.[4] Chapter 3 ends by looking at how all this converges in Deleuze's concept of concepts. Chapter 4 connects these Deleuzian concerns with Godard-Miéville's Sonimage work, centering on its general problem space and on specific embryonic cinecepts as also concerned with complexities and blockages in conceiving of the new.

   While my re/examinations of Deleuze's notions of concepts and novelty regard his thought as a whole, with much focus on *What is Philosophy?* and *Difference and Repetition*, his thoughts on cinema are a central target of reinterpretation and reimagination. The secondary literature on Deleuze's cinema books is large and varied.⁵ While informed by aspects of this literature, this study brings out and critically explores issues in Deleuze's conception of cinema, regarding the film/philosophy relation and the problem of the new, which the previous literature has left unacknowledged or underexamined (see also Nilsson 2014; 2018).

2. *Godard and Miéville.* Chapter 2 explores how two later-half 1960s Godard films (*2 or 3 Things I Know About Her* and *Le gai savoir*) and the first finished Sonimage film (*Ici et ailleurs*) develop a formal logic of montage and a set of concerns around novelty production, which prepare for the embryonic cinecepts (more on the term embryonic below) and the general problem space of later Sonimage. Chapter 4 directly explores these aspects of later Sonimage, that is, problems and embryonic cinecepts in Godard-Miéville's works between 1974/5 and 1977/8. Chapter 5 juxtaposes Deleuze's conception of concepts and Godard's later idea of montage as *rapprochement*, and also briefly discusses the montage forms of *Histoire(s) du cinéma* (1988–98) as a formal resource for cinecepts.

3. *Video essays and contemporary media.* Chapters 6 and 7 connect the theory of cinecepts to a contemporary media environment. Chapter 6 looks at the world of video essays made by film and media scholars and ongoing debates about what it means to be scholarly in this form. I critically examine arguments and assumptions in these debates, spanning artistic research, image/word differences, clarity, medium specificity, and the essayistic. This leads up to a set of criteria for how these kinds of video essays could develop also in a cineceptual direction. Chapter 7 relates the cinecept to current audiovisual media more broadly. Here I address key reasons for why full cinecepts remain as a potential, consider philosophy channels on YouTube, and discuss audiovisual media as a tool for seduction and deception as well as rigorous nuance. I also make further specifications on how the cinecept can function in practice as multimedia philosophy.

Cinecepts Are a Promise, But Embryonic Cinecepts Exist

On the one hand, I consider cinecepts to be an existing potential, something not yet fully achieved (in some ways similar to how Godard regarded filmic montage to not yet have been achieved). On the other hand, I examine what I call *embryonic* cinecepts in parts of Godard-Miéville's 1970s video works (my use of the term embryonic here has principal similarities to Eisenstein writing about "still embryonic attempts to construct a really quite new form of filmic expression" [1998 (1929): 110]). These works provide certain preliminary conditions for cinecepts (partly similar to how most of the first breaks with the movement-image in Deleuze's periodization delivered the preconditions for but not the time-image itself). But they also contain some fascinating direct cineceptual tendencies. These tendencies, which appear at a few select points in their work, are what I refer to as embryonic cinecepts. This does not mean, then, "preconceptual" sketches that, as D. N. Rodowick writes, "may inspire philosophy to give form to a concept"—implicitly meaning the form of (a) word/s written or spoken outside of the videos (2015: 138, 139, 165, 179, 229)[6]—although these video works could certainly do that too. Instead, *embryonic* means here that more fully realized cinecepts would have the same actual form: *compounds of moving images / sounds / voice / texts / graphics / montage*. (A bit further down I will address how the cinecept as a worded concept developed in this book relates to actual cinecepts remaining as a promise.)

Why Deleuze?

The idea of film as philosophy, found in a by now extensive literature, can only really make sense if in each case it refers to a specified definition of philosophy—whatever the definition (pre-existing or not). So why is Deleuze's definition at the center of this study? Four basic reasons: First, this definition of philosophy has not really been dealt with in the film as philosophy literature, including in the field of film-philosophy for which Deleuze is the main inspiration. As Thomas Elsaesser writes, "it was the wide reception of Deleuze's cinema books, once they had been published in an English translation in the late 1980s […] that provided the major impetus for the whole field to emerge in its current form" (2019: 20, see also 41). Second, Deleuze's cinema books are central for film theory more generally—Elsaesser and Hagener describe them as "the single most important resource in film theory of the last two decades" (2015: 178). Third, Deleuze's definition of philosophy, while hardly dominant, is among the most influential or at least recognizable in post-war (non-analytic) philosophy, and perhaps more so in the broader humanities—see for instance its centrality in Mieke Bal's study of "concept-based methodology" and interdisciplinary travels of concepts (2002: 50ff, 23, 316). Fourth, this study aims to contribute clearly new understandings of Deleuze's philosophy as concerning film/video and concepts.

Why Godard and Godard-Miéville?

Not only was Godard among the most philosophy-driven of filmmakers, he was intensely concerned with the formal renewal of film as a medium for thinking. This concern has partly resulted in works with arguably unique relevance for a theory of cinecepts: I have explored alternatives throughout this study (mainly among essay films and theory-driven video art) but have yet to come across work with cinceptual tendencies as clear as in Godard-Miéville's Sonimage period (1974–79).

Moreover, counterintuitively, not *that* much has been written about Godard's films compared to filmmakers of similar film historical stature,[7] and most is focused on Godard's famous early period ending around 1967. Godard's later phases are still quite under-researched (with *Histoire(s) du cinéma* as a relative exception). This is especially the case with the Sonimage period, which Michael Witt in 1998 described as "largely unexplored" (1998: 13). Barring significant—albeit mostly brief—exceptions (earlier: Bergala, Daney, Deleuze; later: Drabinski, Morrey, Steyerl, White, and Witt himself), this is not that far from still being the case, an assessment that is echoed in Jerry White's 2013 monograph on Godard-Miéville's work more generally, and reaffirmed by Witt in 2014: "in spite of the quantity of critical writing devoted to Godard, the Sonimage work ([…] the television series in particular) still remains comparatively understudied" (2014: 319).

Furthermore, Godard is relatively underexplored as a film philosopher. While not seldom referred to as doing philosophical or theoretical thinking in film—David Sterritt for instance writes in passing that Godard is "fond of using cinema as a philosophical tool rather than an entertainment machine" (1999: 3)—studies that explore what this means are still rare. In a book-length study, Volker Pantenburg examines how Godard and Farocki develop theory in and through film, but he largely equates this with filmic and pictorial self-reflexivity (including when internally comparing itself to other arts).[8] Two statements by John Drabinski are of more direct relevance. In the introduction to his book on Godard (2008), which sets out to treat his 1970s video works as "primary texts in philosophy", he points to a 1968 statement in which Deleuze heavily implies that Godard has created new means to think philosophically in and through film (a statement I return to below and examine more extensively in Chapter 1). Drabinski comes even closer to my concern in an editorial for a special issue on Godard two year later: "If philosophy, as Deleuze has it, is primarily concerned with the creation of concepts, then Godard's cinema can be said to create concepts in sound and image" (2010: 4). Yet, these two passages are all Drabinski says with reference to Deleuze about Godard as film philosopher, so neither is developed nor investigated in relation to Deleuze's writings.

Other theoretically driven studies on Godard tend to be unclear about whether original philosophizing (of some kind, that is, in a much broader sense than cinecepts) occurs in and through his films. In the most noteworthy Godard scholarship in which the film-as-philosophy question is somehow broached, it is either placed outside of the delimitation (Morgan 2012: 25f)[9] or affirmed with a certain wavering and without addressing its formal implications (e.g. Morrey 2005).[10] Furthermore, in the introduction to Michael Witt's comprehensive *Jean-Luc Godard: Cinema Historian* (2013), Godard is described as a philosopher (as well as a filmmaker, poet, critic, essayist), but in reference to his complex intermedia production including his writings, so that it is not entirely clear to what extent and in what sense the original philosophizing occurs in the films themselves.

Still, *any* implication that Godard's films are in some sense inherently philosophical can be seen to partly alter a more established understanding of the relation between philosophy/theory and the Godardian and Godard-influenced "counter-cinema" of the late 1960s and '70s: that is to say, such cinema seen more exclusively as "practical experimentation motivated by theoretical presuppositions" (Loshitzky 1995: 26) or as having existing (written) theory "inform the objectives, logic, and aesthetic strategies" of the films (Rodowick 1994 [1988]: 4). As Drabinski (and partly also Morrey) reveals, Godard never fully fit that mold even in the 1960s, and more importantly from the 1970s and onwards he produced increasingly original philosophy in and through film, which was a kind of parallel philosophical work to, and not unlikely an intellectual influence (however small) on, that of contemporaries like Deleuze and even Foucault—just as he was clearly influenced by them.[11] As Michael Witt writes in a text on aspects of Godard-Miéville's 1977/8 television series *France / tour / détour / deux / enfants*:

> is Foucault as Godardian as Godard and Miéville is Foucauldian? Rather than assuming that Godard and Miéville are simply adopting Foucault, [Foucault's own] *Discipline and Punish* could [reversely] be considered an extension of [aspects] in Godard's science-fiction films from the 1960s [...] This position is perhaps a little too far-fetched. But the point is that, in their respective projects, Godard-Miéville, Foucault, and indeed Deleuze/Guattari were all working on parallel tracks. Godard-Miéville's enterprise, however methodologically unconventional, is every bit as serious as that of their contemporaries. (2007 [2004]: 210)[12]

Witt also argues that the Sonimage work in the 1970s "constitutes a self-contained critique of communications processes that *precedes* and *foresees* the influential subsequent work of theorists such as Jean Baudrillard" (1998: 15; see also 2014: 326).[13]

In any case, and whether labeled philosophical or not, Godard was at the forefront of developing film as a form for advanced thought. If Deleuze is the philosopher who has written most influentially about film as thinking in recent decades, it is not by accident that Godard is so central for Deleuze in this regard. Not only are his cinema books "shot through with references to Godard", as Witt writes, *Cinema 2* "could almost be read as a book on Godard" (1999: 111).[14] Intriguingly, and with reference to aspects of Deleuze's conceptualizations, Witt adds that

> it is unclear that Deleuze is doing very much more than stating the obvious: his formulae are extremely close to those proposed by Godard himself, who has talked

of the "BETWEEN" in virtually identical, and equally impenetrable, terms, both in his work, and in the metadiscourse he has spun around it. Thus this summary by Deleuze of Godard's "method" could equally well have been taken from one of Godard and Miéville's films or television series of the 1970s. (1999: 111)

The "impenetrable" part aside, Witt has a certain point about Deleuze's indebtedness to Godard-Miéville having quite well themselves already theorized their logic and ideas within their own work (I return to this issue in Chapter 4). However, Deleuze appears in some ways to shift his views on Godard as specifically concerning filmic thinking and philosophy. Above I mentioned a brief interview statement made by Deleuze in 1968 that implies Godard had singularly developed means to do philosophy in and through cinema (DI 141). In *Cinema 2*, Deleuze instead points to Godard's cinematic thinking as a kind of *contrast* to philosophy, and philosophy then defined as concept creation. Although Deleuze now explicitly claims that Godard is a philosopher/theorist, this is said to be the case only when Godard "talks" about films (not within them). If a main problem animating the 1968 statement is how philosophy can be renewed (in both form and content) beyond its traditional forms and images of thought, Deleuze around the cinema books seems more concerned with articulating the specificity of philosophy in a time when all philosophy is increasingly relegated to the margins. If the first period is expansive, the second appears more protective. In the present study, these two different concerns are equally maintained: the concern with formal development of philosophy and the concern with the specificity of philosophy as a conceptual venture.

Approaches, Methods, Selection of Films/Videos

A cinecept 1) is abstract philosophical form/structure (it organizes conceptual components in a virtual "consistency", as I explore in Chapter 1), which was articulated through and is now carried by 2) literal audiovisual form. This does not mean, however, that a theory of cinecepts, or the analysis of existing cinecepts (whether embryonic or full), can avoid 3) philosophical content. For Deleuze, as further explained in Chapters 1, 2, and 5, concepts are particular determinations of *problems*, and problems provide concepts with meaning. Concepts, as we will also see, are formulated on larger planes of thought (planes of immanence) that can be called problem planes or problem spaces. Accordingly, I will examine Sonimage's embryonic cinecepts along with the larger problem plane on which they are formulated, as well as the specific problems that each embryonic cinecept helps determine on this plane. I will call the larger plane for Sonimage a *problem space*, mostly due to its many spatial manifestations and the thematic centrality of a black background.

While Chapter 2 focuses on a gradual advancement of a formal logic of filmic thought in Godard's *2 or 3 Things I Know About Her* (*2 ou 3 choses que je sais d'elle*, 1967), *Le gai savoir* (1969 [1968]), and the first completed Sonimage film *Ici et ailleurs* (*Here and Elsewhere*, 1975), this chapter also looks at these films as part of developing Sonimage's problem space. The developed problem space itself is examined in the first part of Chapter 4 with a focus on Godard-Miéville's *Numéro deux* (1975). The rest of Chapter 4 explores six embryonic cinecepts found in their two television series *Six fois deux (Sur et sous la communication)* (1976) and *France / tour / détour / deux / enfants* (1977/8), and with some references also to their 1975 film *Comment ça va*. Since the embryonic cinecepts are themselves semi-philosophical expressions, and as their larger problem space has to a large extent already been examined by then, much of the philosophical meaning of each embryonic cinecept is revealed through ekphrastic description and analysis of what we see and hear. Some of them also help explain each other, as they interrelate as if part of a set of embryonic cinecepts that belong to the same theory/philosophy. Each of them will nonetheless also be subjected to philosophical interpretation and discussion (while more interpretational assistance may be required by the absence of conventions for perceiving *cineceptual* articulations, we should bear in mind that interpretation is an unavoidable part of examining any philosophy). Altogether, Chapter 4 looks at 3) the problem contents and the problem contexts of each embryonic cinecept, 2) their concrete, actual forms, and 1) their organization of abstract conceptual components.

Chapter 5 mostly examines ideas *about* form: here I juxtapose the logic of montage that Godard calls *rapprochement* with Deleuze's descriptions of the abstract logic of concepts. Chapter 5 thereby ties things back to similar juxtapositions between Deleuze and Godard made in Chapters 1 and 2. Here I also briefly approach *Histoire(s) du cinéma* as furthering the formal renewal of montage in ways that are relevant for cinecepts.[15] While shown to be a *formal* resource *for* cinecepts, however, *Histoire(s)* does not itself contain cinecepts (neither embryonic nor full). The Sonimage works, of which some do contain embryonic cinecepts, include explicit analytic and philosophical reflections in which the essayistic, poetic, and experimental are slightly more in the service of the critically analytic and philosophical than the other way around. While the *forms* of filmic thought continue to develop in video works made by Godard-Miéville and Godard after the Sonimage period—particularly in *Histoire(s)*—this relationship between the philosophical and the poetical tends to become more reversed. That is, Godard himself and Godard-Miéville tend to now put the philosophical comparably more in the service of the poetic (or to think philosophically more exclusively in and through poetry).[16] Or even the musical: since 1980 Godard "has worked increasingly in the manner of a musician", Michael Witt says, partly structuring films like a composer would a piece of music (2018: 26:10–26:24; see also Witt 2013: 3, 202; and Godard and Ishaghpour (2005 [1999]: 24). He appears increasingly driven by his influence from the German Romantics in the sense of their quest to reach poetic artistic truths beyond words and who often considered music to go furthest in this regard. Similarly, Jerry White (while locating this shift a bit later) finds the films Godard did together with Miéville after *Soft and Hard* (1985) to be "of a distinctly different sort", "more fragmented", a product of them favoring what he calls "more alienated strategies" (2013: 129).

Certainly, continental philosophy in general—with roots going back to Plato's dialogues, the Presocratics, and beyond—tends to utilize literary craft as part of philosophical expression. Distinctions can still be made, however, between art as part of philosophy, and philosophy as part of art. This is a key distinction for Deleuze in *What is Philosophy?* Particularly relevant for cinecepts is its distinction between A) sensations or artistic aspects of concepts, and B) artistic structures that (without synthesis) mix in *non-conceptual* philosophical properties (more on this in Chapter 1). A *cinecept* is a filmic figure of thought in which sensations or artistic aspects are subordinated to philosophical determination. Compared to later works by Godard in which philosophy becomes too subsumed into and too governed by artistic figures of thought, philosophy is somewhat more, and more systematically so, in the driving seat in parts of the Sonimage works.

These works are also—to use Serge Daney's (1976) description—more *pedagogical*, and in the sense of analytically probing and revealing of problems (in Chapters 1 and 5 this is connected to what Deleuze later referred to as the pedagogy of concepts in philosophy). If the earlier Dziga Vertov Group works led Godard a bit too far into the more dogmatic or theoretically static, and the later *post*-Sonimage films tended to be more poetically governed, the Miéville-collaborations in the 1970s can be seen as a middle ground that this study finds to be a productive milieu for embryonic cinecepts. Anne-Marie Miéville appears particularly important here. She seems to have been a key creative force in general for the Sonimage films, and as part of *all* aspects of the filmmaking process (Witt 1998: 10–12; 2014: 319).[17] She also seems to have been vital for striking this analytic/pedagogic balance somewhere between the Dziga Vertov Group's explicit critical expositions and Godard's later more essentially poetic films.[18] Miéville gives Jerry White "the impression of being generally less distracted than Godard and more willing to dig deeply into texts and ideas" (2013: 127, see also 161). At the same time, this analytic/pedagogic balance does not necessarily mean that the Sonimage works are less formally complex. White describes these films as "in many ways their most formally ambitious and experimental" containing "formal gestures that [...] come to form the heart of many of the analyses" which make "the most of the medium of video" (2013: 62).[19]

On the one hand, as I established above, the examination of a cineceptual formation must entail three intertwined aspects: 1) analyzing its organization of abstract components, 2) its literal audiovisual form, and 3) exploring the larger problem context and the specific problem(s) conceptualized. On the other hand, on a purely *metaphilosophical* level of cinecepts, the Sonimage films are primarily approached as form, in the sense of an interrelation between the abstract form of concepts and concrete audiovisual cineceptual form, rather than specific philosophical content. In this regard, there are some principal similarities to how Deleuze approaches philosophers in *What is Philosophy?*: not so much for their individual concerns and topics as for their formal expression of philosophy taken on more of a (both descriptive and prescriptive) meta-level. Here Deleuze mainly investigates the generalizable abstract forms of philosophy (excluding twentieth-century Anglo-American logic, which he argues is outside the realm of philosophy, mainly by turning concepts into functions).[20] General thought-forms, that is, which distinguish philosophy from (but also connect it to) closely related modes of thought, primarily art and (hard as well as a certain social) science. *What is Philosophy?* is only secondarily concerned with explicating and evaluating the content of the philosophies discussed.[21] Therefore, when Deleuze brings up differences between philosophers such as Descartes and Kant in this book, or even when he emphasizes their respective flaws, this is part of a more primary concern with what characterizes philosophy in general and how it differs from art and science. Descartes and Kant created different (or partly different) planes of immanence, conceptual personae, and concepts (all with their respective limitations), but both created planes, conceptual personae, and concepts—in brief: both did (what Deleuze calls) philosophy. The theory of cinecepts, however, has other conditions and a different task: Cinecepts rely on Deleuze's abstract definition of philosophy, but there is no long history of cinecepts from which generalizations can be made, comparable to the history of written philosophy comprehended by Deleuze. Rather, this study relies also on case studies of rare—and, furthermore, embryonic, not fully developed—cinecepts. For these reasons it is more necessary to examine not only the interrelation between 1) abstract philosophical form and 2) concrete audiovisual form, but also 3) philosophical problem content.

The Cinecept as Articulation of Potential

The cinecept as developed in this book is a concept in a Deleuzian sense, and, again, for Deleuze a concept is "the contour, the configuration, the constellation of an event to come" (WP 32f). This does not mean prediction, prophetism, or causing future effects. It means a particular philosophical articulation of potential. The cinecept is a philosophical articulation of potential rooted in examinations of existing cineceptual *tendencies*.²² The film critic and former *Cahiers du Cinéma* editor Jean Narboni²³ described a "feeling that the movement and logic of Deleuze's thought often anticipate [specific cinematic formations] before the filmmakers get around actually to inventing them" (relayed in Rodowick 1997: xvii). Perhaps actual cinecepts will appear or even become prevalent, perhaps not, but this book helps us conceive of them.

Cinematic thought-formations not yet fully realized are also a Godardian preoccupation. On the one hand, Godard sees certain types of early cinema as ripe with potential, for instance German interwar cinema as a site of formal renewal due to a pursuit of philosophical thought articulated through images (Witt 2013: 145). On the other hand, he was famously fixated on how film never realized its thinking potential (e.g. Godard and Ishaghpour 2005 [1999]: 73f; see also Morgan 2012: 168f), which largely means that the promise of *montage* has not been realized; he even said that montage "never really existed, like a plant that has never really left the ground" (Witt 2013: 112f, 117, 124, 149).²⁴ My concern with cinecepts is based on a similar (while less categorical or hyperbolic) presupposition about a not yet fully actualized potential for philosophical thinking in and through film / video / audiovisual media.

Philosophical Rigor and Clarity of Argumentation

If the Sonimage works strikes an analytical and pedagogical balance between the relatively dogmatic and the too poetical, as explained above, how can this be understood in relation to more traditional notions of argumentative clarity? While this is explored at greater length in Chapter 6, certain key points should be introduced here: On the one hand, Laura Mulvey and Colin MacCabe are right to describe the montage in Godard-Miéville's *Numéro deux* as follows: "Using two video monitors with voice-over commentary and written titles, Godard brings together an assortment of ideas and images that are suggestive rather than coherently argued" (1980: 96). On the other hand, "coherently argued" can mean many different things, and it is unclear what metric Mulvey and MacCabe use for making this assessment. (Could, say, Deleuze's cinema books be deemed "coherently argued" using the same metric? And if not, are they merely "suggestive"?) The idea of coherent arguments, furthermore, is not only *broad*, it also says nothing about whether the arguments are *philosophical*. Making an argument backed by evidence to convey a particular viewpoint is for instance part of an established academic definition of the regular documentary (e.g. Nichols 1991: 125). Something similar goes for journalism. What about scholarly coherence and clarity? While the cinecept is neither reducible nor anathema to more traditional ideals of coherence or clarity, it is generally aligned with notions of clarification and rigor in continental philosophy and more specifically with Deleuze's conception of concepts as clarifications and determinations of problems (as explored in Chapter 1). Godard-Miéville's cinecepts are "embryonic" not because they fail to live up to traditional ideals of clarity of argumentation, but because they do not entirely live up to Deleuzian notions of clarifying rigor either, as they lean a little too much into poetic association at the cost of philosophical determination, even at their most cineceptual. (As stated, I discuss clarity and modes of argumentation further in Chapter 6, and explore concepts as philosophical determination and clarifications of problems most directly in Chapter 1.)

Film / Video / Audiovisual Media as Formal Means (Not Thought Disciplines)

The embryonic or still "too poetical" character of the cinecepts in Sonimage, furthermore, is not due to its media form(s). The theory of cinecepts is based on a rejection of ideas about what category of thought media forms are supposedly destined to express. In this study, film / video / audiovisual media are regarded as formal means that can be used to basically express anything, as opposed to being inherently prone (or restricted) to some given discipline or mode of thought (art, philosophy, documentary, narrative, skepticism, etc.).[25] In contrast, Deleuze himself (as well as much film-philosophy) perceives cinema/film as a distinct discipline, however heterogeneous and evolving; for example:

> It is perhaps the question for literature, or philosophy, or even psychiatry. But in what respect is it the question for the cinema; that is, a question that touches on its specificity, on its difference from other disciplines. (C2 168)
>
> There are [...] ideas in cinema that could also work in other disciplines. (TRM 316)
>
> Contact can be made only when one discipline realizes that another discipline has already posed a similar problem, and so the one reaches out to the other to resolve this problem [...] I was able to write on cinema [...] because certain philosophical problems pushed me to seek out the solutions in cinema. (TRM 284f)

It is as "another discipline" that Deleuze compares cinema to philosophy. And they are seen as disciplines of *thought*, which is clearer if we turn to *What is Philosophy?*, in which "art, science, and philosophy"—as clarified in Chapter 1 below—are described as three different "forms of thought" in the sense of "disciplines", where each "remains on its own plane and utilizes its own elements", and "philosophy is the discipline that involves creating concepts" (WP 202, 217, 5). Deleuze's differentiation between cinema/art and philosophy, then, implies them sharing the category of being thought disciplines. The present study has a very different premise: while philosophy is still seen as a thought discipline, film/video is removed from that category and seen more concretely as moving images with sound, etc. Film/video is thereby put in the category of media forms, which it shares with other widely defined media forms like the written word. The written word is obviously used for any of the mentioned thought disciplines, and this study considers film/video to be just as unrestricted in that regard.

How is film/video defined as a media form in this study? One key basis is found in D. N. Rodowick's treatment of Noël Carroll's notion of a media category called moving images. Rodowick redefines moving images as a plural and variable general medium (without static essence) that includes all forms of moving images: celluloid, analog video, digital, etc. (2007: 38, 41, 86). The definition used in the present study adds to Rodowick's an emphasis on the internal multimedia aspect and uses words like film or video to point to moving images and montage that usually also include sounds, voice, and perhaps also texts and graphics. Following Rodowick's definition, furthermore, the differences between celluloid, video, and digital will be of minor importance. While Godard-Miéville's works in the 1970s, as Jerry White writes, "exist in a curious state, between [celluloid] film and video" (2013: 2), this is only relevant secondarily and to the extent that the film/video relationship is conceptualized (and concretely mixed) in a work like *Numéro deux*. We can also note that for Godard himself there are no big categorical differences between film and video, although video allows the filmmaker to do things the former does not (see e.g. Godard and Ishaghpour 2005 [1999]: 32).[26] And while the new formal possibilities afforded by video technology are certainly relevant for cinecepts, this does not make the film/video difference categorical.

The cinecept, furthermore, is not in a separate category from words: All films/videos and embryonic cinecepts examined in this book contain an abundance of spoken and/or written words.[27] These words, moreover, are parts of audiovisual complexes with other forms. The words are themselves audiovisual: by being incorporated into (or appearing along) a time-based medium and becoming aural or visual in other ways, and through their meanings being co-determined in the interplay with the other parameters.

Media Affecting Thought and the Fact That This Is a Book

While a medium is a formal means and not a restriction to a given thought discipline, work within a discipline is still affected by the medium or media used. If a philosopher changes from one medium to another while continuing to do philosophy, this shift will impact their thought work. Deleuze's main media in this regard—however otherwise influenced by art, affects, events, etc.—is speech (lectures, seminars, conversations) and reading/writing (books, articles, letters). Godard certainly also speaks, reads, and writes, but he thinks to a great extent in and through his work with audiovisual media—certainly at the editing table where he is famously "thinking with his hands".

Thinking in and through audiovisual media will also spill over to thinking when not directly using such technology. It will even influence ways of thinking in and through words and writing. This is clear with Godard's writing. And as Witt points out, Godard has an extraordinarily expanded idea about "cinema" that seems to partly include his texts (2013: 7; see also 2004). Relatedly, the Godard-influenced filmmaker/theorist Harun Farocki says while writing in front of an editing table at the beginning of his video *Interface* (*Schnittstelle*, 1995): "I can hardly write a word these days, if there isn't an image on the screen at the same time." And as Nietzsche wrote after switching to a typewriter in 1882: "Our writing tools are also working on our thoughts" (quoted in Kittler 1999 [1985]: 200).[28] Deleuze wrote with a pen. Aside from notes written with a pen as well as on a smartphone, this book was written on a laptop, on which I also watch a lot of moving images, sometimes while writing.

You are reading a book, nonetheless, which tracks with the general aim and delimitation: I investigate the conditions of possibility and lay a theoretical ground for cinecepts, but as a transmedia potential cinecepts are in the end conceived here from a words-only perspective (like Astruc writing a text instead of making a film about the camera pen). This potential can be developed into a concrete practice only through work in audiovisual media, by philosophers/theorists trying to formulate actual cinecepts through such media, or by philosophically/theoretically inclined video/multimedia artists taking their work in cineceptual directions. This book provides a framework for such development. To fully function as an academic practice, however, cinecepts would also require scholarly infrastructures that facilitate their production, dissemination, and reception. I return to these kinds of issues in Chapter 7.

Notes

1 Why *cine*cept instead of *video*cept or *film*cept? Cinecept, along with being easier to say, has etymological advantages: the cine- prefix connects with the more literal original meaning of the French word *cinéma* as a shortening of *cinémato-graphe*, which fundamentally means movement writing or writing through movement (*cine* and *graphe* connect with terms in the Latin/Greek heritage that mean movement and writing respectively). Cinecept can from this perspective be seen to have a literal meaning of concept movement or concept in movement. The -*cept* part of cinecept simply keeps the connection to the word con*cept*—although we can note that the Latin meaning of *cept* is to seize, hold, or take (similar to *griff* in *begriff*,

the German word for concept). This is only an explanation for the word choice, not a definition of the cinecept as a concept.

2 Conceptual art has little direct relevance for a theory of cinecepts for the following reasons:

   A. Deleuze recognizes conceptual art—at least as initially practiced and defined—as a recent attempt "to bring art and philosophy together", but he is highly critical of this attempt. He argues that conceptual art "create[s] sensations and not concepts", despite its ambition to express concepts instead of sensations. And when concepts are in some sense involved, it is an impoverished notion of concepts, concepts reduced to "doxa" (WP 198), or "abstract and signifying Forms" that have merely traded one kind of representation of the given (figurative givens) for another (conceptual givens) (FB 103). Deleuze also argues that conceptual art dematerializes art through generalization in ways that neutralize art's "plane of composition." The plane is made "informative" since the sensation becomes dependent "upon the simple 'opinion' of a spectator who determines whether or not to 'materialize' the sensation,' that is to say, decides whether or not it is art" (WP 198). While this latter critique of spectator activism concerns the art side rather than concepts per se, for Deleuze concepts are equally "not in your head: they are things, peoples, zones, regions, thresholds, gradients, temperatures, speeds, etc." (DI 312, note 3).
   B. What we today tend to call conceptual art—which compared to its 1960s definitions is a much broader category, containing various (more or less) theory-driven mixes of sensations, observations, and ideas—is too undefined and inclusive to be relevant or helpful for something as specific as cinecepts.

Furthermore, when the term conceptual art is used in writings on Godard it tends not to reference the kind of filmic montage or montage logic that is explored in this book, or, when it does, it is still used broadly without further definition or elaboration—e.g. Michael Witt's description of Godard as being already from the beginning a "conceptual montage artist" (2013: 11).

3 The film-philosophical literature that explicitly works with Deleuze sidesteps such questions either by following Deleuze's own separation between cinematic thinking and philosophical conceptualization and focusing on other issues concerning the film and philosophy relation (e.g. Sinnerbrink 2011), or by assuming/implying that Deleuze claimed that film was philosophy, which he did not (e.g. Frampton 2006; Sorfa 2015). A limited few have brushed up against one of these questions while appearing not to recognize it as a question (e.g. Baross 2017; Herzogenrath 2017), recognized it somewhat without subjecting it to examination (Drabinski 2008), or almost examined it but in unclear and partly contradictory ways (Rodowick 2015). I examine these aspects in Bernd Herzogenrath, John E. Drabinski, and

D. N. Rodowick in Part 1 of Nilsson (2018). The gist of it: Herzogenrath claims in passing that if/when film is philosophy, this equals what Deleuze calls the creation of concepts (2017: xii). Yet, he does not examine any of the implications of this connection to conception creation and he references Deleuze's general ideas about a new image of thought instead of his definition of concepts. Drabinski, more relevantly, offers this suggestion: "If philosophy, as Deleuze has it, is primarily concerned with the creation of concepts, then Godard's cinema can be said to create concepts in sound and image" (2010: 4). However, Drabinski does not develop or investigate this suggestion in relation to Deleuze's writings. Rodowick's arguments about film as philosophy from a Deleuzian perspective are more developed and sophisticated but also more ambiguous and even contradictory. He argues for the following three positions: 1) "film is philosophy" (2015: xv, 158, 179); 2) film is "a becoming-philosophy tending toward conceptual formation" (158); and 3) film as that which "may inspire philosophy to give form to a concept" but whose own figures of thought are always "preconceptual" (138, 139, 165, 179, 229). Sidestepping the peculiar generalization of film in positions 1 and 2: the relation between position 1 (film is philosophy) and position 3 (film as preconceptual) would not necessarily be contradictory if Rodowick did not explicitly argue that the first position was also claimed by Deleuze: "Deleuze and Cavell", he writes, "comprehend cinema as expressing ways of being in the world and of relating to the world such that cinema is already philosophy" (179). He then qualifies this to mean that cinema thinks similar problems as philosophy, and that it does so "preconceptually in aesthetic form." But this is actually a shift rather than a qualification since it does not explain how *Deleuze* could have "comprehended cinema" to be "already philosophy" given that cinema—however advanced in its thought—is preconceptual and philosophy is chiefly defined by its creation of concepts. Rodowick similarly writes about "an active philosophy immanent to the Image—a philosophy of the image given in or through images", with the implication that this is Deleuze's position (158). But how could it be his position, given that it would amount to philosophy without concept creation? At times Rodowick seems to try to solve this through sentences that make ambiguous Deleuze's division between cinema and philosophical concept creation (a division Rodowick is carefully upholding at other times): "Deleuze sees conceptual creation in the movement- and time-images", he writes at one point (161). (I can add—to my 2018 article which this note rehashes—that there might be a back door for merging what Rodowick wants to merge here, beyond what he says and my critique of it: There is a certain inconsistency in *What is Philosophy?* between saying on the one hand that philosophy is concept creation, that "Philosophy appears in Greece" and "philosophy is Greek" (WP 96, 87), while also claiming that the Greeks "did not yet 'have' [concepts but rather] contemplated them from afar, or sensed them" (WP 108).)

4 I laid the ground for parts of this reading in Nilsson 2014 and 2020.

5 For the sake of a generalizing overview, the literature can be separated and pressed into five categories (with some works more clearly belonging to more than one):

 i. Works that delve into aspects or the whole of Deleuze's cinema books with the main aim of explicating what they say. While many do so in excellent, original and developing ways, they mostly harmonize with at this point fairly established readings (e.g. Rodowick 1997; Flaxman ed. 2000; Bogue 2003; Marrati 2008 [2003]; Colman 2011; Rushton 2012; Deamer 2016).
 ii. Exegetic explorations of the more specifically philosophical meanings of Deleuze's cinema books seen from the perspective of his overall philosophy (e.g. Rodowick 1997; Pamart 2012; Thomas 2018).
 iii. Works that primarily use the cinema books as a frame for analyzing types of films, areas, or periods that Deleuze did not himself go into, which may critically modify certain categorizations and approaches in *Cinema* while not necessarily expanding significantly on Deleuze's philosophical ideas (e.g. Pisters 2003; Martin-Jones 2006; 2011; Sutton 2009; Martin-Jones and Brown eds. 2012; Deamer 2014; Nevin 2018).
 iv. Works that cross-read the cinema books with other aspects of Deleuze's work that are not discussed or developed in the cinema books, such as his and Guattari's notions of schizoanalysis or his more expanded work on affect (and often applied to spectators, of which Deleuze said little) (e.g. Buchanan and MacCormack eds. 2008; Shaviro 1993; Kennedy 2000; Powell 2007; del Rio 2008).
 v. Studies that provide some wider philosophical reflections and/or expansions on the ideas in Deleuze's cinema books that are less easily categorizable, and which thereby have principal similarities to the present study, but that nonetheless mostly keep more or less within established parameters of how Deleuze's cinema books are understood (e.g. Rodowick ed. 2010; Pisters 2012; Boljkovac 2013).

6 It is quite common to reduce film-philosophy to film stimulating philosophizing and conceptualization in the theorist/philosopher or the viewer more generally. This includes film-philosophical interpretations of Deleuze: Gregory Flaxman for instance writes about "the profound role that these arts [among them cinema] play in Deleuze's work as conceptual provocateurs" (2011: xx).

7 As late as 2009, Zsuzsa Baross goes so far as to argue that (at least compared to his peers) "Godard, or rather his cinema, is also the least known, seen, screened and, perhaps, understood" (2009: 134).

8 Pantenburg (2015 [2006]: 23, 49, 53, 60–3, 71–4, 79, 83, 96, 124, 135, 177, 213, 255). A few times Pantenburg also talks about films as containing or giving rise to theoretical "concepts", but the term (when implicitly defined in ways relevant for

the cinecept) mostly appears to mean abstract ideas, often in a loosely Eisensteinian sense; and, even more significantly, the concept is conceived of as "a leap [...] that has to take place in the viewer's mind", something that is thereby—Pantenburg quoting Alexander Kluge—"not materially concentrated in the film itself" (204, 44, 27, 151f). (For a similar spectator-centric stance in the Godard literature, which also adds a more radical aversion to the very idea of filmic thought—apparently based only on the fact that the film technology itself is not the literal thought agent—see Vaugh 2013: 2, 32, 27.) The cinecept, in contrast, *is* "materially concentrated in the film itself", *before* meeting viewers, a stance that follows a Deleuzian (distinctly non-spectator-centric) conception of both art and philosophy (e.g. WP 164, 175; DI 312, note 3). I return to this aspect of Deleuze in Chapter 3, note 20, and Chapter 5, note 9 (see also notes 2A and 6 above, and Preface, note 10).

9 In Morgan's case, however, this is not because he does not see philosophy at work in Godard's films—rather, the philosophy at work in some of Godard's late films is basically his object of study. Yet Morgan presents his study as avoiding the film-as-philosophy perspective because he sees a risk—and with references mostly to analytic philosophy of film and little film-philosophy—that it can lead "to the reductive thought that the only philosophically significant elements of Godard's films and videos have to do with conversation and dialogue" and to thereby miss "a sense of the subtle texture of the images and sounds that make up a film and the way Godard's philosophical ambitions emerge out of these explicitly formal concerns" (2012: 26). While film-philosophy could perhaps become more aesthetically engaged in certain regards—or at least such criticism would make sense—film-philosophy overall clearly does not equate philosophy in and through film with "conversation and dialogue." Morgan's statement therefore appears more as a result of an insufficient familiarity with the field—at least as it exists outside analytic philosophy—than as a solid reason to avoid its central question. His highly interesting study of late Godard, despite this positioning in the introduction, is in many regards in line with, and a good contribution to, film-philosophy. (See also second part of note 11 below.)

10 At one point in Morrey's excellent overview of Godard's oeuvre, at least some of Godard's earlier films are described as "providing a practical illustration" of "the revolution of French though brought about by the works of Derrida, Deleuze, Foucault, and Althusser in the mid- to late-1960s" (2005: 90). At another point it is said that Godard later addressed the same problems as such philosophers but through filmic means, and here it seems implied that he did so also with some philosophical autonomy (109). At yet another point, Godard's own conception of film as a "mode of thinking" and referencing of himself as a philosopher or scientist seem to be interpreted as a montage method that "sparks off a process of thought in the observer" in which the spectator is "invit[ed]" to "construct the meaning of a given association" (227f), which makes the philosophy of the film itself unclear, while the conclusion still states that Godard's is "cinema *as* philosophy" (242).

11 Deleuze and Guattari's influence on Godard-Gorin and on Godard-Miéville as well as Foucault's influence on Godard-Miéville during the 1970s is fairly well established if not exhaustively investigated; see e.g. Morrey (2005: 115–30, 240); Witt (1998: ch. 1). See also Godard and Ishaghpour (2005 [1999]: 76f) on a key Foucault quotation in *Histoire(s) du cinéma*—emphasized also by Rancière in his discussion of *Histoire(s)* (2009 [2003]: 37f, 59, 62)—which is relevant also for the following issue:

While I agree with Morgan's problematizing of reductions of Godard's films to the philosophies of his French contemporaries, and the importance of regarding Godard as an original thinker, Morgan goes too far in the other direction. Based almost entirely on the claim that Godard does not cite such philosophers directly in his films, Morgan not only finds Godard to be "fairly indifferent to these thinkers and the schools of thought they represent", he also argues that they "simply are not his interlocutors, not the texts his films draw on, and [that] this is important for understanding what he takes himself to be doing" (2012: 65f). This argument is not convincing. Contrary empirical evidence aside, if this is the criterion by which to judge whether there is influence, then none of these French philosophers influenced each other, since they seldom directly reference or engage comprehensively with each other in writing. Even Deleuze and Foucault (apart from Deleuze's late book on Foucault and Foucault's preface for *Anti-Oedipus*) seldom directly referenced each other in their books. The point is that they still deeply influenced each other, and direct citations are not the only metric for determining whether that is the case.

12 Witt goes on to say here that Deleuze had claimed in "Three questions about *Six fois deux*" that Godard with *Six fois deux* made a "full and original contribution", with the implication that this contribution was philosophy in Deleuze's mind (Witt 2007 [2004]: 210). However, while Deleuze clearly always considered Godard as thinking filmically, and in that text explicates ideas at play in this work, he does not actually say anything explicitly about a particularly *philosophical* contribution in and through video. Deleuze's statement in that text is arguably closer to how he positions Godard in the cinema books than to the way he talked about Godard in 1968—more on these differences in the last paragraph of this section.

13 On Godard-Miéville's relation to Julia Kristeva and Luce Irigaray in these senses, see Chapter 4, note 19.

14 Witt's extraordinary Godard scholarship notwithstanding, it is worth noting that in his early writings he was not a very close reader of Deleuze. In this article from 1999 he largely dismisses Deleuze's cinema books as incomprehensible. Moreover, despite it being part of his aim to examine Deleuze and Guattari as an important intellectual context for the Sonimage films, Witt does not really engage with Deleuze and Guattari in his dissertation (1998), beyond some schematic and brief passages.

15 To clarify: the philosophical themes in *Histoire(s)*—aside from certain directly relevant ideas such as *rapprochement*—are thereby outside of the delimitation: e.g. doing historiography through film, the holocaust, various theses about film history (the literature on these themes is of course already quite large and the present study does not aim to make a contribution in this respect).

16 This differentiation is an overall generalization, and not absolute: there are many aspects of the Sonimage films where the poetic is in the driving seat perhaps as much as in *Histoire(s)*, and there are aspects of the latter that can at least be analyzed through a cineceptual lens. While *Histoire(s)*'s poetic-essayistic-symphonic reasoning is philosophically dense, however, this density does not in the same way tend directly towards the cineceptual.

17 Witt: "In view of the frequent underestimation and misrepresentation of the scale of Miéville's contribution, let us note here that she co-directed, co-authored and co-edited all of the Sonimage works listed above [*Ici et ailleurs*; *Numéro deux*; *Comment ça va*; *Six fois deux*; *France tour détour*], with the exception of *Numéro deux*, which she nevertheless co-authored and co-edited" (2014: 319).

18 This is not to take anything away from Godard himself, who as pointed out by Jerry White (2013: 41) had developed much of the concerns and foundations for the formal approaches already in *Le gai savoir* (1968) and partly during the Dziga Vertog Group period (see Witt 1998: 14f).

19 White, however, also considers these works as "precursors" to Godard-Miéville's 1980s films that he regards as being just as philosophical but more "fully realized aesthetic objects" and more "mature" (2013: 62, 94, 99, see also 107). In contrast, the present study regards the Sonimage films as precursors or "not fully realized" in the very different sense of precursors to cinecepts. And from this standpoint, the post-Sonimage films that White finds more "fully realized" and "mature" instead appear *less* "fully realized."

20 Deleuze devotes chapter 6 of *What is Philosophy?* to detailing how this kind of logic turns concepts into functions in propositions (see also WP 22). (Cf. Deleuze's much more affirmative view of what he calls functives in science in the preceding chapter.) This is mainly about twentieth-century logic after logical positivism and starting especially with schools around Wittgenstein (ABC Letter W)—so, not necessarily all, and perhaps especially not all *early* analytic philosophy (Deleuze seems for instance to have admired some aspects of Russell, see e.g. LS 85, note 2, 96).

21 Deleuze makes a certain distinction between form and content in this sense, e.g. DI: 140).

22 There are similarities here to Astruc vis-à-vis the camera pen: "Perhaps it could simply be called a tendency […] Of course, no tendency can be so called unless it has something to show for itself. […] the strange paradox of whereby one can talk about something which does not yet exist" (2014 [1948]: 607).

23 For a biographical overview of Deleuze's close relationship to certain parts of the French world of film critique and scholarship, including Narboni, see Dosse 2010 [2007]: 398–405, see also 411–14.

24 See also Godard (1992 [1988]: 161). He sometimes implies that Hitchcock, Welles, and Ray are exceptions; see Godard (1985 [1980]: 405); Witt (2013: 137; 2000: 43).

25 And if *philosophy* is formulated in and through such media, then the philosophy should in principle be able to concern anything, just like philosophical writing can concern anything and not just writing itself. Reducing film as theory/philosophy to theory/philosophy about film itself is fairly prevalent in contemporary discussions about film as theory/philosophy, notably in Pantenburg (2015 [2006]), who transposes the Romantic idea—originating in Lessing and expressed by Schlegel and Novalis—that a theory or a critique of the novel should come in the form of a novel. The present study argues that this is too narrow a frame for what is at stake with film as philosophy: film as philosophy should not be reduced to a philosophizing about film.

26 To which we can add Serge Daney's claim that "Godard's lead over other manipulators of images and sounds stems from his total contempt for any discourse on the 'specificity' of cinema" (Daney 1976).

27 On the proliferation of visible text in Godard's video works see Lahey Dronsfield (2010) and Leutrat (2000: 179). While not about text *in* the videos, we may also note Raymond Bellour's argument—which references Godard among others—that video *itself* "is more deeply rooted in writing than is cinema" (1990: 421).

28 For a historical and empirical overview of how this can work more generally—focusing on how various writing technologies (from a Sumerian cuneiform script ca. 3500 BC to alphabetic writing to printing to electronic media) "restructure consciousness"—see Ong (2012 [1982]: ch. 4).

1 | Towards a Theory of Cinecepts: A Reorganization of Deleuze's Categories

THIS CHAPTER LAYS the ground for a theory of cinecepts. It does so through a gradual synthesis of what Deleuze separated:

1. "[P]hilosophy is the art of forming, inventing, and fabricating concepts" (WP 2),
2. and "those of you who do cinema […] do not invent concepts—that is not your concern" (TRM 314).

Deleuze upholds this separation, as we will see, no matter how much the two positions might *appear* to blend. Since the cinecept—an actual blend of these positions—is based in Deleuze's philosophy, I will proceed through a close critical examination of parts of said philosophy. Part One of this chapter looks at his definition of concepts—its underlying logic and scholarly implications—along with its relation to art and cinema. Part Two treats these aspects of Deleuze's thought in ways more explicitly critical and speculative, and with a more direct focus on cinema. Bits of his philosophy will be "reorganized"[1] so as to allow and support the idea of "forming, inventing, and fabricating concepts" in and through audiovisual media. The result is a setup for a theory of cinecepts, which will be further explored and developed in subsequent chapters.

PART ONE

How Deleuze Distinguishes between Philosophy and Cinematic/Artistic Thinking

In and around the cinema books Deleuze conceives of cinematic thinking and philosophical thinking as formally different, even though they can share concerns and characteristics, and the main formal difference has to do with concepts. In *What is Philosophy?* Deleuze describes concept creation as the exclusive right of philosophy, that which secures a function for philosophy (WP 8). In *Cinema 1* filmmakers are said to "think with movement-images and time-images *instead* of concepts" (C1 ix, emphasis mine). In a 1987 talk at a film school, Deleuze says, to repeat, "those of you who do cinema [...] do not invent concepts—that is not your concern" (TRM 314; see also ABC Letter I).[2]

At the very end of *Cinema 2* he says the same thing but in ways that appear to invite misunderstanding, so let us examine what he says here: "Cinema's concepts are not given in cinema"—however much it "gives rise to" them—and cinema's theory is something "philosophy must produce as conceptual practice" (C2 280). While the concepts thereby produced "are cinema's concepts, not theories about cinema", this means only that philosophy must produce them in accordance with the specificity of cinema's structures and logics of expression, instead of applying ready-made concepts from other areas (C2 280; N 57–9). Cinema's concepts should closely resonate with the film's signs, images, and thought structures, but philosophy still produces them. This entails extracting filmic structures or ideas onto a philosophical plane on which they are recomposed according to its particular aims and problems and a philosophical logic of determination, while also staying true to the specificity of what is conceptualized (more on this conceptual procedure below). The concept is its own creation; it wasn't simply already there in the film.

The preface to the English edition of *Cinema 1* also seems to invite misunderstanding, as it famously states that "it is not sufficient to compare the great directors of the cinema with painters, architects or even musicians. They must also be compared with thinkers" (C1 x). What does "compare" [*confronter*] entail here? The word "thinkers" [*penseurs*] certainly means philosophical thinkers, and a main premise of the cinema books is thereby introduced: great filmmakers work on a level of advanced thought comparable to philosophers—there is no intellectual hierarchy between them. As Deleuze clarifies in a 1983 interview conducted by Serge Daney: "The great cinematic authors are thinkers just as much as painters, musicians, novelists and philosophers (philosophy has no special privilege)" (TRM 210; see also WP 8). Deleuze is *not* saying that the work of thinking and the thought products of filmmakers are the same as that to which they are compared—whether compared with the work of painters, architects, musicians, novelists, or philosophers. For Deleuze, rather, ("great") cinema and philosophy are comparable thinking modes with key formal differences having most significantly to do with concept creation. Deleuze is clear about this in and around the cinema books: filmmakers do not create concepts. Granted, *What is Philosophy?* hardly mentions cinema in its separation between philosophy as concept creation and a generalization called art, but cinema can be seen as implicitly subsumed into the latter category in *this* sense: a particular set of thought modes that do not involve concept creation.[3] So let us look closer at the distinctions made in this book between philosophy and art.

As Deleuze famously argues, philosophy has three basic elements: 1) A *plane of immanence*, which is a prephilosophical thought terrain made up of assumptions about what it means to think, intuitions, and specific problems, on which 2) *concepts* are created (and on which they can make sense),[4] and 3) *conceptual personae* that are intermediaries between the other two elements in ways that help dramatize the problems to be conceptualized.[5] Art has its own three elements: a *plane of composition* on which *percepts/affects* as well as *aesthetic figures* are created. This division between philosophy and art can maintain itself while allowing crossings and mixtures: Philosophy and art can "intersect and intertwine", but always "without synthesis or identification" (WP 198f). And when one of them takes a component from the other this reconstitutes the component. For instance, an artistic affect that becomes the sensation of a concept.[6] Deleuze discusses three other kinds of intersections between art and philosophy, in which the distinction is still in the end fully maintained:

1. Art, science, and philosophy tend to become indiscernible at the point in which they intersect with the chaos with which they all grapple, but this does not speak against Deleuze's many declarations of their distinct properties beyond that intersection (WP 218).
2. An "intrinsic type of interference" occurs when concepts and conceptual personae like Nietzsche's Zarathustra are placed on a plane that is "difficult to qualify" (WP 217). But difficult to qualify does not mean cannot be qualified, and Deleuze qualifies Nietzsche's plane as a philosophical plane.
3. Trickier are the literary writers Deleuze calls "half philosophers" (like Herman Melville), who mix artistic and philosophical elements in a particular and systemic way: they do not reconstitute components to fit the mode of thought they are taken into, but rather take some elements from philosophy and some from art and create hybrids. Still, the differences are preserved between the elements: they make hybrids of art and philosophy but "do not produce a synthesis" of the two (WP 67).[7]

While some ambiguities may remain concerning the half philosophers, Deleuze is particularly strict regarding one element: concepts. The half philosophers either place conceptual personae on planes of composition or aesthetic figures on planes of immanence. But their hybrids are never described as forming or expressing concepts. As Deleuze writes: "only philosophy creates concepts in the strict sense" and the "exclusive right of concept creation secures a function for philosophy" (WP 5, 8).[8] How, then, does Deleuze define concepts?

Deleuze's Concept of Concepts

As stated, and as further explicated below, Deleuze sees concepts as philosophically determined problems or multiplicities (and as constellations of potential). Clearly, as Daniel W. Smith writes, this "differs significantly from previous conceptions of the concept" (2012b: 62). Deleuze's prominent critique in *Difference and Repetition* of a traditional manner of thinking that he calls representation includes a critique of representational concepts. Creative representational concepts can be seen as multiplicities too, beyond their immediate function in given philosophical contexts (*What is Philosophy?* is generous in this regard). But Deleuze is still firm in his distinction between representational concepts—in which there is "conceptual identity or sameness of representation"—and concepts with internal movement (DR 17). He sees a shift in philosophy from representation to movement happening simultaneously with the development of moving images: "Motion was brought into concepts at precisely the same time it was brought into images. Bergson presents one of the first cases of self-moving thought. Because it's not enough simply to say concepts possess movement; you also have to construct intellectually mobile concepts" (N 122). In what sense do representational concepts lack movement? There are different kinds of representational concepts, of which some are more obviously static while others can *seem* to include movement. The more obviously non-moving concepts are self-same in relation to an identity that the concept references, and/or self-same through the concept's difference to what it is not (a simple prephilosophical example: a cat, not a bird). Such concepts can appear as terms with given places in syllogisms or as functions in propositions. They abstract the essences of things, phenomena, or ideas according to a logic of (static) identity and opposition/difference in relation to other concepts. The component parts of each such concept are themselves presupposed as identities, with the head concept bringing them together in a more generalized, abstracted identity. Then there are more internally dynamic and complex representational concepts—and we will now look at Hegel as the paradigm case—but for Deleuze all such concepts, simple/static or complex/dynamic, subordinate difference to identity and hide real movement and what Deleuze calls difference in itself.

In *Difference and Repetition*, Deleuze distinguishes Hegel (along with Leibniz) from more classical systems of representation, and partly works out his own concept of difference through a critique of aspects in their philosophical logic that can appear close to his own.[9] It is outside the scope of this study to examine the complex relations between Deleuze and Hegel and even more so to substantially interpret Hegel's own philosophy.[10] But I will juxtapose key points in their respective philosophies of difference, (mostly) from the perspective of Deleuze's critique of Hegel, for the purpose of clarifying foundational aspects of Deleuze's logic of multiplicity, which underlies his concept of concepts, and as an entry into a more direct discussion of these aspects in Deleuze.[11]

The core of Deleuze's critique: Hegel subordinates difference to identity through a reduction of concepts, movements, and becoming to abstract generalities and negative contradiction between opposites. For Deleuze, Hegel's concept of "difference implies the negative, and allows itself to lead to contradiction, only to the extent that its subordination to the identical is maintained" (DR xvii). Let us gradually explicate what this means and how Deleuze's thought differs. In *Bergsonism* Deleuze comments on philosophies that "clai[m] to reconstruct the real" and its movements "with general ideas", as exemplified by "Being passes into nonbeing and produces becoming" (B 44). He continues:

> in this type of *dialectical* method one begins with concepts that, like baggy clothes, are much too big. The One in general, the multiple in general, nonbeing in general ... In such cases the real is recomposed with abstracts; but of what use is a dialectic that believes itself to be reunited with the real when it compensates for the inadequacy of a concept that is too broad or too general by invoking the opposite concept, which is no less broad and general? The concrete will never be attained by combining the inadequacy of one concept with the inadequacy of its opposite. The singular will never be attained by correcting a generality with another generality. [...] Bergson criticizes the dialectic for being a false movement, that is, a movement of the abstract concept, which goes from one opposite to the other only by means of imprecision. (B 44)

In *Difference and Repetition*, Deleuze develops a more detailed critique of a Hegelian logic of identity, negativity, and contradiction driving such false movement. First some basic parameters in Hegel relevant for our concerns: Things aren't just what they are on their own, since identities are constituted by relations. Things, phenomena, or ideas are conceptually determinable by containing relationships to what they are not. P is not A, B, C, etc., and at the limit, it is *not* non-P, its opposite—and this is the "essential distinction" that, as driven to contradiction, makes the parts "quickened and alive to each other" (Hegel 2010 [1812–16]: 384). For Hegel, therefore, "the most important aspect of [the] dialectic" is "grasping opposites in their unity" (35). Between them there is a "reciprocal exchange of determinatenesses", a "being-for-each-other" in which one "only has its determinateness through the other" (Hegel 2018 [1807]: 84). Each opposite thereby becomes part of the other's essence. The tension between them as contradictions, however, demands a resolve. Hegel conceives of the resolve as sublation [*Aufhebung*]: the two opposites are reconciled in a higher identity, in which they are both preserved and exceeded (and the higher identity then faces its own contradiction with an opposite on this level, and as already containing the prior level's contradictions). This is how things move, become, develop—albeit, then, through the "false" movement of contradictions and negations (leaving aside the question of in what sense this is, or is not necessarily, part of a larger process of teleological unfolding).

For Deleuze this is to reduce difference—and the greatest and most essential difference—to a logical difference, to a "simple confrontation between opposing, contrary or contradictory, propositions", which subordinates difference to identity; a line of thinking with a history going back to Aristotle that "attains its extreme form in Hegelianism" (DR 11, 203; see also WP 80). While this "extreme form" involves complexities I cannot fully go into here—in Deleuze's reading this includes organic representation becoming "orgiastic" by being extended to infinity, contradiction-based dynamic movements, a ground, and a concept as the Whole (DR 52–6, 59–65; 331–3, 342f)—difference remains reduced to negativity and subordinated to identity.[12] Deleuze:

> It is said that difference is negativity, that it extends or must extend to the point of contradiction once it is taken to the limit. This is true only to the extent that difference is already placed on a path or along a thread laid out by identity. It is true only to the extent that it is identity that pushes it to that point. (DR 60f; cf. 40)

> Hegelian contradiction appears to push difference to the limit, but [...] [i]t is only in relation to the identical, as a function of the identical, that contradiction is the *greatest* difference. The intoxications and giddinesses are feigned, the obscure is already clarified from the outset. (DR 331f)[13]

It is "clarified from the outset" by "confusing the concept of difference with a merely conceptual difference" (i.e. "conceptual" as representation)—however much "each of the contraries [...] was already contradiction"—which reflects only Hegel's "own thought and its generalities" (DR 30, 55, 11). This is a false movement that conceals "far more subtle and subterranean differential mechanisms" composed of what Deleuze calls positive difference or difference in itself (NP 157).[14] Deleuze's philosophy is focused on such subterranean mechanisms, and I need to continue to be a bit technical in describing their essential properties.

These mechanisms consist, most fundamentally, of differences that differ in themselves (they can also be understood as intensities, or repetitions of pre-individual and non-localizable points). Virtual Ideas, Problems, or multiplicities, are Deleuzian terms for distinct systems in which such differences reciprocally determine each other (and that furthermore contain "singularities" with "complete determination" that correspond to remarkable points in these relations between differences).[15] Ideas / Problems / multiplicities are structured through a logic of progressive or positive determination (even in its "complete determination"), beyond negation and negative contradiction.[16] These systems are made up of differential relations between intensities instead of identities, that is, between components that already differ in themselves.[17] Intensities connect with other intensities through processes of "autounification" forming systems of *potential*.[18] The differences may be in tension within such systems, but as each differential element is self-differing or intensive, and as each part is a divergent series (thereby relating as incompossibilities), the overall determination is mobile, dissymmetrical, and metastable. On the one hand, the "reality of the virtual is structure": "the virtual is completely determined", which gives each Idea its "distinctness" (DR 260). On the other hand, virtual Ideas are and remain *disjunctive*: there are no reconciliations in higher identities, neither within themselves nor in what they lead or give rise to.[19] Given their dynamic constitution, however, Ideas do still itch towards solutions/actualizations. And here Deleuze introduces another register: solutions/actualizations involve another realm of intensity, which creates further difference that wasn't simply (like the tree in the seed) prefigured in the Idea. The process of actualization draws out aspects of the Idea and "dramatizes" them into more actual things, qualities, and differences, something more spatiotemporally narrowed down, symmetrical, compossible. This does not in any way exhaust the Idea: the Idea is preserved and subsists during and after actualization, although with an at least partly altered "problematic" determination (which in turn modifies the solution it seeks, *ad infinitum*). Virtual Ideas subsist, however, only as fully connected to or implicated in the actual. They are thereby the open genetic conditions of actual identities (and their relations of negative difference: the actual reality of thing X not being thing Y).[20] I will return to the logic of Ideas as part of the discussion of Godard in Chapter 2, and more extensively to their differenc/tial—and for Deleuze increasingly strained—relation to the actual in Chapter 3.

None of this is to deny the existence or even the value of negation, negativity, opposition or contradiction, only their status as fundamental forces or structures.

In *Difference and Repetition*, negativity, negations, oppositions, and contradictions are likened to "ripples in a pond", described as epiphenomena or "surface effects" that "are dissipated by capturing the problem of which they reflect only the shadow" (DR 65, 337, 77, 143). But the dissipation is only a shift in perspective from actualization to problem. The positive differences remain *in* the problem, but in its actual effects those differences are objectively "cancelled".[21] When Deleuze talks about "illusion" in conjunction with the actual, this is not about the actual itself as illusion, but about confusing the cancellation of intensive difference on the actual plane with difference being cancelled also on the virtual plane (DR 300). On the actual plane, "in actual terms and real relations", "[f]orms of the negative do indeed appear", Deleuze writes, although "only in so far as these are cut off from the virtuality which they actualise, and from the movement of their actualisation". Yet, "the process of difference and of differen*c*iation is primary in relation to that of the negative and opposition", so that the "negative is always derived" and in reality never fully "cut off from" that from which it derives. Even the most seemingly static is thereby also changing if only on the subtlest of microlevels (DR 258, 294f; FLB 90). In *A Thousand Plateaus*, in which certain actualities are even more in focus and appear as having even more consistency, Deleuze and Guattari acknowledge contradictions as part of what defines social reality. But they also maintain the same basic position: "[S]ociety is defined by its contradictions [...] only on the larger scale of things"; "[f]rom the viewpoint of micropolitics, a society is defined by its lines of flight, which are molecular" (ATP 218; see also N 171).

Negative dialectics can be a useful method for analyzing "the larger scale of things,"[22] and more static representational terms can be useful for referencing everyday actualities as well as the empirical facts and functions that are (albeit in complex and creative ways) the objects of science (WP ch. 5). Both are inadequate, however, as means for understanding the subrepresentational or problematic (as always intertwined with the actual), which for Deleuze is the main concern of philosophy. And in this concern the "most important task [is] that of determining problems and realising in them our power of creation and decision" (DR 337).[23] How does Deleuze's concept of concepts extend from all this?

In *What is Philosophy?* Deleuze more explicitly and systematically provides his own definition of concepts as philosophical determinations of virtual multiplicities and constellations of potential (rather than abstract universals or representations of empirical facts or actualities), and as also involving other elements: planes of immanence and (perhaps somewhat less necessarily) conceptual personae. The concept itself condenses a finite number of "intensive" components—of which each, being either a concept or some other abstract component, already condenses intensive components, *ad infinitum*.[24] (A concrete and convenient example is the key components in Deleuze's own concept of concepts: consistency, intensive components, zones of neighborhood, a surveying point, etc.—more on each below.) These components "are processual, modular", "neither constants nor variables but pure and simple *variations*". This may sound a little loose and undetermined. But each variation is a "distinct" component, and they are all "inseparable" from each other in an "ordered" way (WP 20).[25] A concept is determined as a "consistency" both internally and externally. Internally: First, in the sense of having reached a "point of closure or saturation so that we can no longer add or withdraw a component without changing the nature of the concept" (WP 90). Second, through an "ordering of its components by zones of neighborhood", in which each component is distinct while also inseparable from another component in partially overlapping areas: "an area ab that belongs to both a and b, where a and b 'become' indiscernible". All such areas within the concept help "define [its] internal consistency" (WP 20). Third, through a main point "in a state of survey" that "at infinite speed" is "endlessly traversing" and "trac[ing] the contour of its components" (WP 20f, 214). Deleuze uses the I in Descartes cogito as an example of such a main point at which the "concept condenses" and which itself "passes through all the components" (the other components: doubt, thought, being). Externally, a concept is given consistency through its determined coexistence with other concepts on the same philosophical plane.[26] But also through the *problem(s)* to which the concept responds and without which it would have no concreteness or meaning (WP 24f, 32, 16; see also DR xix; ATP 22).

Concepts, however, also *create* meaning: they sketch their own spheres within reality. They make us see things in new ways or see new things. This is one aspect of what Deleuze calls the "pedagogy of the concept". This means that "philosophy must teach us to conceive", whereas the pedagogy of art means to "awaken us and teach us to feel" (WP 218). There is also a more precise and perhaps more important aspect of philosophical pedagogy that has to do with how concepts articulate and determine problems. Concepts reorganize problems, classes, or categories, and bring distant things together, or pull apart what appears close. They can also delink or bring different potentials together to form new constellations of potential. Key for forming concepts is to determine problems *properly*, to articulate new problems or reformulate old ones that have been badly posed or poorly understood.

Furthermore, the often many-years-long work of articulating and determining problems in these regards *involves standard scholarly conducts*. Deleuze may reimagine things like problems, concepts, and tasks—and especially with Guattari he aims beyond *certain* academic formal constrictions—but scholarly rigor itself is certainly not lessened (I will return to the question of scholarly conduct in the discussion of contemporary video essays in Chapter 6.) Which scholarly conducts are involved in philosophical work according to Deleuze? Some pillars:

- *Previous research.* There is the creative working through of previous intellectual material: "Before knowing how to invent concepts or to succeed in doing so, an enormous amount of work is necessary" (ABC Letter H). A large amount of scholarly material is treated throughout the work, even if only a selection is explicitly referenced in the published material.[27]
- *Problems.* The aspect most vital to and inseparable from concept creation: the articulation of problems, which Deleuze describes (with reference to Kant but also extended in his own conception) as "the constitution of a [...] systematic field which orientates and subsumes the researches or investigations" (DR 215).
- *Purpose.* Interrelatedly, there is the need of a purpose—"everything that I learn", Deleuze says, "I learn *for* a particular task"—which drives the work and determines what is relevant to include (however much the task is more sensed than cogently delineated through parts of the process) (ABC Letter B).
- *Aim and contribution.* Deleuze: "[Y]ou do not write a 'worthy' book unless: 1) you think that the books on the same subject or on a neighboring subject fall into a type of overall *error* (polemical function of the book); 2) you think that something essential has been forgotten in relation to the subject (inventive function); 3) you believe yourself capable of creating a new concept (creative function)" (LOT [1986] 86).
- *Scholarly context.* Working out ideas also in relation to A) interactions with students and B) responses from peers.[28]

Nevertheless, concepts themselves determine problems in ways that stay true to a logic of multiplicity—a conception of a scholarly practice that is certainly less of a standard. If the concept loses its subrepresentational internal dynamic, it becomes exhausted: opinion, doxa, cliché (although it can be revitalized in another philosophical context).

While concepts "speak the event" (more on this in Chapter 3) rather than static essences, they are inseparable from concrete, non-philosophical actual facts, identities, or phenomena—but the latter, of course, are not self-identical starting points or end goals.[29] Concepts extract from identities, facts, or actual phenomena the problematic structures that are their generative conditions, and which make up potentials for the new. And concept creation involves *co-creation* through whatever problems it grips and whatever existing potentials it brings together outside of itself: the particularities of existing problems and potentials are brought onto a philosophical plane and reconfigured through a new determination in a concept, and with a main purpose of maximizing the potential for change—whether in thought, in the actual world, or both (as they are intertwined as two facets of the same ontological plane of immanence).

All these aspects finally point to the difference between concepts and ideas: While Deleuze reimagines concepts and ideas in similar ways, as having a logic of multiplicity, a concept is a particular kind of determination resulting from creative philosophical work. An "idea is [...] not a concept, it is not philosophy", Deleuze underlines, "[e]ven if one may be able to draw a concept from every idea"; and reversely, while concepts are multiplicities, "not every multiplicity is conceptual" (TRM 318; WP 15). In the most general sense, virtual Ideas are everywhere. They are for Deleuze an immanent organizing principle of the universe (Deleuze reimagines the Platonic notion of Ideas as radically immanent to our reality and as having the logic of multiplicity).[30] Ideas are "problematic" also in how they are experienced or sensed: they may be encountered in things or situations (or ourselves) as that which seems most profound in them—and as such they are all "in need of interpretation" (DR 27). Some may appear demanding and disturbing and force us to really think (PS 95–100; DR 176, 296f, 345; WP 55). Responses to encounters and engagements with problematic Ideas can obviously vary in kind and lead to different results. If philosophy's response is problem work on a plane of immanence that can lead to the creation of concepts, for Deleuze, artists or filmmakers respond with problem work that leads to blocks of sensations or movement/durations.

Note on the Term "Concept" in (Deleuze's Discussion of) Eisenstein

Above, we established that Deleuze distinguishes firmly between philosophical thinking through concepts and cinematic thinking through movement- and time-images, with reference to various statements around the cinema books and at the end of *Cinema 2*. Yet in the seventh chapter of *Cinema 2* ("Thought and Cinema"), Deleuze writes about cinematic expressions of "concepts". Concepts are discussed here as part of a representational thought logic underlying the classical cinema of the movement-image as exemplified by Eisenstein. Such films—however formally inventive and dynamic—tend to indirectly represent an organic totality, a rational whole in the sense of a "concept" that "is presupposed", both as "the logos which unifies the parts" and as a more vague, affective sense of a coherent totality (C2 159). Even "the fundamentally open character of the whole does not compromise [this organic] model, on the contrary", Deleuze writes, since the plurality of images is "internalized in a concept as the whole which integrates them" along with "the ideal of knowledge as harmonious totality". That is, a whole that "forms a knowledge, in the Hegelian fashion, which brings together the image and the concept as two movements each of which goes towards the other" (C2 210, 161; see also 213).

Deleuze, then, uses the term concept in chapter 7 with reference to his notion of representational thought: an understanding of concepts in conflict with his own.

He also references Eisenstein's own use of the term. In Eisenstein concepts appear to come ready-made from the outside and the term seems to have a wide and shifting meaning: he writes about "the transmuting to screen form" of mostly pre-existing abstract conceptions, ideas, viewpoints, or conventions (1949: 125; cf. 25, 30, 37, 58, 60–1, 63). As Peter Wollen notes: "Eisenstein repeatedly tried to cram and squeeze concepts into an artistic form he had already semi-intuitively […] elaborated" (2013 [1969]: 54).[31] While various such conceptions in/for Eisenstein tend to fall under a head concept like the "cosmic celebration of the workers' triumph", the latter is at its most defined a general or abstract idea.[32] And for Deleuze, as stated, philosophical concepts "must not be confused with general or abstract ideas" (WP 24).

PART TWO

The Peculiar 1968 Comment on Godard's New Means

If from his cinema books and onwards Deleuze becomes quite strict about the differences between cinematic forms of thought and philosophical concepts, there is a certain opening for a more radical relation between cinema and philosophy in an earlier comment on Godard he made in a 1968 interview (referenced in the Introduction above):

> Godard transforms cinema by introducing thought into it. He didn't have thoughts on cinema, he doesn't put more or less valid thought into cinema; he starts cinema thinking [or more aptly translated: "he makes cinema think"—*il fait que le cinéma pense*], and for the first time, if I'm not mistaken. Theoretically [*A la limite*], Godard would be capable of filming Kant's *Critique* or Spinoza's *Ethics*, and it wouldn't be abstract cinema or a cinematographic application. Godard knew how to find both a new means and a new "image." (DI 141)

What is said here? The implication seems to be that Godard found new means to do philosophy in and through film. But in what sense? Would the definition of philosophy as concept creation apply here? Or is this statement rather in line with *Cinema 2* in which Godard is central in Deleuze's discussion of the new image of thought in modern cinema, which precisely does not include concept creation? While Deleuze at the end of *Cinema 2* attributes to Godard and other "great cinema authors" the status of philosophers/theorists,[33] this is only in what they say or write outside of their films: "in talking", Deleuze writes, "they become something else, they become philosophers or theoreticians" (C2 280).[34] That is: philosophy can appear when these filmmakers shift to the medium of words, and words only.

The 1968 statement quoted above—which covers the same ground: the relation between thought, cinema, philosophy, and new images—points in a different direction. Although Godard is claimed to have introduced "thought" into cinema, it is assumable that long-time cineaste Deleuze already at this point (later made obvious in his cinema books) considered cinema and its "great cinema authors" to have been thinking long before Godard—representationally or otherwise—and he seems to use the term thought here as a shorthand for philosophical thought, which the references to Kant and Spinoza further indicate. Now, since for Deleuze a philosophical practice contains more aspects than concept creation—conditions for concept creation: grappling with problems, planes of immanence, conceptual personae—Deleuze may have meant that Godard invented filmic means for expressing such other aspects rather than concepts. Or, again, that this concerns the new image of thought that Deleuze repeatedly comes back to in discussions of both philosophy and cinema (while keeping them separated).[35] But that would not really explain the reference to Kant, who for Deleuze especially around 1968 epitomizes the old representational image of thought in philosophy (however much he fractured the cogito through the "pure and empty form of time" or rethought "Ideas as problematising and problematic", for Deleuze Kant's "critique remains dominated by [...] the dogmatic image" [DR 108f, 172, 200, 214ff, 220ff; ECC 29ff; WP 48]). Kant is therefore not exemplifying the new image of thought here, but rather great works of philosophy, and Deleuze describes some of Kant's work in *What is Philosophy?* as "a blast of original concepts" (WP 32). Since Godard did not invent planes of immanence or grappling with problems in cinema, which were already there before, the implication is that he invented means capable of doing philosophy more fully: a plane of immanence "becomes philosophical only through the effect of the concept" (WP 93).

This would only be to say that Godard invented a filmic form with perhaps a yet unrealized potential for philosophical conceptualization (it is therefore not to say that any of Godard's actual films fully realized the potential). If we connect[36] this 1968 statement, then, with Deleuze's later definition of philosophy, we can make a crack in the rationale for his distinction between cinema and philosophy, through which could pass the idea that such filmic new means hold the potential—theoretically, at the limit—for philosophical concept creation. Can Deleuze's definition allow for this? Or does it implicitly tie philosophical concepts to a given actual form, that of words?

The Actual, Concrete Forms of Concepts

This question requires a look at *What is Philosophy?* from an unusual angle. To the three realms defined in relation to each other—philosophy, art, science—we can add a partly implied analytic division between each realm's incorporeal, intensive, or virtual elements and what could be called their actual or material forms. If the incorporeal elements of philosophy include, most generally, planes of immanence, conceptual personae, and concepts, and in art, planes of composition, aesthetic figures, and blocks of sensations, creation in both philosophy and art means (for parts of the process), as Deleuze writes, to "proceed by" some kind of actual form, from which the incorporeal elements are said to be "extracted" (WP 24). Art proceeds by/extracts from many different materials—stone, steel, canvas, paint, etc.—and, slightly less concretely, lines, colors, shapes, etc. The incorporeal elements of a particular painting are unavoidably connected to the paint and the canvas and to its lines and colors—and art is in this way uniquely "preserved" in and through its mostly very concrete material (WP 163ff).[37] And we find a similar structure in the cinema books, in which Deleuze discusses the concrete material forms of the moving image, the film strip, the camera, projection, video technology, etc., in the sense of the "technical means which [for instance] directly carry the time-image" (C2 264). What about the actual forms for the incorporeal elements of philosophy? While philosophy isn't materially preserved in the same sense as art, according to Deleuze, it cannot fully exist (as the art of creating concepts) without being carried by an actual form. Does this form have to be words, and words only?

While Deleuze never addresses this question, he says useful things about the relation between philosophical concepts and words/language. There is the "baptism" of concepts where words come to designate them (words that, outside of or prior to their baptizing function, may be archaic, new, familiar, extraordinary, barbarous, shocking etc.—whatever a specific concept demands) (WP 7f). Philosophy, furthermore, "uses sentences of a standard language", "proceeds by sentences", and "from sentences or their equivalent, philosophy extracts concepts" (WP 80, 24). But Deleuze says nothing about whether words and linguistic sentences are the only actual form available for the baptism and articulation of philosophical concepts. When he argues that philosophy proceeds by sentences, this is part of a paragraph that contrasts how philosophy extracts concepts from language with how science and art extract their incorporeal elements from language. Since art extracts from language only when it uses worded language at all, why would the articulation of philosophical concepts be principally tied to *only* using worded language any more than art? And in stating that philosophy proceeds by sentences "or their equivalent", despite a lack of further elaboration on what such an equivalent could be, do we not have a direct opening from sentences solely made up of words?

Film/Video as Formal Means Not a Particular Thought-Conduct

It makes sense to regard film/video as such an equivalent, as fitting through these openings, only if we think of film/video as a formal means—as moving image with sound, etc.—rather than a field or discipline generalized (with however many subcategories) as cinema or art. If cinema, as Deleuze understands the term, is a category comparable to philosophy, film/video in the sense of moving image with sound, etc., belongs (as established in the Introduction above) to a different *kind* of category—formal means or media—more comparable to a category like the written word. As a formal means, the written word can be used for an open variety of things and by different fields or disciplines—including philosophy, science, and art. The moving image with sound, etc., should be understood to be similarly open to express whatever.

Including original philosophical concepts as Deleuze conceives of them: there is really nothing in his concept of concepts that in principle ties them to words exclusively. They are *implicitly* tied to words only but for no solid reason. And if we define film/video as a formal means, as moving image with sound, etc., instead of as a field or a discipline, then we short-circuit Deleuze's distinction between "having an idea" in cinema/film on the one hand and philosophy on the other (TRM [1987]: 312, 316). This makes it possible in principle to "have an idea" that is philosophically determined as a concept in and through film/video. This would of course entail a renewal of the concrete or actual form of the concept. The abstract logic of concepts, as virtual structures of determination, would on the other hand have to be kept in accordance with Deleuze's definitions, so that it makes sense to call them concepts rather than other kinds of Ideas-multiplicities.

Furthermore, for a filmic structure to be able to carry the virtual levels of a concept (which is what Deleuze actually defines in *What is Philosophy?*) it is not enough to find, as D. N. Rodowick intriguingly does, general similarities between concepts as fragmented open wholes or intensive structures, and filmic or artistic structures (2015: 119f, 127, 133, 136f, 143, 160f). For Deleuze, much in the world is fragmented, open, and intensive, and many things are multiplicities, but few are concepts (as I discussed in Part One above). The cineceptual question would rather be: which filmic structures can create a philosophical film language within film language—to paraphrase Deleuze's notion of a "philosophical language within language" (WP 8)—capable of carrying original concepts (as Deleuze conceives of them)? And instead of talking about film in *general*, or even general image types, we would have to analyze the rare kind of works (or parts of them) that could reasonably be seen as containing such tendencies.

Two Sets of Preliminary Conditions

There are two sets of preliminary conditions or possible foundations for cinecepts implied in statements on Godard in *Cinema 2*. Together they provide a clear setup *for* cinecepts (comparable to how the breakdown of the movement-image, according to Deleuze, provided some of the initial components of the new image of thought, but not the new image of thought itself).

The first set: Deleuze sees a new "analytics" appearing in the works of filmmakers like Godard, Straub-Huillet, and Marguerite Duras. Sound—including speech—stops being a mere component of the visual image and "becomes for itself an autonomous sound image" that also relates more nonlinearly to the visual image. The visual image, on its part, has become readable/legible in itself in its (increasingly layered or stratigraphic) entirety. In the both disjunctive and conjunctive joining of two such autonomous images, auditory and visual, cinema becomes "truly audiovisual" (C2 243–56). Instead of being torn apart by its disjunctive aspect, this audiovisuality "gains a new consistency which depends on a more complex link between the visual image and the sound image", a link that calls to be read (C2 252). The sound-image relation as well as each image individually contain nonlinear links, which make up "differential" connections on various levels capable of expressing virtual or problematic structures. But these expressions are not just following a logic of multiplicity, they also determine multiplicities through an "analytics".

The second set: There are remarkable similarities between Deleuze holding forth classification, reorganization, and recutting as key parts of concept formation (WP e.g. 18; TRM 285–7) and his discussion in *Cinema 2* of Aristotelian categorization as part of Godard's method of filmic thinking (C2 185–7). First, classification and categorization are directly affirmed: they appear as means for a different logic, and not as parts of a mere undermining or parody of traditional representation. In *Difference and Repetition*, Deleuze points to aspects of Aristotle's own conception of categories in which there was "already a new chance for the philosophy of difference" (DR 41). For Aristotle, individual species-differences are all collected under main categories according to a logic of representation. But the main categories themselves relate only under Being, and Being is not a main category in the sense of a genus collecting differences between main categories. The main categories therefore relate as differences without opposition and without a common genus. And while Aristotle still distributes the main categories through a logic of representation in other regards (foremost through analogy),[38] which allows the identities of each to remain, Deleuze finds a fracture here that opens towards a "diversity or otherness" no longer conditioned by representation (DR 41f). In Godard, clearly, the categories are not representationally distributed. They make up divergent series (as made explicit in *Ici et ailleur*: this category AND this category AND…) quite like series of intensive coordinates within mobile systems: problems-multiplicities.[39] Certainly, again, various kinds of Ideas are multiplicities, and only a specific kind of multiplicities are philosophical concepts. But Deleuze says quite a lot that (inadvertently) signals that this *could* be conceptual in nature. On the role of classification in working out a concept, he writes:

> Every classification is similar: they are flexible, their criteria vary according to the cases presented, they have a retroactive effect, and they can be infinitely refined or reorganized. […] In any classification scheme, some things which seem very different are brought closer together, and others which seem very close are separated. This is how concepts are formed. (TRM [1986]: 285f)

Concepts are also formed through cutting and recutting. In *What is Philosophy?* Deleuze specifies how concept formation relates to already existing concepts in this way: "each concept carries out a new cutting-out, takes on new contours, and must be reactivated or recut" (WP 18). Shifting to Deleuze describing categorization and cutting of categories in Godard:

> According to Godard, categories are not fixed once and for all. They are redistributed, reshaped and reinvented for each film. A montage of categories, which is new each time, corresponds to a cutting of categories. The categories must, each time, surprise us, and yet not be arbitrary, must be well founded, and must have strong, indirect relations between themselves […] [And as such they are] categories of problems which introduce reflection into the image itself. (C2 185, 186)

This can in turn be compared to how a concept for Deleuze is "only created as a function of problems which are thought to be badly understood or badly posed"—as we saw above, Deleuze calls this the "pedagogy of the concept"—and to how philosophers "are always recasting and even changing their concepts" because they "create concepts for problems that necessarily change" (WP 16, 21, 28). This can then be further compared to Deleuze's description (with reference to Serge Daney) of a Godardian pedagogy: how Godard is "finding 'theorems' at the edge of 'problems'", is "constantly creating categories", and goes "from problems to categories, even if the categories end up presenting him with a problem again" (C2 185). The Godardian pedagogy means for Deleuze that "we have to read the visual as well as hear the speech-act in a new way" (C2 247). Similarly, a concept, Deleuze writes, "makes us aware of new variations and unknown resonances, it carries out unforeseen cuttings-out" (WP 28). (I continue this comparison, this second set of preconditions for cinecepts, in Chapters 2 and 5).

Curiously, none of this suggests to Deleuze that Godard thereby provides means to articulate concepts in and through film. Godard is instead implicitly fitted into the following general category of time-image thought: non-chronological figures of time and the revelation of a certain "powerlessness" in thought, which is to say, thought's troublesome encounter with the problematic. It seems that Godard must be put into this category for Deleuze's more general distinctions between cinematic thinking and philosophical conceptualization to work. But there is nothing stopping us from "recutting" and "reorganizing" these categories, without really breaking with Deleuze's overall thought.

Moving Images, Sounds, Words, Texts

If concepts determine multiplicities, and if multiplicities are mobile and heterogeneous compounds of intensive components, would it not make sense to conduct the determination also through concrete forms that are mobile and heterogeneous more so than words? At this point it may be easy to say, sure, why not, but we should recall here, with reference to the Preface and Introduction above, that this has nothing to do with opposing images to words. Words are plentiful in Godard, certainly in Sonimage. And not just speech: as Johnathan Lahey Dronsfield (2010) argues, "the written word has been no more fully and comprehensively introduced into cinema than by Godard".[40] To also reconnect with the second set of preconditions above: "It is often the case", Deleuze writes about Godard, "that the written word indicates the category, while the visual images constitute the series: hence the very special primacy of the word over the image and the presentation of the screen as blackboard" (C2 185). When John Drabinski claims that Godard's late 1960s films show "a philosophical promise" that "becomes philosophy brought to a dense, polysemic cinematic language in the 1970s and after" (2010: 4), we can add that many of them also become increasingly saturated with written words within the frame. Not as added to or determining/being determined by the image (in for instance a Barthian sense),[41] but as woven into time-based, moving audiovisual complexes, in which words and texts become more or less filmic components. As Drabinski writes elsewhere, "cinema promises to fold words, images, and things into one another" (2008: 4). Filmic words and texts can thereby take on different senses than in non-filmic forms of speaking or writing. Obviously, none of this necessarily makes things more *philosophical*. Case in point is the comparing of Sonimage with *Histoire(s) du cinéma* (1989–98). In the latter work, written words are plentiful and often part of even more complex audiovisual compounds, but this also pushes the expression of ideas more towards art and poetry. As Georges Didi-Huberman writes about *Histoire(s)*: "Godard is constantly summoning words to be read, to be seen, or to be heard" in a relation that "must then be understood as repeated collision between words and images" in which "images jostle together making words suddenly appear, words jostle making images suddenly appear, images and words collide making thought take place visually" (2008 [2003]: 138–9). While I find Didi-Huberman to overstate the colliding or jostling aspect, he helps underline the centrality of words in this work and how its thought is more poetic than cineceptual. Still, *Histoire(s)*'s formal inventions can serve as a *resource* for the concrete articulation of cinecepts (more on this in Chapter 5), including its manner of integrating words.

Are words necessary for cinecepts? And if so, serving which functions? Perhaps words help make the philosophical/theoretical aspects more explicit: it is hard to deny that words, regardless of their own ways of being polysemous, arbitrary, and shifting in cultural-historical determination, *generally tend* to be more exact, or *less* polysemic than images, and that words in combination with images tend to direct emphasis (although even such a hedging, general division, or should we say dualism, can be deconstructed—and I will come back to a simpler problematization of it in Chapter 6).[42] We are at least used and trained (if not cognitively wired) to practice and perceive words and images along such lines. Words will likely also for a long time remain the clearest links to the history of philosophy—and such links are needed: however original, no concept is original in an *ex nihilo* sense. As Deleuze writes, "every concept always has a history", "there are usually bits or components that come from other concepts", and a "concept requires not only a problem through which it recasts or replaces earlier concepts but a junction of problems where it combines with other coexisting concepts" (WP 15, 18; see also DR xix).[43] As concepts relate to other concepts in this way, words may be needed also since most prior philosophical concepts (still) come in the form of words, and words only.

Overall, film / video / audiovisual media with its multiple parts—images, graphics, montage, sounds, words, texts—could provide means for at least two kinds of formal development of philosophy: 1) Extended parameters for "recast[ing] or replac[ing] earlier concepts".[44] 2) Extended parameters for making up actual structures capable of carrying the virtual components of concepts: from words-only to the more differentiated structure of moving audiovisual compounds, in which various parts of such compounds might carry with more direct nuance the components of the concrete problem and the components as determined in the concept. While they do not directly map on to each other, there might be clear connections between specific actual audiovisual components and specific virtual components, through how the latter are "extracted" from the former—as with Deleuze's example of the "I" in Descartes' concept of the cogito having a specific virtual function (see discussion of this above). We cannot determine in advance or generalize on which audiovisual parameter could do what in such regards. But words, through being generally less polysemic than images and through their natural link to the history of philosophy (and scholarship in general), may function well as concrete carriers of main points around which the cinecept condenses (and which traverse it in a state of survey). This obviously does not mean (given the discussion above) that the word-point is a generality that the other audiovisual parameters fall in line under as affective backing or illustrational extension. It would also not mean assigning the word a strict role in a linear division of labor. Rather, it would be woven into an audiovisual constellation that as a whole carries a conceptual multiplicity.

In a 1976 text, Deleuze says about Godard's "aural images" that on the one hand they "don't seem to have any priority" over visual images, but that on the other hand, "some of [these aural images] have an *other side* you can call whatever you like, ideas, meaning, language, expressive aspects, and so on [and they] are thus able to contract or capture other images or a series of other images" (N [1976] 42, emphasis in original). Deleuze here mostly means how words can dictate our perception, the voice or text steering what is important in the images, and in an ordering and even dominating way (which makes us see less in the images, as opposed to Godard's aim of making us see more in the image). Still, such contraction could be reimagined as indicating the point at which a concept condenses. Although, given the extent to which words and images are at times spiraling around and over each other (albeit less so in Sonimage than in some of Godard's later work), and given his preference for (clear) images and suspicion of dictating text (at least in theory), it would certainly be reasonable to also see images—perhaps interchangeably—as carriers of such condensing main points that traverse the rest (through montage). In any case, given that film/video is a hybrid and temporal medium that is literally in movement, there would be an unavoidable formal renewal in general of the concrete form of the concept.

While Tempted, Deleuze Did Not Make Films

The cinecept reconditions the idea of a formal renewal of philosophy, as described from the Preface to this point, and I will end Chapter 1 with a concrete case that might exemplify why this could be needed. Deleuze's own ongoing quest to find new means of expression culminated in a failure to find a form for a late book on his concept of the virtual. As Raymond Bellour explains:

> In the last words that we exchanged, in the summer before his death, Deleuze evoked […] the difficulties he was having with his book on the virtual, of which only a few pages exist. He said he was looking for a form. To this end, he listened to music (Ravel). And then he said, "I am not going to write fragments after

all." No, not fragments, as this had been done so inventively by Nietzsche, but something new, to go beyond, beyond the shares that had already been touched. (Bellour 2010: 11)[45]

It would be too much of a stretch to speculate on whether film/video could have offered a formal solution for Deleuze in this case. Not just because we do not know exactly what he found so hard to express, but also because he was not trained as a filmmaker. Still, as Godard once quipped with reference to *Cinema* (and with echoes from Alexandre Astruc):[46] "All those philosophers, it's a pity they didn't make cinema ... Deleuze was tempted, but instead of making a film, he wrote 'a book about'" (Godard and Ishaghpour (2005 [1999]: 46). Godard himself—filmmaker extraordinaire and maker of famously philosophically inclined films—may have provided a method for "how film could express something", as Harun Farocki stated in 1981, but as he added, only as an "abstract, empty possibility" and that therefore "the real work has not yet begun" (1990 [1981]: 161). While much work does remain, this book has a more generous conception of Godard-Miéville's Sonimage period: as providing key preliminary conditions for cinecepts and as formulating embryonic cinecepts. This is what I will begin to look at in Chapter 2 and examine more directly in Chapter 4.

Notes

1 For Deleuze reorganization is a key part of forming concepts, and I return to what this entails towards the end of the chapter.
2 While Deleuze does say in a 1983 interview that "concepts themselves are already images; they are images of thought", he still conceives of concepts as images and filmic images as different modalities of thought expression; as he also says here: "Philosophy is about concepts. [...] Film creates another kind [of image]: movement-images and time-images" (TRM 213). Second, Deleuze will in his later more detailed definitions of concepts and images of thought, separate them as different (however intertwined) aspects of philosophy, in which an image of thought is the terrain that orients philosophical ideas as they emerge, most generally in the sense of a set of preconceptual assumptions about what it means to think (the latter of course also refers back to Deleuze's critique of the image of thought in the 1960s).
3 Ronald Bogue suggests instead that the absence of explicit discussion of cinema in *What is Philosophy?* may be explained by "the fact that cinema blurs the line between philosophy and the arts, a line Deleuze [is] intent on sharpening in *What is Philosophy?*" (2010: 128). Bogue, however, does not expand on how such a line is blurred (or why it would be more blurred than the line between philosophy and literature) or, most importantly, how this would relate to Deleuze's definition of

philosophy as the art of creating concepts. Furthermore, in a 1989 interview with Claire Parnet, Deleuze discusses both the ideas of great filmmakers and his work on *What is Philosophy?*, and not only confirms his view that these filmmakers are not doing philosophy, he also clearly implies that what they do belongs to the category of art in the sense of the three-part schema—philosophy / art / science—he is developing (ABC Letter I).

4 Deleuze: "The concept is the beginning of philosophy, but the plane is its instituting. The plane is clearly not a program, design, end, or means: it is a plane of immanence that constitutes the absolute ground of philosophy, its earth or deterritorialization, the foundation on which it creates its concepts. Both the creation of concepts and the instituting of the plane are required, like two wings or fins. [...] Precisely because the plane of immanence is prephilosophical and does not immediately take effect with concepts, it implies a sort of groping experimentation and its layout resorts to measures that are not very respectable, rational, or reasonable" (WP 41). See also Jeffery Bell's reading of the prephilosophical plane of immanence as a problematic structure / space / plane / field (2016: 16, 20, 75f, 85, 93, 102, 124, 134, 160).

5 Conceptual personae are "halfway between concept and preconceptual plane, passing from one to the other." They perform movements and "show territories" on the plane of thought, are "agents of enunciation" as well as "possibilities of life or modes of existence"; they also express the "powers" of the concept, and "through them concepts are not only thought but perceived and felt." Sometimes they have proper names (e.g. Socrates) and at other times they are "nameless and subterranean" (WP 61, 65, 63, 69, 131, 73). While Deleuze states that "concepts need" conceptual personae in the sense that they "play a role in their definition" and that the "conceptual persona and the plane of immanence presuppose each other" (WP 2, 77, 75; see also 160), I find their necessity to be less than entirely clear—*must* there *always* be conceptual personae for there to be concepts or is it more the case that they have tended to play key roles throughout the history of philosophy? Furthermore, conceptual personae seem to refer to four/five different things: 1) actual characters in the philosophical-literary presentation (e.g. Socrates, Zarathustra); 2) a type with a particular function on a given plane (e.g. the Idiot, the Madman, the Friend, the Judge); 3) a character type coinciding with the concept itself (e.g. the respective concepts of the priest in Spinoza, Nietzsche, and Foucault); 4a) the character of the philosophy or mode of the philosopher (e.g. Leibniz as a "lawyer" for God or Kant as an "investigator" in a tribunal), and 4b) the slightly more general and implicit manner that a concept is "signed" by a philosopher (WP 23f). (This can be gleaned also by complementing *What is Philosophy?* in this regard with what Deleuze says in *L'Abécédaire* Letters J, K, L.)

6 How they differ: while "pure percepts and affects" concern "the arts", Deleuze writes, "there are specifically philosophical perceptions and affections" or "sensibilia

of the concept" (WP 130). And although aesthetic figures "are sensations", and "there are sensations of concepts and concepts of sensations", they "are not the same", "not the same [kind of] becoming": "Conceptual becoming is heterogeneity grasped in an absolute form; sensory becoming is otherness caught in a matter of expression" (WP 177). We may also note a similar stance in Adorno. He sees aesthetic aspects of philosophy—as expressed in the form of the essay—as being distinct from artistic expression: "the essay has something like an aesthetic autonomy that is easily accused of being simply derived from art, although it is distinguished from art by its medium, concepts, and by its claim to a truth devoid of aesthetic semblance" (1991 [1958]: 5; see also 18).

7 I read as the cinematic equivalent of such "half philosophy" Deleuze's labeling of Resnais's films as a marriage [*noce*] between philosophy and cinema (C2 209).

8 What about all the philosophical labor that does not amount to concept creation or that does not primarily aim for or center around concept creation, is that not philosophy? Deleuze's answer is two-fold: A) Yes, if you work through the history of philosophy in the sense of an "apprenticeship in [...] the constitution of problems and the creation of concepts", or B) you are doing philosophy badly which is really to say not at all: "The bad [philosopher] creates no concepts, is someone who uses ready-made ideas [...] puts forth opinions", and we "never know what problems they're talking about", "at most, one knows the questions, but not the problems behind certain questions", and if "you have neither a concept nor a problem [...] you aren't doing philosophy" (ABC Letter H).

9 There is in *Difference and Repetition* a closeness in general to certain Hegelian terms and themes. On the one hand this indicates, as Anne Sauvagnargues shows, "how close-knit his thought is with Hegel's" despite their key differences (2013: 47). On the other hand, as Somers-Hall writes, "Deleuze often uses Hegelian language to show that the same problem [...] is being addressed by the two philosophers, but he also often does so in the spirit of parody, with the intent of showing the distance between their approaches to this problem" (2012: 1f). And as Jean-Clet Martin says, "it is impossible to find in Hegel what Deleuze deploys from the perspective of another 'image of thought.' [...] [W]e are on very different terrains, on milieus that cannot be superimposed. The ethologies of their concepts cannot be compared with one another because their images of thought are incompatible"; while also describing Hegel as Deleuze's most "worthy" enemy, who in some respects and in some philosophical situations may even function "as a partner", especially if (re)read "in a Deleuzian way" (2013 [2010]: 226, 230, 243).

10 For comprehensive such examinations, which also go outside Deleuze's own conceptions of this relation, see Somers-Hall (2012); Houle and Vernon eds. (2013).

11 Hegel is also directly important to juxtapose to Deleuze here since Deleuze will later hold up Hegel as one of two (Schelling being the other) "philosophers who paid most attention to the concept as philosophical reality" (WP 11).

12 A general point in Deleuze's critique is that Hegel, to quote Anne Sauvagnargues, "pursues a philosophy of representation despite his claim to be breaking from it" (2013: 43). For a more developed examination of this aspect of Deleuze's critique see Somers-Hall (2012).

13 This kind of preservation of identity includes dividing the genus while "suppress[ing] division in the species" (DR 56). On how Leibniz's version of orgiastic representation contrasts in this regard, and how it even conceives of pure differential relations beyond contradiction, while still in the end converging things into negativity and the subordination of difference to identity, see DR 56–64.

14 A standard defense of Hegel is to reconceive of Deleuze's *divergence* from Hegel as itself a Hegelian negation, so that Deleuze can be seen to merely confirm Hegel's larger system. This defence relies on the negative playing ground that Deleuze undermines and goes beyond (e.g. DR 64ff, 253–60; see also Hardt 1993: xi–xii, xv, 1ff, 28f, 37f, 50ff). That is, Deleuze's critique is part of an effort to undercut the idea of negation as a fundamental mechanism of reality and to establish a terrain of thought with a different logic.

15 DR e.g. 231, 254. In what sense are Ideas / Problems / Multiplicities synonymous here? Deleuze: "Ideas are genuine objectivities, made up of differential elements and relations and provided with a specific mode—namely, the 'problematic'. Problems thus defined do not designate any ignorance on the part of a thinking subject, any more than they express a conflict, but rather objectively characterise the nature of Ideas as such. […] Problems-Ideas are positive multiplicities" (DR 335f).

16 Deleuze: "Problems-Ideas are […] full and differentiated positivities described by the process of complete and reciprocal determination" (DR 336). And as such they combine a "progressive and serial" differentiation with a temporality of "progressive determination" (267, 348, 269). The relations are thereby both determined and unstatic: "[T]he differential relation […] integrates variation, not as a variable determination of a supposedly constant relation ('variability') but, on the contrary, as a degree of variation of the relation itself ('variety') […] If the Idea eliminates variability, this is in favour of what must be called variety or multiplicity" (219). (Cf. Deleuze's later discussion of variation, variables, varieties in *What is Philosophy?*; see note 25 below.)

17 Deleuze: "Intensity is the form of difference […] Every intensity is differential, by itself a difference. Every intensity is E-E´ where E itself refers to an *e-e´* and *e* to ε-ε´ etc.: each intensity is already a coupling (in which each element of the couple refers in turn to couples of elements of another order), thereby revealing the properly qualitative content of quantity. We call this state of infinitely doubled difference which resonates to infinity *disparity*." (DR 281).

18 On "autounification" see LS 118. On these relations forming potentials: "[T]he differential relation presents a third element, that of pure potentiality. Power is

the form of reciprocal determination according to which variable magnitudes are taken to be functions of one another", "where at least one is of a power superior to another"; so that if each "differential is [...] pure power", "the differential relation is a pure element of potentiality" (DR 221f).

19 Interestingly, Deleuze still conceives of this as *dialectics*: one that is "superior" and non-negative. He describes such a dialectic as "the art of problems and questions"; "the internal character of the problem as such [...] its intrinsic genetic power: that is, the very object of the dialectic or combinatory, the 'differential'"; "this is the aim of dialectics as a superior calculus or combinatory." Deleuze still of course firmly upholds his critique of *negative* dialectics: "Whenever the dialectic 'forgets' its intimate relation with Ideas in the form of problems [...] and falls under the sway of [...] a simple confrontation between opposing, contrary or contradictory, propositions", the "dialectic loses its peculiar power" (DR 196, 226f, 198, 200f, 203f, 237). On Deleuze affirming a dialectics of problems, see also Smith (2012 [2001]: 59) and Sauvagnargues (2013: 43). Relatedly, in need of further examination is Deleuze's quick but intriguingly favorable referencing in *What is Philosophy?* of Adorno's concept of negative dialectics (WP 99).

20 Deleuze: "A problem does not exist, apart from its solutions. Far from disappearing in this overlay, however, it insists and persists in these solutions. A problem is determined at the same time as it is solved, but its determination is not the same as its solution [...] it consists in a system of ideal liaisons or differential relations between genetic elements" which "are incarnated in the actual relations which do not resemble them and are defined by the field of solution" (DR 203, see also 231).

21 Deleuze: "[I]t is entirely true that difference is cancelled qualitatively and in extension. It is nevertheless an illusion, since the nature of difference lies neither in the quality by which it is covered nor in the extensity by which it is explicated" (DR 335). But actualization still entails "movement by which difference in intensity is cancelled", and it is not "apparently cancelled", it "is really cancelled, but outside itself, in extensity and underneath quality" (300).

22 This is not to say that Deleuze ever adopts such a method as part of his own thought. Benjamin Noys, relatedly, finds aspects in post-1968 Deleuze that affirmatively engage or connect with Marxist thinkers of negativity that "could perhaps have enriched" the "strategic possibilities of Deleuze's thinking." This does not happen, Noys argues, since Deleuze continued with a "language of the positive" and "dubious affirmation of ontological power" (2010: 70; 51–74). Noys, however, appears only to recognize what goes beyond his own frame of the negative through that negative frame: what goes beyond is an opposite—pure positivity. What cannot be seen through this frame is how Deleuze is hardly affirmative as a mere opposite of negation, and how he alters the logic of things like critique and polemic away from a logic of the negative (although negativity is certainly kept in the broad sense of examination from a stance of conflict and challenge) to critically

grasping problems that have been badly understood—more on this in the next paragraph—but also through creation in the mode of the *untimely* or what he would later refer to as utopian resistance to the present (more on the latter towards the end of Chapter 3).

23 For Deleuze this is also an ethical and political concern: "none of this would amount to much were it not for the moral presuppositions and practical implications of [the negative] distortion. We have seen all that this valorisation of the negative signified, including the conservative spirit of such an enterprise [...] Contradiction is not the weapon of the proletariat but, rather, the manner in which the bourgeoisie defends and preserves itself, the shadow behind which it maintains its claim to decide what the problems are. Contradictions are not 'resolved', they are dissipated by capturing the problem of which they reflect only the shadow. The negative is always a conscious reaction, a distortion of the true agent or actor" (DR 337).

24 WP 19. This logic of *ad infinitum* is spelled out in more detail in *Difference and Repetition* (143–4); regarding intensities specifically, see 281. That book, furthermore, already conceived of "concepts [as] intensities from the point of view of philosophical systems" (144). The view of concepts as intensities in a more general or affective sense was there from Deleuze's first academic encounter with philosophy as a teenager: "When I learned [...] that there were such strange things called 'concepts,' that had the same effect on me as, for some other people, the encounter with [...] a great literary character from a novel [...] When I learned that, I don't know, even things like 'What did Plato call an "idea"?,' that seemed to me to be as lively, as animated" (ABC Letter E).

25 This order generally accords with the previously established logic of multiplicity, including the lack of spatiotemporal coordinates: The "reciprocal determinations" within the virtual Idea are said to be "non-localisable" also in *Difference and Repetition* (231). For how Deleuze distinguishes between how "chaotic variability" is respectively wrested into the determined "variations" of philosophical concepts, the determined "variables" of scientific functions, and the determined "varieties" of artistic sensations, see WP 202f, 204–11, 215. (Cf. note 16 above.)

26 "Here concepts link up with each other, support one another, coordinate their contours, articulate their respective problems, and belong to the same philosophy, even if they have different histories" (WP 18). It seems that such coexistence of concepts can also include a kind of supporting concepts that are not quite full philosophical concepts on their own. This is implied for instance in Deleuze's descriptions in *L'Abécédaire* of his and Guattari's respective concepts of territory and deterritorialization: "we really created a concept, nearly a philosophical concept, with the idea of territory"; and later on he implicitly contrasts this with a related concept that is more fully a philosophical concept: "we constructed a concept [...] of 'deterritorialization.' [...] a beautiful case of a philosophical concept"; and "there is no territory, territorialization without a vector of exiting the territory [...] that

is, deterritorialization" (ABC Letter A). This aspect of external determination of concepts in Deleuze, furthermore, has some similarities with Adorno's notion of how each concept in a philosophical essay is "articulated through its configuration with the others" and how the concepts together form a larger "constellation" that is "a force field" (1991 [1958]: 13, see also 16f).

27 For some concretion about this aspect, see the bibliography for *Difference and Repetition*, which Deleuze starts with a long note discussing how he selects which references to include in the finished work despite having treated and only implicitly referenced much more material (DR 381f).

28 A) Deleuze had a documented way of working out ideas through teaching classes about subjects he wrote about. B) His famous aversion to discussion aside, there were certainly direct and indirect critical examinations by peers, of which a published formal example is a seminar talk on aspects of his work in chapters 4 and 5 in *Difference and Repetition* followed by questioning by senior scholars (DI 94–116, 300).

29 For Deleuze virtual events (that concepts "speak") are "inseparable from the state of affairs, bodies, and lived reality in which [they are] actualized or brought about" (WP 159) and concepts "refer to things that are extremely simple, extremely concrete […] There are no philosophical concepts that do not refer to non-philosophical coordinates" (ABC Letter D). But concepts are not themselves actual: "through concepts, philosophy continually extracts a consistent event from the state of affairs—a smile without the cat, as it were" (and, in contrast, "through functions, science continually actualizes the event in a state of affairs, thing, or body that can be referred to") (WP 126).

30 Deleuze: "problematic Ideas are precisely the ultimate elements of nature" (DR 205). For how Deleuze actually salvages a lot from Plato in this regard, see DR 71–7, 206; on what is still "overturned", see 79ff, 110, 154–6, 177ff; and for his own worked out concept of virtual Ideas see Chapter 3 below as an extension of what is said above in this chapter, and DR chs. 4 and 5; see also Smith (2006a). To set the general move in relation to Plato into further relief, we could also briefly compare it with contrasting ways of undermining more classical ideas of essences beyond phenomena, whether in the Platonic sense of the Forms or the Kantian thing in-itself beyond what we can experience or know: to instead say that they do not exist, that there is *nothing* there. Such a claim is commonly attributed to Hegel, see for instance Slavoj Žižek's—albeit somewhat idiosyncratic Lacanian—early interpretation of Hegel that discusses both Plato and Kant in these senses (2008 [1989]: 222–5; 231–3). In contrast, Deleuze undermines the classic idea of essences by conceiving of them as mobile virtual multiplicities, "the noumenon closest to the phenomenon", as being immanent parts of our reality, but also as being reachable and philosophically conceptualizable (DR 280; DI 115).

31 Wollen furthermore argues that this eventually led to a "full-scale retreat from" Eisenstein's ambition to "express scientific concepts in film" and an increased focus on "affective logic" and "Pavlovian reflexology" in combination with a "Hegelian dialectics, mechanically applied and eventually degenerating into an empty stereotype" (2013 [1969]: 56f, 37).

32 Ronald Bogue provides this as an example of such an overarching "concept" (2003: 169). Or as Roland Barthes writes, "the obvious meaning, in Eisenstein, is always the revolution" (1977 [1970]: 56).

33 Deleuze here basically equates philosophy and theory. As Rodowick writes: "A slippage is obvious here, with theory standing in for philosophy" (2015: 109).

34 In contrast, after having just talked about doing philosophy through forms *beyond* words, Godard himself says in 1980: "I am a philosopher" (1985: 411).

35 For comprehensive discussions of Deleuze's notions of new and old images of thought in both philosophy and cinema, see Rodowick (1997: 170–93); Paola Marrati (2008 [2003]); Bellour (2010); Lambert (2012); Nilsson (2014).

36 This connection—following a brief suggestion by Drabinski (who also references Deleuze's 1968 statement on Godard)—is additionally supported by Ian Buchanan's idea (setting up his quest to re-read Deleuze's cinema project from the perspective of schizoanalysis) that "we reject this specious segmentation of Deleuze's corpus and instead take seriously Deleuze's demand that we take an author 'as a whole'", so that there "is nothing to stop us as readers from joining the dots ourselves" (2008: 14, 2).

37 What about conceptual art? See note 2 in the Introduction above.

38 And altogether through what Deleuze calls "the four iron collars of representation: identity in the concept, opposition in the predicate, analogy in judgement and resemblance in perception" (DR 330).

39 On series, and "resonating" or "communication between heterogeneous" or "disparate" or "divergent" series, as a key part of Deleuze's logic of problems or virtual multiplicities, see DR 143–51.

40 Lahey Dronsfield, in a close but also critical dialogue with Deleuze, goes somewhat further than Deleuze in ascribing importance to the written word as seen in the frame in Godard. Lahey Dronsfield argues that the disjunctive-conjunctive relation is not only between the audio image and the visual image (with uttered words part of the former and written words as part of the latter), which according to Lahey Dronsfield is Deleuze's conception. Lahey Dronsfield sees the disjunctive-conjunctive relation as including a third (at least partly) autonomous image of the written word, which concerns "showing words on the screen" that are "repeating as an image a word spoken" in a manner that "displaces the word" as speech act (and vice versa), and that through a "play of the separateness and non-separateness of image and text" along such lines, in which images "have to pass through the word" and vice versa, "the text is confronted with itself as an image" and vice versa,

in ways that make "sensible something about the text[/image] that would be otherwise invisible or inaudible", all for the sake of trying to "renew it in its possibility" (Lahey Dronsfield 2010). On the centrality of worded language in all its forms in Godard's films, see also Leutrat (2000: 179).

41 That is, they would not simply serve as anchorage or relay in the Barthian sense of words restricting or steering the meaning of otherwise polysemous images (Barthes 1977 [1964]: 38ff). See also Wollen (2013 [1969]: 99f).

42 A key premise here is not so much how images can carry defined meaning—e.g. various film-theoretical ideas about how cinematic images can articulate meaning by being their own kind of language and/or sign systems—as how words are not always more defined in their practical use. Pasolini, for instance, argues on the one hand that filmmakers create "meaningful im[age]-signs" that make up languages (albeit without a fixed "set of grammatical rules" or even an ability to express abstract concepts), through the means of "brute reality"—in contrast to the writer who makes new meaning from words already found in dictionaries and that make up an "already extremely elaborate" and "historically complex and mature system" (2005 [1965]: 169–72). But on the other hand, even though cinematic image-signs are thereby formulated from a material that is "pregrammatical" and even "irrational", Pasolini underlines how words in film do not necessarily make things more clear or literal: he reminds us of "the 'ambiguity'" and the "polyexpressiveness of the poetic word", and how poetry means "semantic expansion" which "derails, deforms, propagates [...] meaning" (2005 [1969]: 264f). And as Rancière, from a different theoretical (and historical) perspective, writes about images and words in art: "There is visibility that does not amount to an image; there are images which consist wholly in words [...] Words describe what the eye might see or express what it will never see; they deliberately clarify or obscure an idea" (2009 [2003]: 7).

43 A concept is a distinct consistency that is also subject to change on several levels. First, a concept "has a becoming", Deleuze writes, "that involves its relationship with concepts situated on the same plane" (WP 18). Second, concepts are themselves becomings or "pure events" in the sense that they have a virtual rather than an actual or historical constitution (WP 110). Third, concepts are "dated, signed, and baptized" while also "remaining subject to constraints of renewal, replacement, and mutation that give philosophy a history as well as a turbulent geography" (WP 8). So concepts "constantly change" in this sense: over time there have been points of renewal, replacement, and mutation, which, I should add, is not the same as constant flux: when a concept is renewed something happens that is not quite the same as the becoming of concepts between points of renewal (the kind of differentiation I just made there is explored further in Chapter 3). See also Smith (2012b: 62–73).

44 WP 18. The cinecept as *a formal structure* could also be used as a means to retrieve aspects of the history of philosophy—I thank one of the reviewers of the proposal

for this book for this suggestion—and without necessarily forming new original concepts, but rather as new form for learning and working through. Not, then, in the sense of using old concepts to create a new concept, as Deleuze describes here: "the history of philosophy is completely without interest if it does not undertake to awaken a dormant concept and to play it again on a new stage, even if this comes at the price of turning it against itself" (WP 83). But rather something humbler: in *L'Abécédaire* Deleuze recognizes the following as a kind of exception to the requirement of concept creation: the working through of the history of philosophy in the sense of an "apprenticeship in [...] the constitution of problems and the creation of concepts" (ABC Letter H).

45 Although according to Dosse (with reference to David Lapoujade), the book had a working title (*Ensembles and Multiplicities*) and its two first chapters were written: his final text published as "Immanence: A Life" and a text in the appendix to *Dialogues* called "The Actual and the Virtual" (see Dosse (2010 [2007]: 454f). It seems clear, however, that the latter text is only a rough draft; see D 171, translators note 1.

46 In his famous essay on the camera pen, Astruc argues that "a Descartes of today would already have shut himself up in his bedroom with a 16mm camera and some film, and would be writing his philosophy on film: for his *Discours de la Methode* would today be of such a kind that only the cinema could express it satisfactorily" (2014 [1948]: 605).

2 Setting the Stage: *2 or 3 Things, Le gai savoir,* and *Ici et ailleurs*

> Godard is perhaps the only director today who is interested in "philosophical films" and possesses an intelligence and discretion equal to the task. Other directors have had their "views" on contemporary society and the nature of our humanity; and sometimes their films survive the ideas they propose. Godard is the first director fully to grasp the fact that, in order to deal seriously with ideas, one must create a new film language for expressing them—if the ideas are to have any suppleness and complexity.
>
> Susan Sontag (2001 [1964]: 207)

This chapter examines three films that were key for the development of the formal logic of Sonimage. As indicated by the 1964 quote from Sontag above, Godard showed already from the beginning an unusual ability to create new filmic forms for expressing philosophical ideas. In the films between 1960 and 1966, however, the philosophy was—*relative to* his own later work—expressed more through characters and themes in partly more narrative works. Two of the three films examined in this chapter are from the period just after the first—*2 or 3 Things I Know About Her* (*2 ou 3 choses que je sais d'elle*, 1967) and *Le gai savoir* (1969 [1968])[1]—and the third is the first completed Sonimage film, *Ici et ailleurs* (*Here and Elsewhere*, 1975).[2] They each add to the development of a logic of formal organization that makes possible embryonic cinecepts in (later) Sonimage.

A Complex Is Not Chaos: *2 or 3 Things I Know About Her*

2 or 3 Things is a semi-narrative essay film that bridges Godard's new wave period and his increasingly non-narrative and more explicitly philosophical later periods (it was also released the year before Deleuze implied that Godard had invented a film language capable of directly carrying original philosophical thought—see Chapter 1). The film deals with relations between seeing, words, and thinking, and how we can know things. The "her" in the title refers to the main character, the actress who plays her, the suburban call-girl, a Paris housing project, Paris at large, the Vietnam War, the circulation of ideas, consumer capitalism, and the cosmos. My main concern here, however, are the ways through which advanced thought is directly expressed. There are concrete aspects such as Godard's whispered voice-over, him feeding lines and questions to the actors wearing earpieces, and the montage of images, sounds, and voices. But the primary focus here is the general *logic* of how the ideas and forms are woven together (*Le gai savoir* and *Ici et ailleurs* are subjected to more formal analysis below). *2 or 3 Things* is art, I should first say, just as much as it is a partly new kind of philosophical essay film. Some of the audiovisuals are semi-interruptive, on a purely visceral level, and some of the ideas and thinking patterns are improvised and nonlinear. Douglas Morrey makes some similar observations in a perceptive text about ideas in the film, while also, however, implying that its structuring of thought is comparable to chaos:

> Thought emerges not as an ordered sequence, but as a chaotic jumble; it seems impossible to fix attention on one thought without another interrupting it. And this sense of chaos and interference constantly greets the spectator seeking knowledge […] Rather than present us with images, sounds and ideas that can be immediately recognized and assimilated to our pre-existing categories of understanding, [*2 or 3 Things*] forces us to confront the difficulty of making sense of the world, the violence which accompanies the process of learning. Often Godard will cut into an image or a sound that is not instantly recognisable and present us with a pure, unassimilable difference. (Morrey 2005: 68)

While *2 or 3 Things* may have some such qualities, its thought structures are clearly not reducible to them.[3] First, this film is hardly *that* jumbled—no more so than many of Godard's earlier films, or in comparison to the discordance of certain later films like *Film Socialisme* (2010), *Goodbye to Language* (2014), or *The Image Book* (2018). More significantly, thought that does not follow an "ordered sequence" and cannot be immediately "assimilated to our pre-existing categories of understanding"—even if a bit audiovisually interruptive at times—is not always best described as "chaotic".[4] Thought in *2 or 3 Things* is structured rather according to what Godard at the time (with loose inspiration from mathematics) called a *complex*. A look into what he means by this will begin to point us towards a definition of the basic tenets of a logic of structure that will be formally refined in Sonimage.[5]

Godard famously does not write scripts in any usual sense of the term, and *2 or 3 Things* is perhaps unusually characterized by the approach of "improvis[ing] as shooting goes on" (Godard 1986 [1968]: 238). Two clarifications must be made here, for which Godard's own contemporaneous statements are useful:

1. Such on-set "improvisation", he says, "can only work if the ground has been thoroughly thought out in advance, and it needs absolute concentration" (2020 [1967]: 37). He describes the preparation for *2 or 3 Things* as "much more ambitious" than a film he did simultaneously (*Made in USA*), thematically and "on the level of pure research". Such intellectual preparation is required, then, for the "concentration" in the filmmaking. The research also continues throughout the filmmaking and with audiovisual means, and through philosophical questioning and reflexive directions, to the point that Godard says *2 or 3 Things* "isn't a film" so much as "part of my personal research" (1986 [1968]: 238, 239).
2. Perhaps most importantly, in Godard a significant portion of the thinking occurs at the editing table. This is not only key for tying the research and on-set thinking into larger filmic structures of thought; thinking also continues here or in some regards even begins here (as indicated by the well-known Godardian notion of "thinking with the hands"). Later Godard works, certainly the Sonimage videos, are increasingly created at the editing table.

These two things are important to keep in mind: 1) the seeming "jumble" of thought-ingredients improvised during the shooting of *2 or 3 Things* are improvised in ways that concentrate and extend the ambitious research (a bit similar to how improvisation in jazz is rooted in deep familiarity with the material and in clear, however intuitive, ideas about where to take it, rather than a mere mess-making of a previous order); 2) Godard's on-set improvisations are later subjected to further thought at the editing table and woven into larger audiovisual idea structures.

This can be regarded as a setup for producing thought that is both coherent (or at least not incoherent) while also not directly recognizable in its structure. How could such thought be understood as *structure*? I will move towards an answer first by continuing with Godard's own statements on *2 or 3 Things*. The film approaches *things* as complexes and is itself composed as a complex. As he says, even on the level of telling a kind of story:

> the story of Juliette [...] will not be told continuously, because not only she, but the events of which she is part, are to be described. It is a matter of describing 'a complex'. This 'complex' and its parts (Juliette being the one I have chosen to examine in greater detail, in order to suggest that the other parts also exist in depth) must

be described and talked about as both objects and subjects. [As] all things exist both from the inside and the outside. (Godard 1986 [1968]: 239)

The film contains two kinds of such descriptions, objective and subjective: 1) "objective description of objects: houses, cars, cigarettes, apartments, shops, beds, TV sets, books, clothes, etc." and "objective description of subjects: the characters, Juliette, the American, Robert, the hairdresser, Marianne, the travelers, the motorists, the social workers, the old man, the children, the passers-by, etc."; and 2) "subjective description of subjects: particularly by way of feelings [and] through scenes more or less written and acted" as well as "subjective description of objects: settings seen from the inside, where the world is outside, behind the windows, or on the other side of the walls" (Godard 1986 [1968]: 241).

These two descriptive movements are then woven into two more conclusive structural movements. Movement 3:

Search for Structures [...] the sum of the objective description and the subjective description should lead to the discovery of certain more general forms; should enable one to pick out, not a generalized overall truth, but a certain 'complex feeling', something which corresponds emotionally to the laws one must discover and apply in order to live in society. [And] what we discover is not a harmonious society [...] This third movement corresponds to the inner movement of the film, which is the attempt to describe a complex (people and things), since no distinction is made between them [...] I do not neglect [consciousness/conscience],[6] since this is manifest in the cinematographic movement which directs me to these people or these things. (1986 [1968]: 242)

Movement 4:

having been able to define certain complex phenomena while continuing to describe particular events and emotions, this will eventually bring us closer to life than at the outset. Maybe [...] at least in certain images and certain sounds [the film will reveal] what Merleau-Ponty calls the 'singular existence' of a person—Juliette's in particular. Next, all these movements must be mixed up together. [A] film like this is a little as if I wanted to write a sociological essay in the form of a novel, and in order to do so had only musical notes at my disposition. (1986 [1968]: 242)

Evident in Godard's description of the last movement, although he clearly exaggerates, is that these complexes are hardly just philosophical but at least as much artistic. A distinction between philosophical and artistic thought, however, while key for the cinecept as explained in the Introduction and Chapter 1, does not at this point matter as much as the basic logic of the "complexes" involved. If they are neither "ordered sequence[s]" assimilable "to our pre-existing categories of understanding" nor a "chaotic jumble" (to reuse quotes from Morrey above), how are we to understand the logic of these complexes of thought? Here we can be assisted by what Deleuze and Deleuze and Guattari say about the relation between philosophy, art, and chaos.

"A work of chaos", Deleuze and Guattari write, "is certainly no better than a work of opinion; art is no more made of chaos than it is of opinion". Art harnesses, frames, and articulates segments of chaos, turns them into a consistency, a "composed chaos" (WP 204). This is obviously not about assimilating chaos into representation. It is also not a variation on the standard idea of finding a language capable of expressing the "unrepresentable". Are there other options? Deleuze's philosophy at large can be seen as such an option: it is concerned with how to think determination, distribution, structure, and organization differently than in representational images of thought, but also from usual ways of conceiving of what is beyond representation. As John Rajchman writes: "Outside established identities, divisions, and determinations, logical and syntactical as well as pragmatic, it has often been assumed that there is only chaos, anarchy, undifferentiation, or 'absurdity.' Deleuze tries to expose this illusion", which is to say, he "would try to relieve the philosophy of his French contemporaries of the temptation to reinstall transcendence—in particular, in the form of a peculiar mysticism of […] the Unrepresentable and its supposed Law" or "attempts to turn the voids or silences in modern work[s of art] into a mystical metaphysic of the Unsayable or the Invisible". Deleuze aimed instead "to advance a conception that allows for a layer of sense prior to code, even a structuralist one" (Rajchman 2000: 18–19, 125, see also 61, 141).[7] For Deleuze, as we saw in the previous chapter, the "reality of the virtual is structure", it "is completely determined" (DR 260). Which is to say, it is structured and determined according to a logic of multiplicity, and in Deleuze not only "multiplicity" but also, as Rajchman writes, "'logic' takes on a new sense" (2000: 50ff).[8] In Deleuze, the traditional meanings of terms like "determination", "structure", and "problem" (the latter being a way of conceiving of virtual multiplicities) have definitions that can appear unorthodox, with roots in twentieth-century French epistemology, minor philosophies, and experimental strands of mathematics rather than traditional or contemporary logic. While I explore the philosophical details of such structures in other chapters (1 and 3), I can briefly say here that this means most basically that the constituent parts of structures no longer have identity as their core. Distinctions between art and philosophy still aside, what is important at this point is the general logic of structure as something distinct from 1) representation, 2) the non-representable, and 3) the chaotic. If there is something like such a logic that determines both the artistic and philosophical structures in *2 or 3 Things*, the Sonimage videos develop this further on the level of formal film-philosophical articulation.

Images Swirling over a Black Ground: *Le gai savoir*

In between there is *Le gai savoir*, which is an even clearer forerunner to the Sonimage films both thematically and formally. It can also be seen as a sequel to *2 or 3 Things* that takes things in more unabashedly non-narrative and philosophical—and politically militant (it was shot just before and edited after May 1968)—directions.[9] Godard starts *Le gai savoir* by whispering *à la 2 or 3 Things*: "12.247 images speak of her", and his whispers continue throughout the film. *Le gai savoir* also continues the studying—as one of the two main characters, Patricia, says—of "links, relations, differences" in the social fabric, with a focus on language, images, and sounds and how they interrelate. The studying is now more explicit, however, and it occurs on two intertwined levels: the film itself as a study and a study conducted by two fictional characters. The character's study is first planned and then done over what is said to be a three-year period (although carried out in the fiction over seven nights). During the first and second years, images are picked up and recorded and then criticized, decomposed, and reduced; in the third year, images and sounds are recomposed with the aim of articulation according to a different logic. On both levels, the studying involves an effort to do more systematically what Godard had mentioned before: to go "back to zero" (I will look at how this connects to two scenes in *2 or 3 Things* in a moment). According to the characters, this concerns "dissolving" things, man, language, images and sounds and their relations, in order to find "traces" for new solutions (08:23–09:11). The film takes on these issues through audiovisual montage and mixes and shifts between two distinct formal modes:

1. Reduction: the two main characters appear alone (at times with an object like a book or a bicycle) on a dark soundstage. They are (partly) lit, and surrounded by darkness.
2. Analysis of audiovisual materials that are both inside and outside: constellations of images, texts, and sounds are interlaced with the dark soundstage scenes, as the characters/film analytically rearrange material from the popular, political, and social present.

Both these formal modes are key for what is to continue in Sonimage. Let us start with the first and work our way to the second. Early in *Le gai savoir* we get quick verbal biographies of the two characters, which aren't fictional biographies so much

Figure 2.1 *Le gai savoir*

as cheeky crystallizations of types and ideas. Each character is a contemporary revolutionary actor of sorts. Patricia is a child of Lumumba and the Cultural Revolution, and Émile is the great-great-grandson of Jean-Jacques Rousseau. They also appear like archetypical intellectual student-movement-related young Parisians, which the two actors (Juliet Berto and Jean-Pierre Léaud) also were, and they are played with a kind of new wave theatrical subtlety and ease. The characters function moreover a bit like attitudes and movements of thought—in what they say, but also, to reference one of Deleuze's takes on Godard in *Cinema 2*, in their bodily movements.

The dark stage appears to express three/four interrelated things here: 1) consciousness; 2a) consciousness as a scene for flows of images and sounds, or 2b) a blackboard on which they are studied; and 3) a ground of revolutionary intensity. It seems to demonstrate a conception of consciousness similar to the one in Deleuze's Bergson, not as a beam of light but as a "black screen" that stops or reflects images/light (C1 61f). Montage sequences constantly intersect like the outside world whose images the two characters try to seize and reflect upon. Although of course the outside is also part of their insides—as Patricia says: "if you want to see the world. Close your eyes" (24:35–24:40). And what they see is hard to capture: Émile says after one montage section: "The images are going by too quickly. We have to react." To which Patricia responds with a call for patience: "You are too romantic. A cultural revolution does not happen in one day" (22:11–22:19).[10] The characters try to "react" to the image flow as best they can through analysis, dismantling, and reduction, with the purpose of a possible redistribution. The first year, Patricia says, "[w]e'll pick up images, we'll record sounds [...] It will create unorderly experiences. [...] The second year we'll criticize it all. We'll decompose, we'll reduce, we'll substitute, and we'll recompose" (16:13–16:39). And, again, this study is done on two levels, by the characters and by the film, and the film both shifts between and blends these levels.

The dark stage is thereby interspersed with an abundance of images and sounds and texts. We see images of suffering, political leaders, popular culture, comic strips, war, art, ads, political struggles, and pornography, either in succession or sharing the same frame. Most of these images also have added handwriting. Some collages of images within the same frame are also reminiscent of the multi-screen montage of—then more often moving—images in Sonimage (although already here there is a brief shot of two monitors in a dark room showing moving images which will be the main visual template of *Numéro deux*). An example: a photo in the top left corner of what looks like Vietnamese families huddled together on the ground with "Hitler" handwritten over it, and below that a photo of a Vietnamese boy and his mother with "Johnson" (as in Lyndon B.) handwritten over it, and sort of hovering over both on the right side of the frame a blonde woman in a laced bra over which "être libre" is handwritten (30:30). At times there are quick flickers between images, such as between a photo of a pinup and what looks like a young Mao, followed by similar rapid shifts between a cartoon square with scantily dressed female bikers and a photo of black child in what may be war-related distress.

The handwritten words all interact both playfully and thoughtfully with images and sounds, but some constellations appear more theoretically substantial than others. While in one "Hegel est" is written over the crotch of a man in an underwear ad, others indicate more elaborate ideas relating to the character's discussions. An example of the latter: The characters discuss circularity and coming back to the "starting point" not as "identical to ourselves" but "symmetrical to" "what we were before". They then ask: "To what can we link this?" Émile says "To this", after which an image is shown with drawings of two nudes with a set of arrows in various directions indicating a linking of Freud to seeing and the mind, and Marx to the materiality of genitalia and re/production (see figure 2.2b). Patricia disagrees and says it should rather be linked "to this", followed by a photo of a female pinup lying back resting on one elbow with legs spread apart (away from the viewer), with "Freud" handwritten next to an arrow pointing to the head, and "Marx" with an arrow directly pointing between the legs (57:12–57:54). The politics of reproduction/production will be central in Sonimage, along with female emancipation as connected to such issues,

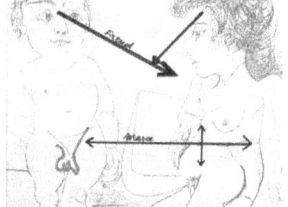

Figures 2.2a–c *Le gai savoir*

for which *Le gai savoir* also plants a more specific seed (which is provocatively stated here but not to be taken too literally or even at face value): "The freedom of woman is in her womb" (44:30). However, what is of interest at this point is just to note the general effort towards slightly new formal structures for expressing semi-theoretical thought—and we can do so here regardless of whether these particular sketches appear theoretically crude or cleverly simplifying diagrams connected to efforts in French philosophy at the time to rethink the capitalist economy as intertwined with a libidinal economy.[11]

Much also happens on the soundtrack. Sometimes sounds and voices separate, and sometimes they interweave, compete, contrast, or complement each other. A host of concerns about how to analyze relations between sounds and images are established or developed here that will be furthered in Sonimage: The idea that sounds and images are the same thing, while analytically separable (11:33–11:58). The concern that follows from that claim—"Analysis of sound *through* image" (39:14, emphasis mine).[12] How images, instead of presenting things, can reduce themselves to the representation of a given sound (50:26–50:31). The view that "within an image and a sound, nothing is stable", which means it is about "grasping a movement". How an "image is never an image, but a contradiction of images", and "it's the same for sound" (47:40–47:50). The concern with complexities and nuances of even the simplest of sounds and verbal utterances in voices as means of transmission between people. The very setup of two characters analyzing sounds and images and their relations (*Ici et ailleurs*, *Comment ça va*, *France tour détour*).

Furthermore, some of the sentiments and rhythms of *Le gai savoir*'s general montage are reminiscent of Sonimage (partly even *Histoire(s) de cinéma*). To some extent the film lays out a basic template for what is to come, in some regards lacking only the video technology that would provide the means for a more fully realized new formal logic.[13] But *Le gai savoir* is also its own thing, and carries out its own kind of study. Let us look at a few of its particularities: what are the basic moves and philosophical aims of this "study"?

Le gai savoir was commissioned by the French television company ORTF as an update of Jean-Jacques Rousseau's *Emile, or On Education* (1762) (the book was immediately banned in France on publication, just as Godard's film was rejected by the television company and banned in French theaters). Rousseau's semi-fictive treatise concerns how education could be re-envisioned to nurture a human state of nature, rather than foster its corruption. Godard might be said to reimagine aspects of its premise to advance his own thoughts on how *studying* might take us beyond current social and political conditioning, without this being about some given, original state of human nature (as the film taking its name from a book by Nietzsche should clearly signal in advance, along with smaller direct signals in the film like references to Derrida's Rousseau-treating *Of Grammatology*). Godard is concerned here, as indicated, with a kind of scaling back to a ground zero. This is not only in order to critique and bypass current social-conditioning formations of words, images, and sounds, however, but also about reconnecting with a ground of potential.

A concern with such a ground extends to the blackened soundstage itself. The dark room is not only like a consciousness analyzing interior and exterior images, it joins inside and outside also in a different sense. Consciousness—passing through an unconscious—connects with a more general ground, what Godard's whispered voice-over calls a "black earth". During a several-minutes-long fairly abstract (and pseudo-bombastic) poem, Godard whispers about a "West" in which there has been a "massacre" of a "red earth", compared to an "East" of "accumulation of history and the black earth" where "violence [...] springs at a future moment, and surges from the swamp of time, and gradually covers the opponent from whom hope has been taken". In the "West" there are "the masses", "images", "signs without roots" and without "any hold on the deep axis of the outside", reflecting instead "the tiny interior of skulls, at the nervous torsion". In the East, in which we find "the people" and "the scene", the past is "erased" by an "invisible force" which is a "simple indestructible force of the line" that "glides and crosses the years and centuries" and which "created and fueled" things but "for you has become [...] superficial". Still it amounts to "a revolution" that will emerge and involve "continents and entire texts", and which will make you "no longer recognize the world of your language", "walk far from these long and discreet signs", and find yourself "at the crossing of unleashed forces", where you are required to see them "sink in their grouped and differentiated multitudes". But you cannot forget the line that is an "infinity" and "an immense animal" with no "determinate figure or senses with which to report back exterior things to itself". "From this perspective, the circular motion around a center disappears, like the movement of rocks, corals, and birds", and through which "the story continues" as a "double trajectory, risen from a force without guarantees" (17:43–20:46). A later whispered voice-over segment adds that "the earth can have a second layer that reinstates critique in life", part of a long exposition which is constantly interrupted by recordings of speakers from contemporaneous revolutionary meetings and with the visual track first showing the two characters on the stage listening but after a while only a completely black image (01:09:25–01:18:42).

At the limit of the analytic reduction of the study, then, we find a ground of intensity or a raw plane of immanence. Let us examine this ground a little further, first by looking at how it connects back to *2 or 3 Things* (how it more obviously extends forward to the black screens in Sonimage—referred to as a "fetal blackness" by Serge Daney—will be examined extensively in Chapter 4). It connects with two scenes in *2 or 3 Things*: the final sequence and the famous coffee cup scene. The final sequence has three shots: an extreme close-up of the burning end of a cigarette forming a big fireball against a dark background (see Figure 2.3b), then a close-up of the word "idées" from the cover of a Gallimard book of essays, followed by the end shot—a zoom out from one to reveal several commercial house products (each their own little image) in a geometric formation on grass. Godard's whispering voice *over the cigarette fire close up*: "I listen to commercials on my transistor [...] I forget Hiroshima and Auschwitz. I forget Budapest"; *over the idées shot:* "I forget Vietnam and minimum wages. I forget the housing crisis. I forget the famine in India"; over the *end zoom out, starting from a package with the word Hollywood*: "I've forgotten it all, except that since it takes me back to zero, I have to start from there." This sequence in *2 or 3 Things* spells out the need to go back to zero,[14] but it also sketches what will be *Le gai savoir*'s basic components for doing so:

1. A ground zero of intensity that is also the ground for new ideas (the inclusion of fire in the black ground here furthermore resonates with Morrey's reading of such motifs in Godard's mid-1980s films: "fire and water are *elemental*, immemorial, and imply a time scale and a rhythm that do not belong to capitalism, that do not belong to anyone" [2005: 190]).[15]
2. Ubiquitous images and sounds that construct our external and internal worlds (news, commercials, Hollywood, etc.).
3. The need to subject these images and sounds to analytic structuring as part of an effort to reconnect with the ground that might allow us to construct new ideas, new articulations of images and sounds, beyond all these clichés.

That is, these are also the three stages of the "study" in *Le gai savoir*.

Then there is the coffee cup in *2 or 3 Things*. While this famous scene may be in no need of a general introduction, here is an overview from the more unacknowledged angle of its connections to the black ground. The main character Juliette sits down at a table in a bar as the focus suddenly shifts to the coffee cup of a man at a neighboring table, with Godard whispering poetic-essayistic statements. Through some brief interchanging images of things and people, we inch closer into the cup until the coffee covers the whole image. We see moving foam formations that create an impression of swirling galaxies. After the foam dissipates, a piece of sugar is dropped into the liquid making it appear instead as a primordial soup from which life starts to bubble forth. These appearances—cosmos and primordial soup—are generated also through the essayistic-poetic voice-over, the second half of which is the most relevant:

> The world itself. Nowadays, when revolutions are impossible and bloody wars loom, when capitalism is no longer so sure of its rights and the working class is in retreat, when the lightening progress of science makes future centuries hauntingly present, when the future is more present than the present, when distant galaxies are on my doorstep. My fellow creature, my brother. [*Pause. The piece of sugar is dropped into the coffee.*] Where to start? But start what? God created heaven and earth, of course, but that is a little too easy. We must be able to say it better: Say that the limits of language are the limits of the world, that the limits of my language are the limits of my world, and that when I speak, I limit the world, I finish it. And that one day, logically and mysteriously, death will come to abolish these limits, and there will be no questions or answers. It will all be a blur. But if by chance things come into focus again, it can only be with the appearance of consciousness. Everything will follow from there.

As the voice delivers the final lines, we see a round bubble formation that has slowly emerged, which rhymes with the round cigarette glow in the last section of the film: a big ball of fiery intensity, a ground from which new things can emerge, but from which we are also limited or barred to a large extent. How can we productively reconnect, if possible, with such a ground so as to be able to create new forms of life?

If this is the question also animating *Le gai savoir*, for most of that film the ground appears more like an obscure black background in consciousness in which cultural

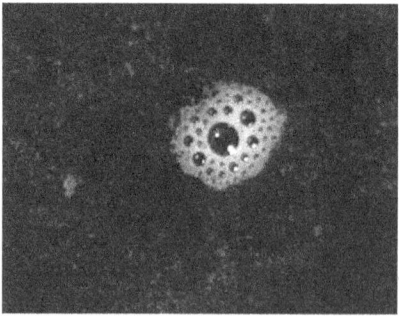
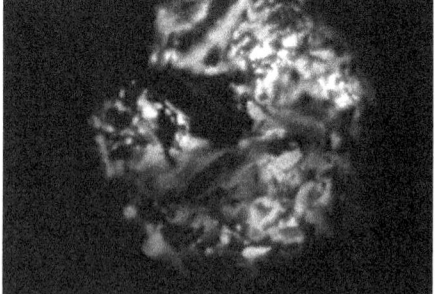

Figures 2.3a–b *2 or 3 Things I Know About Her*

images and sounds are swirling around—as Deleuze reads the monad-subject in his book on Leibniz: a local folding of the universe that expresses only specific aspects clearly with the rest appearing as chiaroscuro "dark background" (FLB 26–9, 36). It also functions like an analytic blackboard for the study the two characters (and the film) conduct. As a ground of intensity, however, the background seems in this film to be sort of sealed off, or as if its force was recuperated for the purpose of powering the current socioeconomic system studied by the characters. But the ground also rumbles underneath as a potential that could be activated in other ways, if the characters can just work to find a right way back to it, through the veil of current images, sounds, and texts.

What is the position of Godard's whispering voice within this multileveled fictional space, with its black background variously expressing a ground of intensity, consciousness, and blackboard over which twirl images, sounds, and texts? The characters tend to listen to Godard's whispers while staring out into the darkness of the room, at least during his longer tirades. But the voice appears to broadcast from some other register, not the black background. The longer rants aside, the voice is often, if not very clear or straight, somewhat teacher-like, strategizing, opinionated, concerned with political theory, and referencing actual events. The voice also comes with loud buzzing and bleeping radio signal noise, the kind that sounds like a 1960s electronica version of a dial-up internet modem or an alien transmission in an old sci-fi film, so that it seems to arrive from some strange underground headquarter or another planet or dimension. The voice can thereby be read as an imperfect (perhaps slightly parodied) mediator or negotiator, like scattered efforts to retain and incorporate revolutionary energy in/to the actual situation of the characters.[16] An actual situation, that is, in which the new appears blocked. The struggle to productively reconnect, if at all possible, with potentials for the new in such situations is key to understanding many of the concerns of Sonimage in which the new—post 1968—seems even more blocked. As explored in the next chapter, such blockage is increasingly important for Deleuze during the same period, and even more evident in what would become his writings on cinema as well as on philosophical concepts. This central thread will be taken up in the next two chapters.

Let us now return to the new kind of articulation developing in Godard. What is the logic of articulation, first, in *Le gai savior*'s many constellations of found images with playfully political handwritings (and drawings)? The influence here from the Situationist practice of *détournement* may seem straightforward. Godard, however, never simply complies with Guy Debord's limitation of this approach to "critique as negation" and a "style of negation" that dialectically turns capitalist symbolic expressions against themselves (Debord 2005 [1967]: §204, §207–8). While somewhat in line with the Situationists' aggressively tongue-in-cheek approach to and focus on a society of images, *Le gai savoir*'s juxtapositions are irreducible to dialectics in the sense of contradiction and negativity. The film actually subjects an image of the cover of Debord's *Société de spectacle* to detouring handwriting: "2éme année suite et fin", that is, "2nd year continuation and end". While on a literal level in the fiction, this is about the continuation and end of the characters' "second year of study", it could more subtly indicate that Situationist approaches can continue to be useful while also being limited or something to pass through in order to go further (57:10). And as shown by Brian Price, *Le gai savoir* also more generally subjects Situationist works and methods to critical detournement, in ways that strengthen their core idea while also exposing their weakness, as well as just doing something more advanced (Price 1997). Why is this important for our concerns? The question of whether Godard uses a dialectical logic of contradiction or not has some bearing on how to conceive of embryonically cineceptual expression in Sonimage, it connects directly with the discussion of Deleuze's concept of concepts in the last chapter, and, as we will see, it is key for several theorists who have discussed the first Sonimage film, to which we will now finally turn.

Deconstruction AND a Different Logic of Articulation: *Ici et ailleurs*

Godard and Anne-Marie Miéville's *Ici et ailleurs* (*Here and Elsewhere*) mainly examines footage by the Dziga Vertov Group, the militant filmmaking collective of which Godard and Jean-Pierre Gorin were the core members (1968–72).[17] Godard and Gorin shot the footage (with cinematographer Armand Marco) between February and July 1970 in Jordan, Lebanon, and Syria, for what was to become a film about the Palestinian Revolution called *Jusqu'à la victoire!* [*Until Victory*], which they were invited to make by the Al Fatah section of the PLO. Back home in France, however, as Godard's voice says in *Ici et ailleurs*: "you don't know what to make of the film. Very quickly the contradictions explode, taking you with them […] It's not going well anywhere" (07:56–08:12). It was going especially badly over there: in what came to be known as Black September 1970, the Jordanian army (with support from Henry Kissinger) killed over 3,000 Palestinians, many civilians and refugees, and almost all of the subjects portrayed in the footage. Furthermore, the making of *Ici* "coincided", as Irmgard Emmelhainz writes in her recent study of Godard's political films, "with the end of the 'French Cultural Revolution,' with the failure of revolutions *elsewhere* and with the beginning of a new reactionary period in general, specifically in France" (2019: 101).[18] All this forced them to fundamentally rethink the footage.[19] Most obviously it was subjected to self-critique. While self-critique was an already established procedure in Godard and militant filmmaking more generally—including presumptions of what it means to speak from a position of being *ici* (here) for those *ailleurs* (elsewhere)[20]—in *Ici* such critique is complexified in many regards, not least through Miéville's input.[21] We now see deepened reflections on how images and sounds are organized around us more generally, and how—formally significant for the cinecept—they might be organized differently.

Before going into how *Ici* establishes such different organization, let us say a bit more about how it differs from the preceding Dziga Vertov Group films. First, we should avoid the common reduction of the DVG films to mere Maoist/Marxist-Leninist dogma that was rectified in Sonimage and onwards.[22] Such a view has been predominant perhaps partly due to those films being largely unavailable until recently, and their release on DVD has at least coincided with increasingly nuanced takes. Witt had already pointed to much continuity in problems and thematic focus: Sonimage's "investigation of various forms and process of communication—notably television, cinema, journalism, and language—had been central to Godard's concerns from the mid-1960s onwards, and is at the heart of essayistic works such as *Le Gai Savoir* [...] and the Dziga Vertov Group films". Witt also argues that the "Dziga Vertov Group work can be viewed with hindsight as a protracted exploratory trailer for the Sonimage project, with 'Communications' coming to belated fruition in the Sonimage work, especially in [...] *Six fois deux*" (2014: 322f). Emmelhainz goes beyond thematic concerns: "*Ici et ailleurs* does not differ drastically from [the] DVG films: it articulates an avantgarde attitude (here, the militant abroad), points at the contradictions inherent in the situation it analyzes, and proceeds to self-critique", with the key difference instead being that "it is temporally and spatially larger in scope than [the] DVG films" (2019: 75; see also 4).

Emmelhainz may however go a little too far, or at least gloss over some important differences. The earlier predominant view of DVG was not baseless. The Sonimage work was "fiercely skeptical of political dogma" and "characterized intellectually by a rejection of the Marxist-Leninist theory that had underpinned the work of the Dziga Vertov Group", as Witt also argues, adding that a "revisionist political agenda is integral to the structure of *Ici et ailleurs*" (2014: 321, 314; see also Witt 2013: 46).[23] Even more to the point of my concerns here: the Sonimage films were more "tentative, searching examination[s]" that came "to more conflicted conclusions", as White argues, and their "didacticism" was about meaning and processes rather than information or knowledge (2013: 87). And as Morrey writes, these works had a more "fruitful dialogue" (2005: 114), which resonates with Nora Alter's claim that *Ici* contains a "multiplicity of voices and [...] stories and perspectives" (2018: 160). How can we understand this shift in *Ici* to the more openly dialogical and multiple in terms of formal logic of organization? And what does formal logic of organization mean here?

In an essay called "The Articulation of Protest", Hito Steyerl explores two different logics of montage, in two different films, as contrasting types of articulations of difference within resisting political formations. The premise is that "the field of politics" is a matter of "how pictures and sounds are organized, edited, and arranged" (2012: 88, emphasis omitted). The first film is a documentary called *Showdown in Seattle* which covers the 1999 anti-globalization protests. Steyerl finds its montage to unreflectively add together diverse groups into a populist unity of "the people", which veils important contradictions and opposing interests. This film's montage and general aesthetics, Steyerl writes, are "a faithful reproduction of the corporate media's manner of production" even though the aim is to counter the "information circulated by" such media (82). It creates a "time-space" that she describes "in Walter Benjamin's terms as 'homogeneous' and 'empty,' organized by chronological sequences and uniform spaces", in which "differences and opposites are leveled for the sake of establishing a chain of equivalencies" (81, 86).

The type of montage we see in *Showdown*, Steyerl argues, is critically analyzed in *Ici et ailleur*. Steyerl finds *Ici* to reveal how the "additive *and*" in such montage combines elements in a "populist chain of equivalencies" that do not actually add up, and which can instead "hinder, contradict, ignore, or even mutually exclude one another" (2012: 85, 89). Displayed thereby, Steyerl adds, is "the void that [the chain of elements] is structured around, the empty inclusivist *and* that keeps blindly adding and adding, outside the realm of any political criteria" (89). *Ici* shows the conjunction *and* as a contradiction-veiling stich in an indiscriminate "inclusion at any cost" (89). Yet Steyerl ends the essay by raising the possibility of a different kind of combination that she implies is not realized in *Ici*: a "different order" of dialectical "oppositional articulations" that "tenaciously pound two [elements] together to create a spark in the darkness" (90f).

For Deleuze, however, Godard not only goes beyond 1) the mere exposing of stiches in naive inclusion, he also exceeds 2) those very dialectical "oppositional articulations" that Steyerl calls for, by following 3) a logic of multiplicity in which the conjunction *and* has a different and autonomous function. As Deleuze famously says in a 1976 "interview"[24] on Godard-Miéville's *Six fois deux* (1976) (which Deleuze considers to be closely aligned with *Ici et ailleur* [C2 179]):

> Godard's not a dialectician. What counts with him isn't two or three or however many, it's AND, the conjunction AND. [...] This is important, because all our thought's modeled, rather, on the verb "to be", IS. [...] Even conjunctions are dealt with in terms of the verb "to be" [...] AND isn't even a specific conjunction or relation, it brings in all relations, there are as many relations as ANDS, AND doesn't just upset all relations, it upsets being, the verb ... and so on.

While this avoidance of dialectics may so far almost seem reducible to deconstruction, Deleuze continues in a partly different direction:

> AND, "and … and … and …" is precisely a creative stammering, a foreign use of language […] AND is of course diversity, multiplicity [and] diversity and multiplicity are nothing to do with […] dialectical schemas […] Multiplicity is precisely in the "and", which is different in nature from elementary components and collections of them. […] I think Godard's force lies in living and thinking and presenting this AND in a very novel way, and in making it work actively. AND is […] the borderline, there's always a border [*frontière*[25]], a line of flight or flow, only we don't see it, because it's the least perceptible of things. And yet [this is where] things come to pass, becomings evolve, revolutions take shape. (N 44f)[26]

(In Chapter 4 we will see how what Deleuze says about the in-between here is said with more philosophical precision in *Six fois deux* itself). Before I critically examine this passage from a cineceptual perspective, we should note that it has been quite influential for the understanding of montage in mid-1970s Sonimage. "[T]his is not really a dialectic strategy. The montage is too multiple", White writes about the form in *Ici*, adding that Godard and Miéville instead "highlight the complexity of the situation"; and further down he explicitly references Deleuze (2013: 66, 68, 82f). Morrey refers to series of images and intertitles at the beginning of the film "as a kind of five-fold dialectic", while also referencing Deleuze's analysis of AND (2005: 106, 108). Alter states that in *Ici* the "conjunction 'and' reflects not the fusion or synthesis of two autonomous elements but […] function[s] as a facilitator of diversity, multiplicity, and heterogeneity" (2018: 160). Alter also claims that Godard "replaced a model of dialectical thought and the montage of Eisenstein with the rhizomatic thought proposed by Deleuze" (164).[27] "Unlike Vertov (and Debord)", Emmelhainz furthermore writes with reference to Deleuze, "Godard is not a dialectician, and in the filmic syntax of *Ici et ailleurs* Godard [instead] *differentiates* [images] so that their signifiers enter into disparity", with "'AND' allow[ing] signification to emerge at the interstices between the images" (2019: 155).[28]

Now, if looked at from a *cineceptual* perspective, Deleuze's descriptions of a logic of multiplicity in *Six fois deux* (and by extension *Ici*) appear both accurate and insufficient. As we saw in the previous chapter, human conducts can create and articulate different *types* of multiplicity. What type of multiplicity is articulated here? The implication is that the multiplicity is an artistic one. The *and*-based montage of *Six fois deux* and *Ici* is described as a "creative stammering" and "a foreign use of language", just as Deleuze finds in the likes of Beckett or Kafka. And the concern with problems in these video works is described as that which "can only be expressed in the form of questions that tend to confound any answers" (N 39), similar to certain time-images in *Cinema 2* that are said to be "problematic rather than theorematic" and thereby "deeper than all the explanations that can be given for [them]" (C2 175). *Cinema 2*, however, tends to equate such cinematic expression, including Godard's, to a "powerlessness" of thought to think a rational whole that opens up a different kind of power of "the unthought in thought" (e.g. C2 175). While important and adequate for most of the films Deleuze talks about, this is restricted as a means for grasping the cineceptual tendencies in Sonimage. Cinecepts are particular philosophical determinations of problems / Ideas / multiplicities (see Chapter 1). In terms of philosophical or conceptual articulation, then, how much can be said to happen in Sonimage if we follow Deleuze, who does not, as we have seen, raise the question of whether philosophical conceptualization can occur in and through film/video?

There are passages in *Cinema 2*, however, that come very close to actualizing this question. As I started to examine in Chapter 1, Deleuze describes Godard's montage as an articulation of problems through open categories that organize series of elements and cuts and recuts in ways similar to how Deleuze also describes how concepts are formed. Additionally, Deleuze says that there is in Godard a synthesis occurring at the end that gives the problems a particular theorematic determination:

> It is not a matter of a cataloguing [or] "collage" [but] a method of constitution of series, each marked by a category [...] It is as if Godard [...] was finding "theorems" at the edge of "problems" [...] [W]hile problems impose conditions of series on unknown elements, [theorems as] overall synthes[e]s [fix] categories from where these elements are extracted [...] Godard is constantly creating categories [...] even if the categories end up presenting him with a problem again. According to Godard, categories are not fixed once and for all. They are redistributed, reshaped and reinvented [...] A montage of categories, which is new each time, corresponds to a cutting of categories. The categories [...] must be well founded, and must have strong, indirect relations between themselves [...] (C2 184f)

Is this not to set the stage for formulations also of *concepts* "at the edge" of these problems? The Godardian categories are said to have something Aristotelian about them, just not in their overall logic. Would it really take that much for us to be able say of Godard's "theorems" that there is something representational about them, just not in their actual logic? Let me elaborate. More generally, theorems are for Deleuze tantamount to what he calls representation (which I discussed in the previous chapter). Theorems "express and [...] develop the properties of simple essences, whereas problems concern only events" and "the genetic point of view". Representation limits or reduces problems *to* theorems—whether in the form of

"Greek geometry", "the Aristotelian dialectic", or the "Cartesian method" (DR 199f). For Deleuze, Godard is like the epitome of precisely going beyond representational thought in film, so why would his "theorems" be an exception? If Godard even weaves "Aristotelian categories" into a logic of the problematic, why could not the theorems at the edge of those problems be part of a subrepresentational logic just as well, while also—to get to the main point—supplying a kind of *determination* that could, through tweaks in the Godardian approach, become cineceptual?

With this in mind, let me repeat key parts of the block quotation above and add some from subsequent pages in *Cinema 2*: Godard finds and articulates problems partly through the categories that he creates (C2 187, 185). The problems are thereby articulated through montage formations of categories. Problems, as we recall from the previous chapter, have a logic of multiplicity. Here they "impose conditions of series on unknown elements" (which "can be words, things, acts, people"), and through each series being "marked" by a category (C2 185f). Each category "must be well founded" and together they must "have strong, indirect relations between themselves", while also being "redistributed, reshaped and reinvented" instead of "fixed once and for all" (185). So what about the theorems found at the edge? While the theorems supply an "overall synthesis" that "fixes categories" of elements, such fixes are hardly any more statically "once and for all" than the categories synthesized (185). The theorems do however seem to provide the problem with more consistency or a slightly different and perhaps more explicit kind of determination. So again, why could they not also point in the direction of something slightly more *conceptually* consistent, something closer to a philosophical-conceptual determination of a multiplicity?[29]

Yet, quickly after this discussion of categories, problems, and theorems, Deleuze states that with Godard "Cinema ceases to be narrative" and "becomes the most 'novelesque'"—now with reference to *Pierrot le fou* (1965). Deleuze does this throughout much of his discussion of Godard in *Cinema 2*: he sweeps across all of Godard's works with no clear differentiation, mostly for substantial reasons rhyming with his general approach of taking on authors and artists as a whole. But this also allows him to pivot from what may come too close to philosophy in Sonimage to the "novelesque" of *Pierrot le fou*. To be fair, Deleuze does recognize that "with electronic procedures", adding to everything Godard had already done, "new possibilities are opening everywhere for montage", and he indeed discusses this in relation to the development of a new analytics of the image (C2 184). But as we saw in Chapter 1, Deleuze also formally separates such analytics from questions of philosophical conceptualization which he implicitly reserves for writing and talking. Looking specifically at the analytics in the Sonimage films, however, it would make more sense to say that "Cinema ceases to be narrative" and (instead of most novelesque) "becomes the most philosophical".

If Deleuze writes with insufficient differentiation between periods about Godardian "categories of problems which introduce reflection into the image itself" (C2 186), Nicole Brenez points to how the into-the-image-itself part is gradually developed. Brenez finds in Godard a general approach to philosophical questions and problems characterized by critical power and experimental openness, and she argues that this became increasingly integrated into the image. She charts an "evolution of Godard's work [that] takes us from the simplest *mise en scène* of the question toward the transformation of the image itself into a pure formal problem" (2007 [2004]: 165). In such images the "question no longer needs a character" or "a questioner-figure even as a voice-off", since the images have "become the protagonists themselves, direct and autonomous", acting as "displacement, a proposition, and an opening" (171). While the details of Brenez's account of this evolution are not so directly relevant here, the general move of pointing to such an evolution harmonizes with the reasoning for this study's focus on a particular period in Godard. I will now conclude this chapter with my own close look at the evolution of form as it appears in *Ice et ailleurs*, which is both a kind of deconstructive process and a probing setup for a new logic of articulation extended in later, more directly embryonically cineceptual, Sonimage works, as explored in Chapter 4.

In the perhaps most recognized—certainly by Steyerl—scene in *Ici* (starting ca. 21:20) we are shown printed-out pictures of images from other parts of the film, lined up in various ways: first put on a wall and then shown by a chain of actors each holding one image and moving in a horizontal row past or in a queue straight in front of the camera, showing how one image follows the next in conventional film. With Godard's voice-over added, this is an overly pedagogical breakdown of how moving images are normally linked. This scene simplifies a deconstructive strand in *Ici*, which in its Hollywood-comparing self-critique almost implies an impossibility of linking images differently. However, this is only half the story. The film's focus on links is combined with efforts to organize elements in other ways (not to be confused with a capacity to show "unrepresentable" voids or ruins of representation). It contains a double movement of deconstruction and a kind of groping towards a new logic of articulation.

Ici begins with Godard and then Miéville stating that the film is called *Jusqu'à la victoire!* in 1970 and *Ici et ailleurs* in 1974/75,[30] while we see a black screen and the green electronic words "Mon. Ton. Son. Image." with the last two words blinking back and forth (such green electronic text on a black background recurs throughout the film as well as in *Numéro deux*). Godard's voice then emphasizes the "and" in this juxtaposition of film titles, and we are introduced to a leitmotif image of big white Styrofoam letters "ET" (the French word for *and*) on a little stage with a black cloth and with a black background. The conjunction "and" is at the center of the film in both words and images. A set of things, events, and ideas are combined in this way. With some intriguing variations: Around 06:25–06:50 the link word shifts temporarily from *and* to *plus*. This thing *plus* ... that thing. At this early point, *plus* is somewhat part of a critique of how "all the sounds and images" of the original material were "organized" in an "order" that was "commanded by the people's logic". But *plus* is thereby also dislodged from such a logic, and it appears to *extend* things, to "proloooooong", as Godard says a few times in the film. And this is followed by the above-described account of coming home to France and finding things no longer making sense: "the contradictions explode, taking you with them". At this point all conjunctive elements (and, plus, or) are temporarily removed: "This, this, this, this"—represented by flows of images and sounds—leading only to death (of the people depicted). When *plus* returns around 12:13 it is even more loaded. We now see a hand adding (although also subtracting) the digits of years for different revolutions or revolutionary outbursts (1789, 1917, 1936, 1968) on a calculator.[31] Around 12:47 the green electronic text spells "Ici + Ailleur" over a black background with the plus sign blinking. What is the general point—aside from thematic ones made about the elements combined[32]—of this blinking shift from *and* to *plus*? I mentioned that this partly functions to dislodge and extend things, but it is done in ways that underline or push further towards multiplicity. Immediately after this, Godard starts to combine a vast array of things, events, and terms using *and* again, but there is now a literal stammering that wasn't there before: "French revolution and, and, and ... Arab revolution" (cut to the styrofoam "ET"). As if the plussing (and partly subtracting) of revolutions just prior revealed a more intense means of connection hidden also within the *and* (something similar goes on with the word-elements combined, when a word is seen on screen electronically and letters within it shift revealing other words concealed within the first, a procedure more extensive in *Numéro deux*).[33] Godard's voice goes on to emphasize *and* in a series of combinations of elements.[34] It is done over images of newspaper front pages or texts with pertinent words in headlines circled with a red pen (interspersed with images and sounds from the original material). One of these circled words is "zero" and it appears as the voice utters the same word. It is part of a cropped headline that reads: "Art de Zéro. Travailler ensemble" [Art of zero. Work together].[35] After a moment, *or* takes over from *and* (14:26), as if the filmmakers were trying yet another tool for dislodging established ways of linking and for experimenting with new ways to do so.[36] This leads up to Godard concluding, over an image of Nixon (15:12), that it is "Too simple and too easy to divide the world in two." He then seems to qualify that this applies only to plain dualisms in which one side of the combination of terms is wholly *this* and the other term wholly *that*. The possibility to conceive of elements differently and to organize them differently is thereby left open.

A few minutes later (ca. 18:00) we see a complex video montage that tries out a different logic of articulation (extending and developing two similar brief efforts earlier in the film starting around 03:20 and 06:42 respectively). It begins with an image of Lenin. Another image breaks in showing men from the French Popular Front at the time of their electoral victory in 1936. This image hesitatingly grows from the top left corner, before taking over. This is quickly followed by Hitler taking over from below, first half, then three quarters of the frame, leaving a hand stretched in the air from one of the Popular Front men in the top corner. Hitler's screaming voice is heard (a sound that seeks to dominate the image). Then the image of Lenin reemerges through superimposition for a second, as the green digital text "Populaire" starts blinking. The blinking word continues over the picture of Hitler and the remaining quarter of the frame shows part of the Popular Front image. There is a cut back to Lenin and what sounds like a song from the Soviet Union, then a shift to the Popular Front image, with "Populaire" still blinking. Hitler's voice returns while an image of a blonde woman with a revolutionary-like facial garment begins to appear through superimposition, which is then swiped over leaving the hands in the air from the Popular Front image in top left corner. After a brief intermission with a calculator (and repeated images of the killed Palestinian revolutionaries), there is a similar montage with even higher degrees of audiovisual complexity, which now links Hitler, Golda Meir, Israel, Moshe Dayan, Brezhnev, voices speaking in multiple languages, a Hebrew song about Auschwitz and Treblinka over images of dead Palestinians, and images (recurring throughout the film) of a French family watching television. While the surface political implications here may sound almost heavy handed, the thought structures are more artistic and scattered than cohering into propositions or linear argumentation, even generously defined continental philosophical argumentation. Yet, these forms also start to indicate that a more coherent, conceptualizing philosophical argumentation is precisely what *could* happen here with some further tweaks.[37]

A later section of *Ici* is also a bit more explicit and methodological in its aim for a new logic of formal organization. This section starts at 24:23—following the above-described scene which deconstructs film as chains of images (21:20)—with "Premiere question" [First question] appearing in green electronic text over a black background as Godard's voice-over asks: "How do you use your time to occupy your space? How do you organize a schedule? How do you organize a chain? Like this?" We see an image of a row of cars in a factory. "Like this?" We see an image of a man carrying a stick over his shoulder from which hangs two severed heads. "Like this?" We see an image of what seem to be Jews behind the barbed-wire fence of a concentration camp. He then asks: "But also like this?", now pointing to a *soft montage*[38]— three TV screens in a blackened room showing different images, through a slightly different logic. Godard now briefly backtracks: "Or like that?" We see an image from an ad with a smiling, stereotypically wholesome family (mom, dad, child) with very white teeth. But this is quickly followed by: "Like this would do," triggering a more analogue variation of the soft montage: slides. First there is a row of three slides shown over a black background, each changed manually by a visible hand. Various images and sounds are connected here, largely along the same lines as before. Hitler, the Israeli army, a tourist ad for Jerusalem, Brezhnev, Moshe Dayan, Nixon, Golda Meir, Pinochet, a tank, fighter planes, and resistance fighters (Chilean, Palestinian, and Vietnamese). We hear sounds of combat, struggle songs in Arabic, songs in other languages, the hymn about Auschwitz and Treblinka, Hitler's voice, etc. This is followed by an even more intricate set of nine slides. And the "second question" is presented: "How do you go about making your own image?"

Around 30:05 Godard says: "Maybe we should abandon this system of questions and answers and find something else. [...] Before producing you must distribute." A few minutes later at 35:00 there is another complex video montage with Kissinger, pinups, electronic text, the letters "SS" flashing, and so on. At this point the image organization appears to reflect "the whole world", as Godard says at 36:05, as a "vague and complicated system" of images, rather than indications of coming embryonic cinecepts, but it is also a probing experimentation with a different logic of articulation or "distribution" beyond the previous "system of questions and answers", which also produces new cineceptually interesting forms. This section is followed by a soft montage of four screens of altering moving images, with increasingly complicated blends of sounds (Godard's voice claiming capitalist wealth is built on the lie that the whole world can be fitted into one image,[39] a football match also seen on one of the screens, a news report on Middle Eastern war wreckage, etc.).

Now, if *Ici et ailleurs* critically deconstructs dominant organizations, as well as tests out and even provides a raw template for a new logic of organization of images and sounds, *Numéro deux*, the second (completed) Sonimage film, and

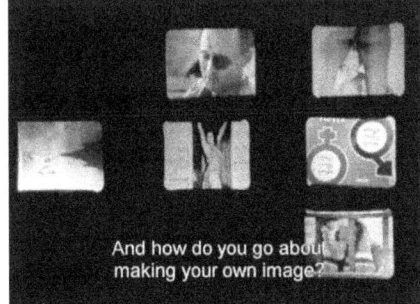

Figures 2.4a–b *Ici et ailleurs*

Godard-Miéville's two television series, *Six fois deux* (1976) and *France tour détour* (1977), are more like direct realizations of such a new organization, and with some embryonically cineceptual parts. To use the frame of the fictional three-year study of *Le gai savoir*: *Ici* focuses extensively on the first and second years, in which images are picked up and recorded and then criticized, decomposed, and reduced. The following Sonimage films then develop more directly what was initiated in *Ici*: the third year in which images and sounds are recomposed, structured according to a different logic—and not only as essayistic art, but as more direct philosophical critique and analysis. And if Miéville in *Ici*—albeit sharing credit on all aspects of the filmmaking—appears to come in a little bit from the side as a refreshingly critical voice, she seems to have been a clearer co-driver of the fundamental ideas in these subsequent works. The philosophical focus now also shifts more towards production and problems in production, and with a recurring focus on the female body as the site of re/production (with resonances not only in Marxist theory and Deleuze and Guattari's *Anti-Oedipus* but also feminist theories like those of Luce Irigaray and Julia Kristeva). In Chapter 4 these works will be examined not only as partly containing Godard-Miéville's most clear expressions of embryonic cinecepts, but also as a more general problem space in which a main concern is the production of the new as a complex struggle or difficulty. In the next chapter I look at some key intricacies in Deleuze's conception of the new, as going through certain changes roughly around the same time (a post-'68 period of disappointment and regrouping), and then leading up to *Cinema 2*, which will be read as a conceptual map of struggles for the new in situations where the new appears blocked. Deleuze's conception of concepts as laid out in *What is Philosophy?* extends many of the same concerns. The next chapter will thereby gradually bring out a central aspect of the concept in Deleuze, as a kind of resistance to a present seemingly rigged against substantial political change. For Deleuze, art, cinema, and concepts are different modes for composing virtual potential, also in situations in which the actualization of potential can seem impossible.

Notes

1 The English translation of the film title *Le gai savoir* was "The Joy of Learning", which not only fails to capture most levels of the title, but also hides the fact that it is borrowed from the title of Nietzsche's book *Die fröhliche Wissenschaft*, of which the French translation is precisely *Le gai savoir*, and the English translation *The Gay Science* (although previously more often *The Joy of Science*, *The Joyous Science*, or *The Joy of Wisdom*). While Kaja Silverman and Harun Farocki give a solid argument for translating the title as *Gay Knowledge* (1998: 236, note 6, see also 117), this seems not to have caught on. I will therefore stick with the French title of the film.

2 I will keep to the French title also of *Ici et ailleurs*, even though there is a perfectly good English translation (*Here and Elsewhere*), because it appears to me to be more established also in the English literature on Godard.

3 Given how Morrey discusses some of Godard's later works, such as *Histoire(s) du cinéma*, there is reason to believe he would agree with most of what follows in this section, but I will still use this aspect of his discussion of *2 or 3 Things* as a means to make a larger point.

4 Daniel Morgan levels a seemingly similar critique of Douglas Morrey's reading of the strip-mining scene in Godard's 1991 film *Allemagne 90 neuf zero*, claiming that Morrey remains "at [the] level" of identifying "confusion and ambiguity" or resistance to the "fixed and easily intelligible", but Morgan's critique seems not to be based on a full reading of Morrey's analysis of that film which clearly goes deeper than that (Morgan 2012: 126).

5 Colin MacCabe suggests that *2 or 3 Things* "anticipate[d] much of the reflective essays produced by Sonimage", but he does not develop this beyond mentioning "Godard's own commentary", "the uncertainty of the 'knowledge' [...] emphasised by the dissociation of sound and image and the increased use of montage", and "the devices of cinema" seen as part of "consumer society" as a "contradictory ground on which Godard can attempt to articulate the terms of the personal and the political" (1980: 52).

6 It seems to me that Godard uses the French word *conscience* here in the sense of consciousness—as indicated by a certain phenomenological framing in this text and even more so by the ending of the central coffee cup scene in the film (which I will look closer at below)—while the English text translates the word to conscience. He may however mean both (we can note that the Latin "conscientia" covers conscience and consciousness but also knowledge that is collective, that goes beyond the individual).

7 As Deleuze himself writes in *the Logic of Sense*: "What is common to metaphysics and transcendental philosophy is, above all, this alternative which they both impose on us: either an undifferentiated ground, a groundlessness, formless nonbeing, or an abyss without differences and without properties, or a supremely individuated Being and an intensely personalized Form. Without this Being or this Form, you will have only chaos" (LS 121, see also 118). And in *Difference and Repetition*: "The ultimate, external illusion of representation is this illusion that results from all its internal illusions—namely, that groundlessness should lack differences, when in fact it swarms with them. What, after all, are Ideas, with their constitutive multiplicity" (DR 347).

8 Some commentators have taken the terminology in *Difference and Repetition* to indicate a "structuralist" phase that Deleuze later abandons. This is to downplay or miss precisely that "structure" in *Difference and Repetition* (as well as in the article on structuralism he wrote earlier) has a "new sense" or logic, with conceptions of

determination and organization that continued to be central for Deleuze, although described with varying terminology.

9   Godard directed or co-directed films in between, including *La Chinoise* (1967), to which *2 or 3 Things* is more commonly seen as a sequel due to its specific political concerns and connections to the student movement.

10 Alain Bergala points to how all Sonimage works continue to find new means to grapple with the same problems having to do with the parade of too many images moving too fast—and the use of slow motion in *France tour détour* is a means to do so—and he connects this with the program laid out in *Le gai savoir* (1999 [1979]: 34).

11 Douglas Morrey makes a connection between one of these sketches in *Le gai savoir* and such efforts in the late 1960s and early 1970s by the likes of Lyotard and Deleuze and Guattari (2005: 89, see also 109, 155ff).

12 Two examples directly follow. Patricia says, as we see a complex poster with writings and illustrations of Third World solidarity: "Here the sound is missing. The CIA killed the sound technician who had recorded the voice of Camilo Torres who denounced the alliance of the Vatican with the American secret service"—playful but also conceptual, in the wider sense of the term. In the following scene, in which the image is all black, Émile says "Here the image is missing, the Anglo-Canadian police gouged out the eyes of a cameraman who was filming the landscapes and faces of a free Quebec."

13 For discussions on how Godard's transition to/inclusion of video meant expanded possibilities for critical reflection, see Dubois (1992) and White (2013: 47; 62). See also Michel Witt, who talks about how video technology "afforded [Godard] considerable economic and creative autonomy", how "the video image can [...] be immediately reviewed and subjected to collective discussion", how it "can also if necessary be wiped and redone", and how "video allowed him to process all manner of types of imagery from paintings and photographs to freshly shot footage, and to combine and reflect on this material through the use of simple vision mixing techniques such as split screen, wipes, superimposition and the use of onscreen text" (Witt 2018: 15:16–16:53). It also provided "some of the independence and flexibility long enjoyed by other artists, such as writers and painters", and "[a]bove all", "video functioned for [Godard] from the outset as a quasi-scientific tool for the processing of found images and sounds, an instrument of thought that allowed him to combine and dissect material from disparate sources",; in Godard's own words: "it permits me to re-inject all the images I want, and allows all manner of transposition and manipulation. And above all it allows me to think in images, not in text" (Witt 2013: 52; see also 2004: 76ff).

14 Douglas Morrey: *Le gai savoir* "marks, within Godard's œuvre, the mythic *return to zero* that had been repeatedly called for over the preceding two years" (2005: 84). See also MacCabe 1980: 54.

15 Daniel Morgan makes a similar point about images of nature more generally in this later Godard period (2012: 118).
16 We can note two different lines of interpretation of Godard's voice-over: Farocki suggests that it "represent[s] something like the political super ego of the movement" and "the subject who says he knows", while Silverman argues against this by claiming that "[a]s the film progresses, Godard's voice is stripped of its pretense to rationality, and becomes more and more free-associative" (Silverman and Farocki 1998: 125).
17 Jean-Henri Roger appears to have had a key role in the first two DVG films, but otherwise it was basically Godard and Gorin. While the nature of their collaboration is a bit hard to ascertain, Gorin seems to have been more in the driving seat than what is often assumed—although how much and in what sense is unclear (MacCabe 1980: 58, 76).
18 Colin MacCabe argues similarly that Sonimage deals with "some of the bitter consequences of the failure of the revolutionary left in Europe during the 1970s" (1980: 74).
19 As Witt writes, "[a]ccording to Gorin, by 1972—well before Miéville and Godard subsequently revisited the rushes—he and Godard had already struggled long and hard with the material and produced several rough cuts" (2013: 46).
20 There was similar verbal self-critique in *Caméra-oeil* (*Camera-Eye*), Godard's (form-wise relatively simple) contribution to Chris Marker's anthology film *Loin du Vietnam* (*Far from Vietnam*, 1967), in which he discusses having to relate to the war from France (after being denied an entry permit). For more on this kind of self-critical awareness in Godard in the late 1960s and early to mid 1970s as being informed by and in dialogue with third-worldist thought and filmmaking, and how this altered along with changing historical conditions at the time of Sonimage, see Emmelhainz (2019: 92–6, 101–8, 77, 21f).
21 We should note, again, that Miéville was involved in all aspects of the film: as co-producer, co-director, co-editor, and co-writer. So, contrary to what is often implied even by those careful to credit her contribution, this contribution is far from reducible to what she says through voice-over. Her voice-over is not even that prevalent: after intersecting with Godard's in the beginning, her voice does not return until the last ca. thirteen minutes of the (ca. fifty-four-minute long) film (although, certainly, she then delivers fairly harsh and revealing critiques of what Godard and Gorin did in shooting and directing the footage as well as how they understood what goes on in it).
22 Examples from two of the Godard scholars recurring in this book: Sonimage serves as a "corrective to the dogmatic rhetoric of the Dziga Vertov Group films", writes Morrey (2005: 114). White not only argues that the DVG films were "unyieldingly didactic indictments" (2013: 87) but also that Sonimage "ended the pseudo-revolutionary silliness of his Dziga Vertov period" (160). Both however also point to differences that are important and easier to agree with, as we will see.

23 Miéville was key also in this regard. In the early 1970s, after she had met Godard but also before they started working together, "[s]he relentlessly criticized the assumptions of the Maoist revolutionary discourse and argued that it had continuously ignored the reality of daily life in France", and that the "response to the inadequacies of the commercial cinema was to be found in the analysis of how the image functioned in daily life", which led to them setting up a video atelier to "investigate the intersection of the political and the personal in everyday life and the place of the image in that intersection" (MacCabe 1992: 20).

24 Why scare quotes? Because Deleuze appears to have written the questions himself for this *Cahiers du Cinéma* text presented as an interview (Dosse (2010 [2007]: 401).

25 In Chapter 4 I will briefly come back to the meaning of the French word *frontiére* when examining the first two of Godard-Miéville's embryonic cinecepts, which are precisely about *frontiéres*, and in which they clearly play with the double meaning of the term as both border and frontier. We can also note that in the English translation of *Cinema 2*, in which Deleuze also discusses this aspect of Godard, *frontiére* is translated as frontier.

26 Cf. Serge Daney's clearly different claim earlier that year (1976) that Godard's approach "consists of taking note of what is said [...] and then looking immediately for the other statement", and in which "the real question is 'what can we oppose to this?'" (1976). While Daney does say that "Godard is speaking to us" from "an in-between", this is an "in-between" of photographs, cinema, television, rather than something in line with what Deleuze is saying here.

27 Jacques Aumont makes similar points about subsequent shifts from a (supposedly) more Eisensteinian montage of the Dziga Vertov Group period (despite their critique of Eisenstein in favor of Vertov), but without mentioning its logic of montage in terms such as dialectics or going beyond dialectics. It is also a bit unclear how the Eisensteinian goes together with Aumont's claim a page earlier that in the DVG films montage was reduced to illustrating a given *verbal* discourse rather than creating sense on its own (2011: 55f). For a more substantial comparison of montage in Godard and Eisenstein—and a more nuanced assessment of what Godard also adopts from Eisenstein (and Vertov), as well as how Godard critiques Eisenstein for not having really achieved montage but rather effects arising from combinations of angles in the editing—see Witt (2000); see also Witt (2013: 12f, 98f, 148f); Morgan (2012: 233–5); Godard and Ishaghpour (2005 [1999]: 15f, 33f, 105–8).

28 For a different interpretation of the "et" (and) in *Ici et ailleurs* concerned with deconstruction and a more traditional continental philosophy of lack and negativity, see Drabinski (2008: 51f). Drabinski's thorough readings of the Sonimage works more generally also deserve a longer comment as they can serve as a clarifying contrast to a Deleuzian perspective. Drabinski convincingly reveals some Derridian and Levinasian aspects in the Sonimage works. These aspects have to do with an ethical concern with developing language capable of expressing the

seemingly unrepresentable, and with focus on the violence and suffering of the other (2008: 36f, 42f, 111, 132ff, 142ff). Much of what Drabinski brings up is also about destabilizing clear or traditional meanings—or forms of representation that expel otherness—by exposing underlying chains of references (2008: e.g. 83–7, 123, 135). A Derridian chiasm, in Drabinksi's terms, "unsettle[s]" and "displace[s]" meaning, and expresses that which is beyond representation only negatively, as a trace at the border between representation and the "non-representable" (78). Derrida, we can add, generally operates through a logic inspired by negative theology: what is beyond representation can appear directly only as a haunting or a ghost (in contrast to Deleuze's direct and positive handling of subrepresentational structure as I discuss above and more extensively in Chapters 1 and 3). More specifically, Drabinski reads the conjunction *and* in Sonimage as "structurally" revealing that "there is no possibility of a relation or correlation." And while *Ici* still aims at "craft[ing] some sort of relation to the Other, even if across an abyss"— and Levinas appears to push a little further in this regard—the discussion keeps returning to "the Derridian *reservation* about language's ability to carry [things] across" without falling back into representation. Furthermore, while the *and* of *Ici* is recognized as a kind of nonrepresentational movement, it is a movement of that which "haunt[s]" rather than presents (51–3, 57, emphasis mine). Similarly, *Comment ça va* is said to be concerned with finding "the image" to represent "the singular", but although "Godard's cinematic grammar gestures" "toward" such an image, it "never arrive[s]." Instead "the image comes to address us in a series of detours and deferrals" showing that "[t]he undecidable is a voracious abyss, but also evasive and oblique" (75f). Overall, and despite a promise of what he calls a "rendering" of the unrepresentable, Drabinski conceives of Godard's "cinematic language" as a "countergrammar" in which what it says "(the scene, the shot) is unsaid in/at the very same moment (unraveled, dissolved)". This is a "site of saying and unsaying", "a representation that is internally ruinous", "a site of representation and its destruction" (132f, 77, 135). Again, this reading sharply contrasts with Deleuze's.

29 I return in Chapter 5 to a comparison with this aspect of Deleuze but with Godard's *own* ideas of montage: montage as *rapprochement*.
30 Looking at how the film is referenced by scholars, there seems to be no full consensus on whether it was finished in 1974 or 1975. However, while most say 1974, and while it was intensely worked on every day across 1973 and 1974 (Witt 2014: 320), the film clearly appears to have been finished in 1975. At the beginning the "now" is said to be 1974, but in the rest of the film it is 1975. Not long after the opening sequence Godard's voice-over says the *Jusqu'à la victoire!* footage is from "five years ago" (it was shot in February–July 1970). In the end Miéville explicitly says the film is called *Ici et ailleurs* in 1975 (for a thematic reading of this temporal "slippage", see Drabinski 2008: 56). In his famous 1976 article on Godard, Serge

Daney says the original footage was "held on [to] for five years" and that the span considered in the film is "between here and elsewhere, images and sounds, 1970 and 1975" (1976). Furthermore, and adding to the referencing difficulty, while *Ici* was the first finished Sonimage work, it was not released in theaters until 1976, after, as Witt writes, "the completion and first screenings of *Numéro deux* and *Comment ça va* as well as *Six fois deux*" (2014: 340, note 6). (Although, as White says, *Comment ça va* was not released in *theaters* until 1978 [2013: 78].)

31   1936 is the year when the socialist movement the Popular Front won the general election in France, so not a revolution per se.

32   For some readings of such thematic points interspersed with formal analysis, see Alter (2018: 161–3) and Morrey (2005: 107f). See also Emmelhainz (2019: 149–51). For a reading of a similar joining together of revolutionary moments in *Histoire(s) du cinéma*, see Morgan (2012: 220).

33   Cf. Serge Daney's more reductive interpretation of the shifting electronic texts in *Numéro deux*: "In between the rare moments where they make sense, the letters inscribe in the heart of the black screen only the enigma of their form: hieroglyphs. Sense becomes no more than a particular instance of non-sense" (1976).

34   Here/Elsewhere; Victory/Defeat; Foreign/National; Everywhere/Nowhere; To Be/To Have; Space/Time; Question/Answer; Entrance/Exit; Order/Disorder; Interior/Exterior; Black/White; Yet/Already; Dream/Reality.

35   The status of the zero in this particular film, however, is quite complex. While I primarily want to point to the connection to a ground zero of revolutionary intensity, as explored above, and its specific attachment here to collective work, zero also appears in *Ici* as part of other functions and measures. Starting at 16:10 there is a brief section in which capital is said to work through zeros, turning us all into hordes of zeros as it multiplies by adding zeros. While this is reasonably read just as well as intensity bound up by capitalism, zero here also functions to indicate lack of hope and agency: at 17:28 Godard adds: "As they're zeros, it multiplies as it cancels out." And "in this place, our hopes have been reduced to zero." But Godard-Miéville then briefly tie things back to the calculator, and the years of prior revolutionary moments.

36   They now combine the following through *or*: Here/Elsewhere; Powerful/Miserable; Today/Tomorrow; Normal/Mad; All/Nothing; Always/Never; Man/Woman; More/Less; To Live/To Die; Poor/Rich.

37   So, while not argumentative, it is not merely artistically associative—Deleuze: "It can, in fact, always be objected that there is only an interstice between associated images. From this point of view, images like those which bring together Golda Meir and Hitler in *Ici et ailleurs* would be intolerable. But this is perhaps proof that we are not yet ready for a true 'reading' of the visual image. For, in Godard's method, it is not a question of association. Given one image, another image has to be chosen which will induce an interstice between the two. This is not an operation of association, but of differentiation, as mathematicians say […]" (C2 179).

38 The term soft montage appears to have been coined by Harun Farocki in a discussion with Kaja Silverman of the (in this sense) formally similar Sonimage film *Numéro deux* (discussed in Chapter 4 below). Farocki: "When Godard shows two monitors, he makes one comment upon the other in a soft montage. I say "soft montage" since what is at issue is a general relatedness, rather than a strict opposition or equation" (Silverman and Farocki 1998: 142). Deleuze, on his part, describes this montage in *Ici* as "placing separate images together in the same spatial field" (C2 162f).

39 Godard: "The whole world is too much for one image. No, it is not, says international capitalism, which builds all its wealth on this truth."

3 The Problem of the New: Ideas, Cinema, Concepts

DELEUZE'S PHILOSOPHY OF concepts is inseparable from his grappling with the production of the new. In this chapter I focus on the latter part. What is Deleuze's conception of the new? How does novelty come about? Is it common or rare? What is the role of art and philosophy vis-à-vis the new? This chapter presents a reading of the new in Deleuze that goes beyond the prevailing understanding. This requires close examination of details in parts of *Difference and Repetition* and *Cinema 2* and of certain changes in between these two works. In the next chapter I return to Godard-Miéville to examine a set of embryonic cinecepts, but we will also see how they deal with the problem of the new in ways similar to the later Deleuze: this even forms the problem space for the whole of Sonimage. We can then draw together Godard-Miéville's embryonic cinecepts with both Deleuze's conception of the new and his concept of concepts.

This chapter explores neglected shifts and complexities in Deleuze's conception of the new. According to a dominant understanding, Deleuze conceives of the new as constantly produced. And there is much to that if we look at the basic ontology: it was evidently foundational for Deleuze to shift to a being of becoming from more traditional views (from older notions of the world as static or circular, to various ideas about changes happening only through grand eruptions in the otherwise unchanging, or as rearrangements into new patterns implicitly already there as possibilities from the start). Yet, there is another order of novelty in Deleuze which is not often acknowledged: events or creations—grand or subtle—that are remarkable and *rare*. This is obviously not about some outbursts of transcendence (WP 47ff): as with many other aspects in Deleuze, the very idea of the new as remarkable and rare is fundamentally rethought, like how he rethinks notions such as Ideas or essences. The mechanisms of all this will be examined below.

Deleuze sees the new as rare with increasing explicitness throughout his works, and without any contradiction with the basic ontology of a being of becoming. We find his most developed exploration of the new as rare in *Cinema 2*, a book that reconsiders a set of problems from *Difference and Repetition*. Deleuze's conception of the new as rare has clearly not been much noted by antagonistic readers such as Alain Badiou, who contrasts himself against Deleuze in this regard.[1] But advanced and pioneering Deleuze scholars (and perceptive critics of related aspects in Badiou's reading of Deleuze), like Daniel W. Smith and James Williams, also tend to reduce Deleuze's thoughts on the new to continuous becoming or differentiation. This chapter shows that such readings overlook complications in the virtual/actual relation as well as certain shifts—at least in emphasis—in Deleuze's thinking during the 1970s and '80s. I will start with a critical examination of Smith's and Williams's respective readings of the new in Deleuze, while also developing a counter-reading with a focus on *Difference and Repetition*. I then shift to a reading of the problem of the new in *Cinema 2*, and finish with a section on how all this is implicated in Deleuze's late concept of concepts.

According to Smith, Deleuze follows Bergson and Whitehead in conceiving of the new as a "fundamental ontological concept: Being = Difference = the New" (2012a: 236f).[2] Not only is difference instead of identity ontologically primary, for Smith difference equals the new. Deleuze himself, however, rarely uses the term new in this way. Smith acknowledges this by saying that "the new is merely an operative concept in Deleuze's philosophy", and that the new is "thematize[d] explicitly under the rubric of difference (*Difference and Repetition*) or the event (*Logic of Sense*) or time (*The Time-Image*)" (237). This, as we will see, is a little misleading. Smith also argues, and this is more clearly the case, that the main Deleuzian question is "What are the ontological conditions under which something new can be produced?" Smith references a statement by Deleuze in *Cinema 1* about Bergson shifting the focus from the eternal to the new in this sense, and Deleuze's 1986 preface to the English translation of *Dialogues* which mentions conditions for the new with regards to A.N. Whitehead (2012a: 237; 406, note 2). Deleuze's focus in these statements, however—as evident in Smith's formulation of the question—is on the *conditions* under which something new *can* appear, and more so than on the new itself (why would there be a need for the words "something" and "can" if not to imply that which does not happen all the time?).

These conditions for the new, as Smith also shows, are virtual structures of potential that are implicated in actual things and qualities. They are Ideas or Problems that are immanent to the world, real, and in themselves made up of (positive, self-differing) differences, which also create new difference. Let us a look a little closer at how this works, continuing the discussion of these structures in Chapter

1 above. Virtual Ideas or Problems are systems made up by "differential relations between genetic elements" and by "mobile singularities" that correspond/correlate with remarkable points in those relations (DR 229, 231, 260, 350f, 274). These systems are intensive, metastable, disparate. Yet, they are also fully determined. First, through reciprocal determination between differential elements, which also "establish[es] a kind of resonance between divergent series" since each differential element is a self-differing intensity. Second, through "complete determination", which means that in these relations between differential elements or divergent series there are "significant points", or "singularities corresponding to" such significant points, and the Idea/Problem makes up a "distribution" of these singularities/significant points (DR 348f, see also 262). This double determination (reciprocal and complete) of "virtual content" Deleuze calls differen*t*iation with a t (258).

The actualization of such "virtual content", however, means the production of *further* difference—differen*c*iation with a c. Actualization is *not* a realization of something preconfigured as a given possibility in the Idea (DR 263f). The Idea functions instead as a "problematic field which conditions" actualization. Its distribution of singularities makes up its "potentiality", which pushes towards "solutions". And "it is the problem which orientates, conditions and engenders solutions" (348, 258, 264, see also 262). Still, the Ideas themselves appear to lack the ability to fully actualize solutions (235). It is rather a second order of intensity "expressed" as "spatio-temporal dynamisms" which "'develops' and […] determines the movement of actualization", like in a growing egg (266, 307). These dynamisms perform "pre-quantitative and pre-qualitative dramatization[s]" of Ideas (266, 274), which "create a space and a time peculiar to that which is actualised": "the developed qualities and extensities of the perceptual world" (274, 351). While these dynamisms are in some sense "internal to Ideas", they also have an autonomous "intermediary" function between virtual and actual. They unleash the "element of potentiality in the Idea" but do so inventively through their "own power of determining space and time" (354, 271, 274).[3] In "correspondence with the differentiation of the Idea", they "creatively specify" its "relations and singularities" (271, 268f). I will return to these mechanisms below in slightly less technical terms, especially in the reexamination of *Cinema 2*, and show how the virtual-intensity-actual relation is not always uninterruptedly productive. I will also look more specifically at *how* Ideas get *their* determinations (which for reasons we cannot yet see is central for conceiving of how art and philosophy can be productive also in situations that appear blocked).

Let us here return to Smith's and Williams's respective readings of the new in Deleuze. For Smith "every process of actualization is, by its very nature, the production of the new" (2012a: 240). What is said here? Is everything that happens new? And what would the term new thereby mean? In his book on Deleuze's (late 1960s) philosophy of time, James Williams appears to claim precisely that everything is new: "Every pace taken by every animal is new. Every roll of every stone is a break with the past"; all in all, "every event is new" even "any habitual gesture and the passing of that gesture". For Williams, the habitual gesture is new in the *same sense* as the French Revolution, although the latter is more "easy to understand" as new (2011: 106, 15, see also 19, 129f, 152). Smith's assessment of the new in Deleuze is similar but slightly less radical: while every event is new, and novelty is a ubiquitous part of everyday processes, not everything is an event. A multiplicity, he writes, is a mixture of both "ordinary" and "singular" points, and it is only with the latter that "something 'happens' within the multiplicity—an event" (2012a: 247).[4] Still, Smith's examples of such events—physical: the point at which water boils; psychic: the point at which a person breaks down in tears, or even just says something or gestures in a certain manner (247, 253)—are not only everyday: the first is a mechanical repetition, locking singularities into a closed system,[5] and the others are strikingly (and likely deliberately chosen to be) trivial.[6] Pointing to the trivial can underline the universality of a being of a becoming. Yet, if there is something that Deleuze contrasts to the new, it is, as we will see, the trivial.[7] Smith and Williams, erudite, thorough, and innovative readers of Deleuze, are still clearly grounded in parts of his philosophy and far from simply wrong, or wrong in any simple sense.

I agree with Williams that everything existing—according to Deleuze's ontology—differs from the self-identical and diverges from the predictable and predetermined. But does this also mean that everything—every roll of every stone and every animal pace or gesture, as Williams writes—is "new"? I will answer this question first by making my own path through chapter 2 of *Difference and Repetition*, the main focus of Williams's reading. In this chapter Deleuze presents three syntheses of time which imply, necessitate, and intervene in each other. The first synthesis pulls time into "living presents" (and thereby serves as "foundation" for time). An animal/organism is a particular living present. From this perspective "the present alone exists": the past and the future are included but only as dimensions of a particular lived present, that is, as former lived presents (past) and as anticipation / exception / prediction (future) (DR 91, 97f). An animal/organism is a cluster of "contractions-contemplations" or passive and active syntheses. Passive: the organism as a preconscious, prepsychological "sum of [material, physical] contractions, of retentions and expectations", which make up a lived present as a linear succession in time. Active: activities that—as both "founded upon" and continuously conditioned by "preceding passive syntheses"—involve "faculties of reflective representation, memory and intelligence". As such, an organism (as with everything else in the world) is a "habit" that "*draws* something new from repetition—namely, difference" while also "assuring the perpetuation" of itself. The first synthesis is thereby both productive and "reproductive", both a "constantly renewed form of a living present" and a "repetition as a binding" (DR 93–5, 99, 101, 120, 122; cf. FLB 88, 90). Habit, therefore, "is *more or less* able to 'draw off difference'" from repetition, and even when *more* able, merely drawing a difference from repetition is contrasted by Deleuze to repetition as difference in itself (117f, emphasis mine).

Organisms draw difference from their own self-repetition in these ways: the passive level constantly both produces and reproduces things like cells and organs—"*the organism as biological Idea*" (DR 233f)—and more wholistically and psychically a sense of a particular self in time. So, if we bracket the reproductive side, the passive syntheses contain a type of constant "novelty" production. Also the active syntheses involve novelty but of the sensory-motor kind: organisms are indeterminate and "delayed" in their reactions—for example an animal responding to incoming stimuli with a gesture: what will the gesture be? They "have the time to select their elements", as Deleuze writes about the same aspect of sensory-motor re/action in *Cinema 1*, "to organise them or to integrate them into a new movement which is impossible to conclude by simply prolonging the received excitation." But, as he adds, such presentation of the "unpredictable or new will be called 'action' strictly speaking" (more on this below) (C2 62; see also DR 96f). Of course, very few actions are new in any other sense than not precalculable, or, to use key criteria of evaluation for Deleuze, interesting, remarkable, or extraordinary. How about the second synthesis?

The second synthesis is the "ground": Memory as Being, a Past prior to any former presents, a virtual Whole of time coexisting with itself on all its levels of relaxation and contraction (Bergson's cone), including the present. The first synthesis, the "life of passing presents" (and its memory as mere present-centered psychological representations of former presents), occurs *in* this deeper Past. The present is here a dimension *of* the Past: its most contracted point. As the Past also "perpetually differs from itself" the present as its most contracted point is constantly made to *pass* (rather than remain as eternal present): each "new present [...] comes forth only by contracting this past" (DR 126, 100ff, 358). The Past also adds underlying differential substance to the mere line of "new presents" or "indifferent instants". Each lived present "contracts a differential level of the whole", a specific set of sub-representational syntheses (or Ideas), although they also link up to the whole of the Past (DR 105f, 110). It is the *third* synthesis, however, that "bends" the temporarily of the pure Past, that disjoints/decenters its orderly/circular relations to the present, makes its Ideas differential rather than self-same, and which drives the actualization of new difference from virtual Problems: it undoes "the identity of the self [and] the world" (DR 111, 344, 364f, 113).[8]

Yet, the third synthesis is itself "empty and pure form", the ungrounded: time "freed from the events which made up its [empirical] content" (and from being the mere measure of its movements). Time, instead, as intensive force. The third synthesis guarantees change, and as such it is (paradoxically) "static": it is "the form of change [that] does not change"—an eternal return of the same as difference (DR 111). The past and present are on this level only dimensions of the future (117). Not the future, then, as a dimension of the first or second syntheses, not the future present in a succession of presents nor the future of anticipation or prediction, but the future as an autonomous force that (from this perspective) precedes the other syntheses. Deleuze calls this "the future as such" and equates it with "the new, complete novelty" (113). How does this complete novelty relate to the other aspects of time? The living present and pure past need the future as such as their basic condition, but the future also needs grounds and living presents: it needs content— however much this "involves their reorganisation" (141). But of course, the content cannot *itself* be the "complete novelty" of the empty form, without dispersing into that empty form. Granted, the pure future is a constant in the functioning of the other two syntheses: it eternally propels their underlying differential mechanisms and interrelations, certainly also in the everyday. But the third synthesis, even in this second chapter of *Difference and Repetition*, is said to "struggle" against the tendencies towards the same in the other syntheses (117), and as Deleuze writes in the conclusion, its "role […] would not be to suppress the other two but […] to distribute difference to them (in the form of difference drawn off or included)" (DR 365). Furthermore, also in the second chapter, Deleuze implies that the third synthesis can align the pure past and passing present in more dynamic and rare ways.

Deleuze uses pivotal Acts in *Hamlet* and *Oedipus* as parables for how the third synthesis connects with the past and present, and as parables they can be interpreted as pointing in both directions: to novelty as ongoing and to the New as rare. For most of their respective play time, Hamlet and Oedipus—however much the Act has also already happened while it has not yet happened or doesn't even need to happen—are either too small for the Act (they remain "in the past and live themselves as such") or they conquer the role of the actor (become "equal to the act" in a self-identity-forming present moment). But it is only in the Act itself that the past and the present align as a "royal repetition" of each other, forming a self-identity-destroying "secret coherence" that "draws together the whole of time" in ways more fully equal to the third synthesis as eternally repeating only difference. As "image" or "symbol", Deleuze continues, the Act can be "expressed in many ways: to throw time out of joint, to make the sun explode, to throw oneself into the volcano, to kill God or the father". These are not everyday events, of course, but "unique and tremendous" ones [*unique et formidable*] (DR 112).[9] Still, a volcano can also be seen as ever active underneath every gesture or pace—and as a *static* identity, the self *is* constantly thrown into it.[10] To expand on the image, however, volcanic *activity* (not to mention dormancy or extinction) does not mean constant eruption—as Nietzsche wrote: "we are all growing volcanoes approaching their hour of eruption; how near or distant that is, of course, nobody knows" (2001 [1882]: 36 [§9]). And later in *Difference and Repetition* Deleuze likens the third synthesis in the form of "the eternal return" to that which "ceaselessly rumbles in this other dimension of the transcendental or the volcanic *spatium*", contrasted with "the laws of nature [that] govern the surface of the world" in which generating intensity "tends to be cancelled" (DR 301f).[11]

The implication in chapter 2's drama parables of a more dynamic order of novelty production, moreover, is underlined by what Deleuze brings up directly after: outstanding events in actual history and how they interconnect; for instance the French Revolution repeating aspects of the Roman Republic. Deleuze's main point here is that the former does not simply repeat historical facts or literal happenings in said Republic but "the historical condition under which something new is effectively produced" (DR 112, 367ff; see also WP 140). That is, remarkable events in history never replicate other remarkable historical events, only their conditions. My point, however, is this: the French Revolution still belongs to the kind of events that are exceptional. The long-time Deleuze reader may here think about the danger of confusing history and becoming or erasing becoming-revolutionary by focusing on the actual Revolution.[12] But rarity and becoming are not mutually exclusive: Deleuze described May '68 as "a becoming-revolutionary without a revolutionary future" and an "intrusion of becoming [...] a gust of the real in its pure state" that "was astounding" (ABC Letter G). The third synthesis, then, may be both constant in its driving of the everyday becoming of everything, *and* propel an underground movement that can develop into a dynamic new potential, which may or may not erupt in the actual. That is, another order of *Future* which may temporarily crack open the womb-crystal[13] of past and passing presents in ways that make its production of the new—not necessarily Grand (as the volcano metaphor implies), it can just as well be subtle or occur only in thought, but—interesting, remarkable or extraordinary, at least at the moment of its birth.

Williams's focus on the novelty of everything, then, makes a certain sense as referring to the open creativity of time affecting everything in time: even the seemingly most predestined in development or static in identity is the outcome of (slow or fast) processes that are distinctive and perpetuating but also openly creative and without a given origin—Deleuze: "The eternal return has no other sense but this: the absence of any assignable origin"; it "does not presuppose any identity"; it "is said of a world the very ground of which is difference" (DR 153, 302). After (and way before) Nietzsche, however, there are many others who have made similar points, and Deleuze's philosophy wouldn't be that original if it could be boiled down to such points. And it cannot: it has complications that go far beyond the open becoming of everything. Once the being of becoming is firmly established, other registers of the problem of the new can come into focus.

In his preface to *A Thousand Plateaus*, Brian Massumi claims that for Deleuze (and Guattari) "the world rarely leaves room for uncommon intensity, being in large measure an entropic trashbin of outworn modes that refuse to die" (1987: xiv). Hyperbolic but not simply inaccurate, this claim is the opposite of Williams's. Yet, they are not mutually exclusive. As Nathan Widder writes, "in the ontology Deleuze advances", "[p]olitics, like time and becoming, consists of multiple dispersed layers that are interwoven and folded into one another", so that "combinations of apparent stasis and fundamental change are to be expected" (2012: 52). Williams draws his conclusions—based on close readings—about omnipresent novelty by focusing too much on the interrelation between the three syntheses as uninterrupted constant production, and by reading as too dominant the side of reality in which only differences return in time.[14] Massumi's claim makes sense only by focusing almost exclusively on the actual realm, spanning a continuum of nature and culture, including "insignificant facts" and "everyday banality", or processes of stratification—"beneficial in many respects and unfortunate in many others"—that Deleuze and Guattari say "consist of giving form to matters, of imprisoning intensities or locking singularities into systems of resonance and redundancy, or producing upon the body of the earth molecules large and small and organizing them into molar aggregates" (DR 171; ATP 40). With a selective focus, then, one might read out of Deleuze's philosophy either the claim that everything is new or that almost nothing is new, without there being a hard contradiction.

Still, there are clear problems with the "everything is new" line. It has most obviously little to do with Deleuze's diagnoses of social, aesthetic, and political areas. This is the case already in *Difference and Repetition*, as is made explicit in this passage from the conclusion on the need for art to intervene in our daily life of "sad repetitions":

> The more our daily life appears standardised, stereotyped and subject to an accelerated reproduction of objects of consumption, the more art must be injected into it in order to extract from it that little difference which plays simultaneously between other levels of repetition [...] Each art has its interrelated techniques or repetitions, the critical and revolutionary power of which may attain the highest degree and lead us from the sad repetitions of habit to the profound repetitions of memory, and then to the ultimate repetitions of death in which our freedom is played out. (DR 365f)

The "everything is new" reading is also more directly and most clearly at odds with Deleuze's conception of thought, and questions of thought and what it means to think are at the center of his work. Even the second chapter of *Difference and Repetition*, the main basis of Williams's thesis, is mostly about thought and its conditions. While that chapter is part of a kind of ontology of nature (i.e. it is wholly irreducible to humans), Deleuze more generally sees "Thought and [...] Nature" as "two facets" of the same "plane of immanence" (WP 38; see also 48). And as Williams writes in passing towards the end of his study: "Acts are event-like not only in bodies, but also in thoughts" (2011: 158). So, if one concludes from *Difference and Repetition*, as Williams does, that everything is new, even the most banal sensory-motor movement, then must not all thought, even the most banal sensory-motor thought, also be new? That is obviously not the case. The "everything is new" conclusion can therefore only be drawn after having taken a wrong turn somewhere.

In all of Deleuze, the new in thought is considered to be rare. Throughout *Difference and Repetition*, including in the second chapter, new thought or thought directly pushed by the third synthesis appears only as a possibility. Exceptional encounters with certain troubling signs can force us to think, but not even such encounters lead to new Ideas with any necessity.[15] To really think, as Deleuze writes in the third chapter of *Difference and Repetition*, is "to bring into being that which does not yet exist" and this happens "rarely" [*rarement*] (DR 185, 168). In a talk given in 1987 on what it means to have an idea in film and in philosophy (respectively) Deleuze said: "having an idea is a rare event [*un evenement qui arrive rarement*], it is a kind of celebration, not very common [*peu courante*]" (TRM 312). And such events can be sudden and explosive: "we must condense all the singularities, precipitate all the circumstances, points of fusion, congelation or condensation in a sublime occasion, *Kairos*, which makes the solution explode like something abrupt, brutal and revolutionary. Having an Idea is this as well" (DR 239.) In his book on Foucault, Deleuze writes about the occasions when thinking "free[s] itself from what it thinks (present) and is able to 'think otherwise' (the future)" by making "the past active and present to the outside so that something new will finally come about" (F 119).

Extraordinary vs. Trivial

No new thoughts, no sign of any subtle change or fold in an old thought.
                                        Nietzsche (2002 [1886]: 119 [§248])

[T]he greatest thoughts are the greatest events.
                                        Nietzsche (2002 [1886]: 171 [§285])

Taking inspiration from Nietzsche, early Deleuze aimed in one sense to shift focus from the Great Historical Event to the "silent plurality of senses of each event" and the evaluation of their internal genealogies of conflicting forces. This, however, is not reducible to saying that every event is *new* (NP 4, 2, 156, 159; DR 202f). Furthermore, while the logic of the Great Event is reimagined with a focus on its underlying conditions, Great Events are not thereby disregarded, and they are not made to be equal in importance to everyday gestures. There is a general difference in value, sense, and even register between the "novelty" of everyday gestures and, say, May 1968, even though they have the same *kind* of underlying conditions of virtuality and intensity. Moreover, Significant Great Events can be *subtle*, occur only in thought, and be hardly noticeable in general, at least at first. So how does Deleuze distinguish between significant and insignificant events beyond their size? For Deleuze it is vital to separate trivial events from extraordinary events also within the silent or small, and extraordinary events—whether physical or psychological, micro or macro, subtle or grand—are uncommon. Deleuze upholds this differentiation on several levels, spanning the actual and the virtual, matter, culture, and thought. "The problem of thought", he writes in *Difference and Repetition*,

> is tied [...] to the evaluation of what is important and what is not, to the distribution of singular and regular, distinctive and ordinary points, which takes place entirely within [...] the description of a multiplicity, in relation to the ideal events which constitute the conditions of a 'problem'. To have an Idea means no more than this, and erroneousness or stupidity is defined above all by its perpetual confusion with regard to the important and the unimportant, the ordinary and the singular. (DR 238)

Looking back at May '68 from 1984, Deleuze claims that "[e]verything that was new has been marginalized or turned into caricature" (TRM 235). A main antagonist in *Cinema 2*, which I will explore more closely below, is the "permanent state of daily banality" of post-war capitalist societies.[16] Crumbled organic conceptions of history, culture, and subjectivity—and the very idea of the "new" recaptured by commodity culture—remain as free-floating clichés, a state of modern/late nihilism from which a certain type of post-war cinema, through the power of the unthought, tries to find "a subtle way out" (C2 170).

Phases

While all this is basically in Deleuze from the start, as shown above, his different writings from the 1960s to the 1980s also cover certain shifts in emphasis. These shifts can be screened through what John Rajchman has called three "periods of invention" in Deleuze's work. These periods do not involve "dramatic turning point[s]", linear development, or a maturity curve, but point to how Deleuze's thought became "more complex and multiple in its implications and its reach, as well as its internal relations" (2000: 24). This periodization (itself brief) can be compressed into rubrics: 1) The texts leading up to and including *Difference and Repetition* and *The Logic of Sense*. 2) Post-1968: the work with Guattari up until *A Thousand Plateaus*. 3) The 1980s and 1990s: a burgeoning neoliberal order during which Deleuze formulates a new problem of belief in the world that "reaches its fullest development" in *Cinema 2* (Rajchman 2000: 24–6).[17]

Rajchman's periodization, interpreted and expanded upon, is of some use also for charting Deleuze's thinking on the new—with the caveats that 1) it is understood to cover phases that on the philosophical level are not bound by chronology: to some extent they can be understood as registers or points of focus that Deleuze shifted between from the start; and 2) the second and third periods are basically two stages of the same post-1968 period—vis-à-vis the new, that is, and regardless of other changes.

As is well known, the shift from pre-Guattari to *Anti-Oedipus*, from the first to the second phase—and the chronological aspect is fairly clear here—means a turn towards the more explicitly political, towards flows rather than depths and surfaces, and overhauling the terminology along with shifts in problems (and Guattari's influence). But many core elements remain, including certainly the notion of genetic conditions that subsist in actualized things and phenomena. The fact that this genetic register of reality is far from always dominant, however, now becomes increasingly emphasized and explored.

The shift from the second to the third period is subtler and much less recognized. The biggest difference is perhaps that Deleuze, after having worked intensely with Guattari, "had to return to [his] own work", so that the conceptual apparatus to a large extent shifts back to pre-*Anti-Oedipus* (TRM [1984]: 240). With regard to the focus on the sociopolitical and the conception of the new, the third period is not markedly different from the second. But if the second period already dealt with various repressive forms of reterritorialization, it also manifests a bit more belief in the creative powers of life, art and philosophy, whereas the third period seems more marked by a wavering in Deleuze's own belief in the contemporary world and the possibility of "creating new forms of life". Other kinds of forces perhaps became more overwhelming. Thinking and believing in the world come to concern struggle even more clearly than before, and what that struggle is up against is not merely representational forms—as tended to be the focus in the first period—but rather an ever more slippery, modulating, rhizomatic form of capitalist repression and capture, as already so perceptively conceptualized in the second period (and extended in "Postscript on Control Societies"), to which the third period adds a focus on an aggressive state of banality and cliché and the problem of belief in the world. It is in this third phase that Deleuze writes his cinema books and *What is Philosophy?*[18]

Cinema, Thought, and Sensory-Motor Novelty vs. Time-Image Novelty

Deleuze: "we create [concepts] as a function of problems. Well, problems evolve" and "doing philosophy is creating new concepts as a function of problems that arise today" (ABC Letter H). *What is Philosophy?* responds to the sociohistorical problem (along with more specifically philosophical problems) of how to conceive of the role and characteristics of philosophy in an era in which philosophy is increasingly relegated to the margin by various forces. *Cinema 2* can instead be seen as Deleuze's return to the concerns of *Difference and Repetition* but re-envisioned from other perspectives, and with the problem of the new at center stage. As film theorist and friend of Deleuze Jean-Louis Leutrat wrote in 1988: "A part of [*The*] *Time-Image* evolved from the second chapter of *Difference and Repetition*" (quoted in Dosse 2010 [2007]: 414).[19] While the complexities of *Cinema 2*'s concern with the new are barely acknowledged, Smith and Williams do mention this book in their respective discussions of the new in Deleuze. Smith, as we saw above, takes the concept of time in the time-image to be a synonym for novelty. Williams devotes some concluding pages in his book on Deleuze's philosophy of time to explaining why his study contains "no references to Deleuze's works on cinema": they "fall short of a satisfactory rendition of Deleuze's philosophy of time", and might even "take away from" the "most consistent and extensive form" given to it in *Difference and Repetition* (2011: 161). Williams's brief dismissal of the cinema books appears not to be grounded in a very close reading. *Cinema 2*, as we will see, further complicates—and undermines more of Williams's interpretation of—how Deleuze conceives of the new.

Cinema 2's complications of the new will be laid out more clearly in the next section, since we need to first look at the cinema books' most fundamental level—their basic ontology as this connects to thinking organisms and thinking in film—and gradually work our way towards the problem of the new. *Cinema 1* presents an ontology, creatively borrowed from Bergson, of movement-images: The universe is an acentered aggregate of interacting images consisting of matter-movement-light. Movement, image, and matter are the same thing, there is nothing more real behind or beyond images, and it has been that way since "the world before man" (C1 56–60, 49, 81f). This ontology short-circuits the dichotomy that places images in consciousness (or in other representations) and movement in quantitative space (images = movement). The "black screen" that constitutes subjective consciousness, however, is a specific interruption and subtraction within matter-movement-image-light, which—in terms of Deleuze's book on Leibniz—*folds* the universe into a local center or point of view, expressing only specific aspects clearly with the rest appearing as dark background (C1 60–4; FLB 26–9, 36). It is a "frame"—returning to the language of *Cinema*—into which selections of images are continuously dragged (a kind of material base level of subjectivity). The frame holds up a gap with an interval of time between acting and reacting images, in which thinking is made possible.[20] The narrative that spans the two cinema books, on this level, reads like a map of dwindling paths from chaotic states of matter-images from which emerge simple subjective centers, whose consciousness hardly transcends action-reaction, all the way to creative nonlinear thought.

So we have now approached thought but not yet novelty, and we need to continue a bit more with the basic ontology: thinking, images, and matter are ontologically of the same stuff, and while "there cannot be anything else" in matter that is "of a different kind", there can obviously "be more in matter than the image we have of it", as Deleuze writes in his 1966 book on Bergson (B 41). The universe of primary movement-images is something "we have to construct [...] since it is given only to the eye which we do not have" (C1 81). But there are other eyes (to connect with speculative philosophy), other framings of images, found within science, scientific technology and art, which exceed "natural" perception and cognition.[21] Film has an inherent potential to go beyond human limitations in its ways of dragging selected images into a frame (a kind of "camera consciousness", as a base level of film thinking).[22] As images produced by, or through, machines, film and especially filmic montage might be used to expand our thinking. Or not. For Deleuze cinema "trac[es] and retrac[es] cerebral circuits", but these can be the circuits of a "deficient idiot brain as well as a brain of creativity" (TRM 284, translation modified).

The two cinema books are divided to cover two generalized moving-image types based on different images of thought: the classical movement-image of organic wholes as based in a representational image of thought, and the modern time-image as approaching something like a new image of thought.[23] The time-image is made possible when thought encounters an inability to think organic (or orgiastic) representational Wholes. But this inability opens towards other possibilities: it is a "powerlessness" that is no "simple inferiority" but a clearer revelation of a fundamental part of thought itself—a "reverse side of thought", its "core" or the "unthought within thought", which "is indistinguishable from the greatest power" of thought. But just as a possibility: the "powerlessness can remain powerlessness, but it alone can also be raised to the highest power" (C2 167; DR 185, 250; see also 166, 181f; 242, 285). It is a realm of potential for the new in thought, which is contrasted to a representational movement-image thought related to an organic "One-Being" (C2 179). Now, to complicate things, before we go further into the problem of the new in time-image thought: the movement-image entails change and novelty in its own ways.

The classical movement-image gives an *indirect* image of a changing whole of time, through its representational logic of combining primary movement-images.

This logic entails the subordination of difference to representation (and not just the subordination of time to movement): while the whole of time itself is open, it is also given on the levels of thought or signification on which it is indirectly represented. The whole is therefore changing while also determined by preconceived meanings having to do with, for instance, a Mythic Past / Universal History / Progress, etc., and/or a grand Idea of organic Unity such as Spirit, the Subject, the People, etc.—which the film (implicitly or explicitly) presupposes, points towards, or gives expression to through organic associations and rational links. This can entail an enthusiastic orientation towards the future, but as tied to an already given "concept" projected forwards. That is, to abstract Ideas which "conform to accepted meanings or established precepts [...] that confirm something, even if it's something in the future, even if it's the future of the revolution" (N 38f).

The movement-image regime can also include the new in two non-given senses, as fitted within a sensory-motor schema (here the latter basically means that "someone on the screen perceives, feels, reacts [...] in a given situation" [N 123]). The three most central sub-categories of movement-images are perception-images, affection-images, and action-images, which form around the center in the interval between perception and re/action. The center is a local folding of the universe not only into conscious perception but "already from the point of view of action". Since the new action is not given but the outcome of a subjective analysis of received perceptions, the center is a "center of indetermination" and the action it selects therefore "present[s] something unpredictable or new" (C2 62; cf. DR 94). But this is "new" only in the sensory-motor sense of a certain (conscious or unconscious) freedom of choice in how to react. As already quoted in the discussion of the first synthesis of time above, which is what we are dealing with here, Deleuze says this sense of the "new will be called 'action' strictly speaking" (C2 62). There is also an affective or experiential form of sensory-motor novelty: the perception-center-reaction schema may include an affection-image that temporarily lingers within the center and expresses a pure quality or affect—"pure" in the sense of a sign that refers only to itself and which, as Deleuze writes, "concerns what is new in experience" (C1 98f; C2 30f). Within the regime of the movement-image, such qualities or affects are measured in relation to the sensory-motor schema (such as a character momentarily shocked by a perception of something—that might be old to everyone else—before taking action) and an organic thought-whole (or a "spiritual" whole) in which time is indirectly represented.[24]

This movement-image logic eventually lost its sway within what Deleuze perceives as the heart of cinema (and for a complex set of historical reasons). The following became increasingly exhausted: belief in individual or collective action as capable of modifying a situation, and belief in organic unity as organized around pre-established, transcendent ideals projected onto the past and/or the future. The first Neorealist films reveal lost or damaged organic links between humans and the world. The world has become "unthinkable" or even "intolerable", not least because of a new permanent state of daily banality (C2 18, 170). Nevertheless, this state also propelled certain film thought—certain time-images—towards exploring the new beyond the crisis of classical or modernistic notions.

This is made possible not least by this basic difference: movement-images show the actual/virtual relation from the perspective of the actual, and time-images show time from the perspective of the virtual. In time-images, time is thereby freed from merely measuring movement and movement can become movement in time. This also frees thought from being limited by representation. Why is that? Thought, as we saw above, first arose within an interval of time. And as time complicates and deepens in its logic and movements, so can thought, which now tends towards the searching, singular, and nonlinear. As time is shown more directly, thought becomes increasingly immanent to the filmic expression, in contrast to images that—as with the movement-image—only create associations or illustrate pre-existing representational concepts. This opens up the possibility of a "new image of thought".

How does one set up a new image of film thought? One that is not quickly recaptured in representation (as its "alternative")? It is not enough to break with representation (or wallow in its ruins). It is also not enough to construct a "pure time-image". On a more technical level, there is a sort of passage from the break with the sensory-motor to a new image, consisting of three—or four—steps/levels. The break itself only provided the "preliminary condition" (C2 3): "faltering sensory-motor connections" that "did not yet constitute [...] the new image" but provided coordinates for the second step/level—pure optical and sound images/signs that make perceptible bits of "time in its pure state". But that too "was not enough: the image had to enter into relations with yet other forces, so that it could itself escape from a world of clichés" (C2 3, 21–3). It had to open to what Deleuze calls "the readable image and the thinking image", where more clearly cuts, camera movements and "reframings [are] functions of thought" and movements in time, more than descriptions of space (C2 22–4). There is also a fourth step, or rather a fourth aspect implied in the new image: the capacity to "put thought into contact with an unthought" or an "outside", which is to say, with the forces of the new (C2 214; see also WP 59f).

Different time-images relate to all this in different ways, and they differ in how close they come to something like a new image of thought. Certain Italian Neorealist films introduced the "preceding characteristics" and had "an intuitive consciousness of the new image in the course of being born", while also retaining much of the organic logic (C1 211f). The New American Cinema as well as parts of the French and German new waves tended to stay "content to parody the cliché instead of giving birth to a new image" (C1 210f). A new image of thought was achieved to a higher degree, in Deleuze's estimation, in Godard (and in the "noo-sphere" cinema of Kubrick and Resnais).

Now, regardless of their levels of success in setting up a different image of thought, a large part of the time-images discussed in *Cinema 2* concerns the struggle for the new itself, the new conceived of as something delicate and rare, and in actual situations that often appear to be the result of an entropic cancellation of potential. Or rather, these time-images concern compositions through virtual potentials that still *subsist* in such situations, but their lines of actualization seem more or less blocked. This is most explicitly explored in the chapter on crystal-images in *Cinema 2*.

Crystal Conception

In the crystal-image chapter of *Cinema 2*, Deleuze can be said to map struggles for the new as seen from the perspective of a virtual past. These struggles appear to aim at reviving or creating channels of actualization between virtual potentials and the seemingly exhausted actual states in which they persist. This involves an elusive third force of intensity: that which can make "the past active and present to the outside so that something new will finally come about" (F 119). Before we go into the details of how this is played out in the films Deleuze discusses, we need to look at some basic temporal parameters of the crystal-image.

The crystal-image contracts the actual/virtual relation to the point that they coexist within the same image.[25] While objectively distinct, the two sides can no longer be discerned as distinct (they chase after each other in continual, reciprocal exchange). At this most contracted point, the present is revealed as no longer a point (in a succession of points) but as a double flow: the present as a constant split between the actual present (which flows to the future) and its coexisting past (which it flows back to). (Differently put: we shift from the first to the second synthesis of time.) The present, as this double movement, is merely the most contracted (pseudo-)point of the whole of the virtual past that coexists with itself in all its levels of contraction and relaxation (as illustrated by Bergson's cone). Expressed thereby is the virtuality that subsists *within* any actual thing or state, any actuality's "own" virtual side that— through the crystalized limit point (the contracted tip of the cone)—opens up to the whole of a virtual past "in general", a "pure" past consisting of elements that have "not yet received a date" (C2 79).

The crystal-image is said to thereby reveal "the hidden ground of time" (C2 98), implicitly referencing *Difference and Repetition*'s description of the second synthesis as precisely a ground of time. Other kinds of time-images give expression to deeper realms of this ground, rather than just its most contracted tip. Such as—coexisting and intercommunicating but non-organic and all-in-all incommensurable—"sheets", "strata", and "regions" that a time-image film may traverse in an open variety of ways (and with varying depth). These sheets and regions consist of variable constellations of pre-individual singularities, which is to say, components for problematic Ideas or potentials not yet actualized. The virtual ground, that is, contains one of the conditions for the new.

Difference and Repetition more directly explicates the other condition: a third synthesis of time, the force of the future, intensity. Novelty entails complex interactions between these two conditions and what they may give rise to: 3) intensity, 2) virtual Ideas, 1) actualization. Ideas contain potential, and novelty can be drawn from them, and then actualized. As empty force the third synthesis depends on the content of the virtual past. As Williams writes, the pure past is a "reserve of difference", which avoids "the need for creation out of nothing" (2011: 136). But in contrast to Williams's view, this does not always mean an ongoing flow of actualized creativity. The processes involved with creating the new can contain systematic hindrances or even blockages. This is explored and made explicit in *Cinema 2* and in ways that directly connect with *Difference and Repetition*.

While in other works, Deleuze can shorthand or simplify his conception of time and/or conceive of time through a different set of concepts, for example the Chronos and Aiôn division (LS 186–93; ATP 262ff), *Cinema 2* rather complicates, re-envisions, and adds disturbances between the two conditions for the new—the second (pure past) and the third synthesis (intensity)—as concerning the possibility of creation within the actual. In *Cinema 2* the pure crystalline past can seem closed in on itself, and the actual present a state of entropic cancellation of generative force. Still, however blocked from actualization, the virtual appears as a realm of potential and creative experimentation.

A "perfect crystal" is a prison with much going on inside. Here the actual/virtual circuit forms a closed circle from which nothing can escape. This is especially the case in the films of Ophüls, in which characters are "imprisoned" and "[c]rystalline perfection lets no outside subsist: there is no outside" (C2 83). Potentials are blocked from being drawn out by the "third" force so as to create something new (and time is here even barred from flowing to the future in the sense of the forward direction of presents caused by the founding operation of the second synthesis, so that the second synthesis seems sealed off also from the first synthesis). Yet, crystal prisons are not sterile, but rather like experiments in virtual Ideas. They tend to display a theatrical uncertainty, where new things are *tried out*, before the right role is found which *could* pass on to new life. And it must somehow: while "we are born in a crystal", a closed crystal which remains closed—like an egg that never hatches—"retains only death, and life must come out of it, after trying itself out" (C2 86). For that to happen in any significant manner, however, there must be an escape from the crystal. Not only from the enclosed past but from the whole crystalline time circuit itself (consisting of flows of presents passing forwards and back to the past). This is possible if the crystal contains a flaw that can function as a "point of flight [*point de fuite*]" (C2 87).

Renoir's crystals are imperfect. His films deal with levels of theatricality "absorbing the real" into a crystal circuit, but they also contain "the third side, or the third dimension", so that the crystal always has a "failing": small cracks through which something can escape (C2 85).[26] *Something*, out of all that has gradually been formed from experimentation within the crystal, may "slip away in the background", and in the sense that "a new Real will come out beyond the actual and the virtual" (C2 85f). What slips away is directed towards a future, not merely in the sense of presents continuously made to flow forwards, but "as a bursting forth of life" that produces "a new distinction [...] like a new reality which was not pre-existent"—all on condition "that it leaves the crystal" (C2 87f).

But such productive intrusions of an elusive third force do not come about easily in any time-image. The new is rare. While crystal-images are more firmly at home in the virtual past/second synthesis, the new is equally rare also in time-images where the past and the outside are in more dynamic and direct contact.[27] In Straub-Huillet the past comes in the form of texts, documents, monuments, and the archeological layers of the earth that bury events, from which a pure, "nomadic" speech-act struggles to "tear" itself (C2 254ff). Whether the tearing will fully succeed is left as an open question. The new is rare also when explicitly manifested, as in the ending of Kubrick's *2001*: Deleuze conceives of Kubrick's cinema (like Resnais's) as expressing an identity between world and brain, as having as its *mise-en-scène* a world-brain, which is not an organic whole but a topological membrane connecting "two forces": an "inside" deeper than any interiority that equals the depths of the past, and an "outside" beyond any exteriority that is the violent force of creativity, evolution, future. The two forces, the two conditions for the new, which at the limit "become ultimately indiscernible", are themselves here "deadly". There is in *2001* only the "chance of entering into a new, incommensurable, unknown relation, which would convert death into a new life" (C2 205f). Over the course of *2001*, that new life is eons in the making, not a common occurrence.

Returning to the chapter on crystal-images, even in the more optimistic and future-oriented of Renoir's films, the "new Real" is what towards the end *may* take flight or sneak out in the background through a crack. The new Real also tends to have a subtle and downplayed position, and in some of his more "pessimistic" films it may never come about. Although directly implied or hinted at by a camera, it is seldom if ever shown as a present actuality (with the last image of *2001* as a kind of, not entirely untacky, contrast), or as a brief poetic gesture (like the camera panning out into the water at the end of *The River*, 1951). Rather, the new Real appears in these time-images more like the hint of an actualized new future as seen from the perspective of the virtual past.

Nonetheless, whether closed or cracked, crystals are always internally productive of potential.[28] In reference to Renoir, Deleuze writes: "Everything happens as if the circuit served to try out roles, as if roles were being tried in it until the right one were found, the one with which we escape." In the experimentation with roles "something *takes shape* inside the crystal which [might] succeed in leaving through the crack" (C2 86, emphasis mine).[29]

In the crystal-images of (later) Fellini the something that "takes shape" is instead more like the whole film or the whole crystal in the process of growing. Rather than escaping *from* a crystal past that can equal death if not creatively opened to the future, it is now the march towards death in the actual, linear time of successive presents—an "incredible entropy"—that must be escaped. Life therefore seeks entryways *into* the crystal, entryways that themselves form "seeds" (some abort while others succeed) and that make up a crystal "in the process of being made" (C2 88, 90, 92, 93). Here it is more clearly *in* the crystal that we see the main creativity of life, instead of in the bursting out from it. The crystal as a realm that "holds in its depths or in its sides the surge of the new reality"—the crystal world, if you will, as a growing egg (C2 268).[30]

Many of the time-image films discussed in *Cinema 2*, then, are deeply explorative and expressive of virtual potential. But the 2) potentials (even including some of their spatiotemporal dramatization, which isn't itself quite the same as the actualization it can lead to) also seem cut off from and struggling to reconnect with 3) lines of actualization, while stuck in 1) concrete sociopolitical situations that can appear like outcomes of an entropic exhaustion of generative difference. Something similar goes for work with philosophical concepts, as described in *What is Philosophy?*, where Deleuze increasingly emphasizes how both cinema/art and philosophy must co-create with and through virtual potential (instead of merely, by going in the opposite direction from actualization, revealing virtual potential). So that even when things may appear blocked, there can be much creativity and experimentation, with the aim of maximizing potentials for change.

What Determines Virtual Ideas?

Before finally looking at concepts from this perspective, a final point on how all this connects with the ontology of virtual Ideas in *Difference and Repetition*, and a final point of contrast with Williams. As described above, *Difference and Repetition* conceives of Ideas as having a double determination: reciprocal determination through relations of differential elements and complete determination as distribution of singularities. Both determinations are described as being at "play *in* the Idea" (DR 349, emphasis mine). In other words, virtual Ideas have determination also autonomously from their actualization. Deleuze even says that Ideas "combine the greatest power of being differen*t*iated with an inability to be differen*c*iated" (DR 235). Still, Williams argues that virtual determination is *only* an effect of processes of actualization. Williams is certainly correct in saying that "the construction of reality" "takes place in both directions": the virtual is partly determined through its relation to the actual (2003: 21).[31] But then he goes too far: the "Idea only acquires the determinacy [...] by being actually expressed", "the chaos of the virtual becomes determined in this way" (186, 21; see also 11, 14f, 164, 176).[32] Williams, then, sees the virtual as mere "chaos" if we take away the actualization (2011: 137). But this is not what Deleuze is saying.

Problems, Deleuze writes in *The Logic of Sense*, are "emissions of singularities" that "possess a mobile, immanent principle of *auto-unification*" (LS 118, emphasis mine). Problems/Ideas, differently put, have their determination also independently of their solutions/actualizations, or as yet even having solutions/actualizations (D 1). Granted, condition (virtual) and conditioned (actual) are said to be "determined at the same time" (DR 203), but this cannot imply that actualization is the only thing that determines the structuring of Ideas, given the many times they are said to be determined otherwise. *Difference and Repetition* clearly conceives of Ideas as also determined through a depth of intensity affecting the virtual *directly*: as the third synthesis intervenes in the second. It is, as Deleuze writes, "the always displaced circle of the eternal return [...] [that] animate[s] ideal problems, determining their relations and singularities" (354). Furthermore, determined "at the same time" does not really specify *what* determines the Idea. It may be less affected by the actualization than by the intensity that *directs* the actualization: "A whole flow of exchange occurs between intensity and Ideas, as though between two corresponding figures of difference", with intensity understood here as "independent of the differen*c*iation by virtue of its own essential process", as that which "direct[s] the course of the actualisation" not the actualization itself (305–7). Similarly, while "the movement of Ideas" is described as "inseparable from a process of actualization", inseparable is not the same as reducible to. There is a "difference and excess of the always positive Idea", and Ideas, as metastable configurations of pure differences, are configured through differential movements on their own virtual plane, autonomously enough for Problems/Ideas to always be "differentiated even though [...] completely undifferenciated" (306, 361, 314). That is, they are always determined in their virtual structure even when entirely un-actualized.

This leads to a larger point: art and philosophy add yet other ways of co-determining virtual Problems/Ideas autonomously from actualization. And art and philosophy co-determine, and thereby form new potential, also in situations where actualization seems improbable.

Concepts as Potentials in a Blocked Present

The second and third phases in Deleuze's thinking about the new belong to a longer period of grappling with the post-1968 period of defeat that continues into our own present. This general situation has been dealt with by innumerable other thinkers. What is interesting here—and there is no need to rehash the famous characteristics of the recent era, whatever we call it (postmodernity, neoliberalism, late capitalism, etc.)—is how we conceive of creativity and potential. Much of the discourse tends to negotiate how not to *resign* ourselves to a sense of lost futures, and to what could be called lost movement-image-notions of the future. In his 2014 book on lost futures, Mark Fisher (born 1968) quotes Franco "Bifo" Berardi (born 1949) speaking of "the slow cancellation of the future [that] got underway in the 1970s and 1980s", but also of how he finds it "very difficult, maybe impossible, to get rid of" the "psychological perception" of time as "directed towards the future", which "reach[ed] a peak after the Second World War" when his "generation grew up". Bifo also finds it difficult to "look at reality without this kind of temporal lens" and says that he will "never be able to live in accordance with the new reality" (quoted in Fisher 2014: 6f). Is it not a lost movement-image kind of notion of the future that Bifo is referring to here, which for Deleuze isn't cancelled so much as it remains as one of those "free-floating clichés" (or to speak with Fredric Jameson, "dead styles of the past")? Beyond such a sad framework that seems so often to lead to resignation, Deleuze's concept of the time-image as well as his notion of the concept in *What is Philosophy?* offer alternative ways to work with *potentials* for the new, also in bleak situations in which the actual new seems blocked.

Concepts—described in more detail in Chapter 1 above—are philosophically determined results of experimental work with virtual ideas / problems / potentials. Concept creation involves grappling with virtual problems already existing in reality, but as material for co-creation which entails reworking them into concepts with philosophical properties. While the concept "extract[s] an event from things and beings", it also "shapes and reshapes the event in its own way", so as to "set up the new event from things and beings" (WP 33f). Concepts do not thereby set up the actual new itself, at least not outside of thought, but "the contour, the configuration, the constellation of an event to come" (WP 21, 32f). The potential thereby formulated as a concept, however, while perhaps spawning new thoughts and perceptions, might not lead to any sociopolitical (or otherwise tangible) actualizations until long into the future, or might never be actualized—and if and when it somehow is, its actualization always means further, unforeseeable, difference from the potential (in contrast to realizing a given possibility).

Although concepts—as potentials—*can* abound also in situations in which the actual new is blocked, creative concepts always tend to be fairly rare. For every concept that is "well formed and attest[s] to a creation", there are many that are "not viable […] arbitrary or inconsistent" or "do not hold up", or, we might add, that are too trivial or merely put a new gloss on established wisdom (WP 3). In contrast to the latter, Deleuze and Guattari see the "creation of concepts" as a *"resistance to the present"* that we generally "lack" and as "calls for a future form", at times even "for a new earth and people that do not yet exist" (WP 108). Concept creation thereby has a "utopian" aspect, through which "philosophy becomes political" and "takes the criticism of its own time to its highest point". Following a logic of "infinite movement and absolute survey", however, this must always "connect up with what is real here and now in the struggle against capitalism, relaunching new struggles whenever the earlier one is betrayed" (WP 99f, 111ff).

Notes

1 For Deleuze, in Badiou's mind, all events are occurring as a "continuous result of becoming", an "indivisible continuum of Virtuality", so that any temporal "separation" or "void" is disallowed, which—seen from the perspective of Badiou's ontology—means an inability to account for the production of the new in actual situations (Badiou 2009 [2006]: 387, 382). This reading allows Badiou to *declare* the following distinction: "Contrary to Deleuze, therefore, I think […] events are rare" (Badiou 2000 [1997]: 74f). This chapter will show that reducing Deleuze's philosophy of events and novelty to constant differentiation is to mislead by merging and concealing certain registers in his thought.

2 Note that the essay referenced here called "The Conditions of the New" in Smith's 2012 essay collection is a slightly rewritten and expanded version of the article with the same title from 2007.

3 The ontology presented in *Difference and Repetition* is hereby not just different/ciation, or the actual-virtual pair: "The totality of the system which brings into play the Idea, its incarnation and its actualisation must be expressed", Deleuze writes, "in the complex notion of '(indi)-different/ciation'" or "indi-drama-different/ciation" (DR 350, 308).

4 In a footnote, Williams corrects Smith on this issue and argues that if we are looking specifically at the philosophy of time in the second chapter of *Difference and Repetition*, there are no ordinary points, only singular points (2011: 187, note 10).

This does not make much sense, however, if we read all the chapters together as presenting one coherent philosophy, and not just the second chapter. When Deleuze in the fourth chapter argues that "the distinctness of Ideas" lies "precisely in the distribution of the *ordinary and the distinctive*, the *singular and the regular*, and in the extension of the singular across *regular points* into the vicinity of another singularity", as the "formation of ideal series around these singularities", this is not only some mathematical specificity to be contrasted to his philosophy of time but a presentation of other aspects of the larger ontology (DR 223, 351, emphasis mine). Furthermore, Deleuze not only frequently comes back to distinctions between ordinary/regular points and singular/distinctive points throughout the book, he also underlines how vital such distinctions are for philosophy (see e.g. DR 57f, 191, 203, 231, 252, 308, 351; on the latter point specifically see 238, 348f).

5 See e.g. ATP on "strata" or "molar aggregates" as "imprisoning intensities or locking singularities into systems of resonance and redundancy" (40). Or from the perspective of *Difference and Repetition*, an "empirical […] partial system, governed in such a manner that the difference of intensity which creates it tends to be cancelled within it (*law of nature*)" (DR 301).

6 Although Deleuze in *Difference and Repetition* says that "[b]eneath the general operation of laws" and "generalities in nature" there "always remains the play of singularities", and despite the "domain of laws" having to be understood "always on the basis of a" realm in which "laws do not yet exist", that hardly means that repetitions of actual laws and generalities are "new"—even though they in the most fundamental sense share conditions with the new (DR 28f).

7 Nathan Widder, on the one hand, brings up the fundamental issue here, albeit mostly with reference to the influential Badiouian critique and in the specific realm of politics: "at this point a difficulty arises" as Deleuze's ontology "seems to offer no criteria for differentiating a banal from an extraordinary change." On the other hand, Widder implies that this is an issue in Deleuze only if we "foist on him a conception of politics that is not his own" (2012: 51), which is to say, Badiou's equation of the extraordinary to the great rupturing historical event, his ideas about voids, separations in time, etc. (which for Deleuze amounts to a kind of transcendence). Yet, we should be careful not to throw out the baby with the bathwater, the bathwater being the kind of understanding of the extraordinary we find in Badiou, and the baby being Deleuze's own (subtle and complex) differentiation between banal and extraordinary, in which the extraordinary event is still rare while irreducible to the great historical or empirical event. I return to this issue below.

8 Deleuze attributes to the *second* synthesis an "ambiguity." It is "attracted by the representation that it grounds" while "drawn towards a beyond; as though it vacillated between a fall into the grounded and an engulfment in a groundlessness" (DR 343).

9 Williams provides a detailed reading also of these acts and symbols which in his interpretation applies to all events (2011: 87–102, see specifically 99ff).

10 "[T]he I and the Self, undermined by the fields of individuation which work beneath them" (DR 190; see also 319ff). Cf. Deleuze on Whitehead's notion of the *superject* (FLB 21).

11 Cf. Deleuze: "the line which comes diagonally from the heart of things and distributes volcanoes: it unites a bubbling sensibility and a thought which 'rumbles in its crater'" (DR 289).

12 On Deleuze's famous separation between the actual Revolution (always going poorly) and becoming-revolutionary, see e.g. ABC Letter G; WP 100f; ATP 292; and on the difference between history and becoming, see WP 111–13, 96.

13 What I mean by "womb-crystal" is clarified in the section below titled Crystal Conception.

14 I should add that Williams does still acknowledge the same in the actual. As in this pertinent passage, which could have had more of an impact on his conclusion about novelty "all the time, everywhere" (2011: 130): "without sameness, for instance as captured in reliable relations of cause and effect, Deleuze would have no actual events to refer to and he would fall into the trap of a world of pure becoming and the paradox that if all is becoming then there is nothing to ensure continuity of reference through time [...] difference as taking a primary but never complete role in relations of determination between actual identities and ideal differentiations" (2011: 42; see also 123).

15 DR 139, 176, 181f, 296f, 345; PS 95–100. In both *Cinema 2* and *Difference and Repetition*, Deleuze also quotes Heidegger saying: "Man can think in the sense that he possesses the possibility to do so. This possibility alone, however, is no guarantee to us that we are capable of thinking" (C2 156; DR 181f).

16 *The Logic of Sense*, on a more strictly artistic note, mentions an event in music (a piece by Stockhausen) that was "quickly covered over by everyday banality" (LS 286).

17 Other periodizations can be made from other perspectives, but they seem to mostly align with this one. For instance, Anne Sauvagnargues's definition of three different periods/stages in Deleuze's numerous writings on art (2018 [2005]: 4–21, 176f), as well as Deleuze's own suggestion of a three-part periodization: "a sort of second period that would never have begun or got anywhere without Félix. Then let's suppose there's a third period when I worked on painting and cinema" (N 136f).

18 Released in between these two books is Deleuze's *The Fold: Leibniz and the Baroque*, with its sixth chapter on Whitehead and the Event. This chapter can be seen to go against my periodization here. It is mainly focused on how everything in the world is an event in the basic sense of a being of becoming. Even "The Great Pyramid" which is "the same over the succession of moments" while also "constantly gaining

and losing molecules" with "bits and pieces continually entering and exiting" (FLB 90). This chapter portrays Whitehead's philosophy, of course, and regardless of how creative Deleuze can be with his philosophical portraits, the point is an old and fairly basic one for Deleuze: Being as flux as a contrast to ideas about Being as identity or eternity. "Leibniz implemented the second great logic of the event: the world itself is an event" in the sense of an "oppos[ition] to the essentialism first of Aristotle and then of Descartes" (60f). Yet, even in this chapter there is an appearance of the new that is subtly but distinctly differentiated from ongoing flux: "For with Leibniz the question surges forth in philosophy that will continue to haunt Whitehead and Bergson: [...] in what conditions does the objective world allow for a subjective production of novelty, that is, of creation? [...] [A world] endowed with a capacity for innovation or creativity" (89).

19 Patricia Pisters has been one of the first to more systematically interpret the connections between the cinema books and Deleuze's three syntheses of time. Despite general points of agreement, however, her reading of this relation is quite different from the one I present below. This includes her interpretation of the syntheses and how they are or are not at play in the cinema books, and her idea of a contemporary image type not written about by Deleuze that gives a kind of direct expression to the third synthesis. I particularly disagree, as evident from the discussion of the syntheses above, that the third synthesis can be involved in visualizations of content "from the future" (Pisters 2012: 136–55).

20 This is implicitly also the only (and very small) place for the spectator in Deleuze's thinking on cinema: the spectator is *another* black screen in the universal interplay of images, and in this way the spectator's "brain is the screen" too. We could add that spectators, just as any other images relating to other images, subtract according to their own needs and prior experiences, but Deleuze also holds a firm line against spectator-activity romanticism: "Nothing happens in the viewer's head that does not derive from the character of the image" (C2 104). To which we can add Deleuze's description in *What is Philosophy?* of art as "independent of the viewer or hearer, who only experience it after, if they have the strength for it" (WP 164). Richard Rushton (2009) asks how Deleuze can have inspired so many theories of cinematic spectatorship when there is no explicit theory of spectatorship in his writings on cinema. A Deleuzian spectator has partly been invented, he shows, in order to fit Deleuze's unorthodox film theories into mainstream contemporary film studies, which after the 1970s' Screen Theory has been increasingly focused on various notions of active spectatorship. See also Introduction, notes 2A, 6, 8 above and Chapter 5, note 9 below (and Preface, note 10).

21 On cinema as exceeding, or even contradicting, natural perception, see C2 201; C1 2f.

22 Deleuze: "we can say of the shot that it acts like a consciousness. But the sole cinematographic consciousness is not us, the spectator, nor the hero; it is the camera—sometimes human, sometimes inhuman or superhuman" (C1 20).

23 This division is the general level of a typology that has a potentially endless array of new subtypes, variations, and mixes of cinematic thought-images (and that might be complemented with some different general image-type). The larger two-part typology also relates to individual films in complex ways. Neither of the two image regimes ever fully exists without the other, but in one film one regime is more dominant. And in an individual film it is the dominant regime that determines the overall sense also of aspects from the other regime, which means that forms or styles that may appear to signal a time-image are really part of a more overall movement-image logic, or vice versa. How do we evaluate which regime is dominant in an individual film? This is not always obvious and can sometimes require a close genealogy-like analysis specifically attuned to the particularities of the film, such as when representational aspects dominate in subtle ways. And there is no easy checklist of filmic form. That is, specific forms aren't necessarily tied to one of the regimes. Forms conventionally connected with one regime can be recuperated by the other. And the classical movement-image, we should note, was "already made up of aberrant movements and false continuity shots", forms we may associate more with the time-image, but without being able to give body to virtual time. In the classical movement-image, instead, "false continuity function as […] voids which are still motor, which the linked images must cross" (C2 213). Throughout its history the movement-image has continued to find new means to be sublime, disjunctive, to reclaim forms that Deleuze associated more with the time-image, to update the sensory-motor in line with parts of contemporary physics, etc., without going beyond a representational image of thought and organic unity (case in point: some of the more dynamically edited parts of the contemporary Hollywood action film).

24 Both the action-image and the affection-image (as well as the perception-image itself) can also drag the logic of the movement-image far towards different limits, and, famously, Hitchcock takes the logic of the movement-image as far as it can go through a "mental image" that introduces "a new, direct, relationship with thought" (C1 196–205). Hitchcock does this by abstracting and externalizing sensory-motor relations, and by shifting from character-subjects as the locus of reasoning to a camera that is said to become more explicitly conscious. Importantly, Hitchcock's cinema here indicates openings for other kinds of thought-images that go beyond, and not merely stretch, the logic of the classical movement-image—openings that are partly passed through in some of Hitchcock's later films, such as *Vertigo*, which belong more to the time-image.

25 In contrast, the movement-image has an internal tendency to expand towards grander "sets" and "worlds", spatially and/or through vast virtual circuits of dreams or recollection which are measured in relation to an actual, present perspective in which they appear as representations (e.g. dream-images anchored in dreamers that dream, recollection-images in characters that remember something in an actual present).

26 Richard Rushton discusses the crack in Renoir's crystals from the perspective of articulating a "Deleuzian imaginary" that he contrasts to the critique of the imaginary in 1970s and '80s film theory (2011: 241–60). See also Nevin (2018).

27 Throughout the latter half of *Cinema 2*, Deleuze discusses much more dynamic incorporations of the outside than in crystal-images, mainly in terms of the interstices that appear in various "differential" connections between images and between images and sounds—the audio can importantly form its own autonomous image frame (no longer a mere aiding component of the visual image) that relates nonlinearly to the visual image, forming new kinds of complexes of audiovisuality, as I discussed in Chapter 1. We must also note, however, that the outside must be carefully harnessed. While there is a need to creatively connect the outside (3) with (virtual) Ideas/potentials (2) and in specific actual situations (1), the outside is also "deadly, too violent and fast", Deleuze says in a 1986 interview, and adds that "we have to manage to fold the line and establish an endurable zone in which to install ourselves, confront things, take hold, breathe—in short, think" (N 111).

28 An exception of sorts is the "decomposing" aristocratic crystal worlds of Visconti's later films that are separated "from life and creation" and that have not yet vanished completely because the crystal is "artificial", and in which the only actualizing, clarifying aspect possible is the realization that it is "too late" for these (aesthetically "grandiose") crystal worlds to escape their own decomposition (C2 94–6).

29 Similarly, in his 1981 book on Francis Bacon, Deleuze not only reiterates his notion of art as making invisible "forces visible" and "capturing forces" that are "nongiven", he also carefully emphasizes that this is not enough and that something must also take shape, "emerge" from the "diagram" of such forces. On capturing invisible forces, see FB 57, 58, 61; on something having to emerge from the diagram, see 103, 138, 156.

30 Looking at this from the perspective of the fifth chapter of *Difference and Repetition*, the egg (being a "theater") is not just the differen*t*iation of the virtual Idea but rather the relation between the Idea and the "spatio-temporal dynamisms" or "differenciating agencies" that "dramatize" the Idea (DR 268f, 347f). The larger point is that in *Cinema 2* they are both seen to be to a large extent blocked from creative actualization.

31 That is, I agree with Williams that reality moves in both directions, contrary to a common reading of Deleuze as exemplified by Miguel de Beistegui's claim that reality only moves "downstream" from the virtual to actual (de Beistegui 2004: 334).

32 Williams calls this "reciprocal determination." John Roffe critiques Williams on this account, pointing to 1) how the term "reciprocal determination" is in *Difference and Repetition* only used for differences determining each other *within* the virtual

Idea, and 2) how the idea of mutual determination between actual and virtual only finds support in *The Logic of Sense*'s descriptions of the creation of virtual sense (Roffe 2012: 149ff). This, however, seems to me to be a false choice: either the virtual is all the way determined by actualization (Williams's position) or there is no mutual determination (Roffe's implication).

4   Sonimage: A Problem Space and Six Embryonic Cinecepts

Between 1960 and 1972 […] there was a new rich period. […] It's a little like […] a period, or a collectivity launches an arrow, and eventually it falls, and then someone comes along to pick it up and hurl it out elsewhere, so that's how creation happens […] passing through desert periods.

Deleuze (ABC Letter C)

We exist in a desert. […] There's nothing left. All the proposals have been tried. They all led nowhere. Now we're waking up. [We must regroup. There are people who fight with their own means. We want to join them!]

France / tour / detour / deux / enfants (1977)[1]

Slowly you create. A script? It yields nothing, it takes … nine months.

Godard in *Scenario du film 'Passion'*

The combination of quotes above indicates a problem: what are pregnancy and birth—as figures for creativity and change—in a sociopolitical desert? Deleuze's *Cinema 2*, as explored in the last chapter, contains much implicit concern with conception in blocked sociopolitical situations. Something similar goes for Sonimage, and with pregnancy and blockage more explicitly at the center—often quite literally (pregnant bodies, constipation). It also takes place in a 1970s desert slightly more specific than the longer post-war period of *Cinema 2*: The start of Sonimage, to repeat a quote from Chapter 2, "coincided with the end of the 'French Cultural Revolution,' with the failure of revolutions *elsewhere* and with the beginning of a new reactionary period in general, specifically in France" (Emmelhainz 2019: 101; see also MacCabe 1980: 24). In other words, it followed a brief period in which it seemed possible to create new modes of existence, new ways to organize society, new ways of being and relating to the world beyond a late capitalist frame (and beyond transformations driven or confined by this frame). This sense of possibility was either beaten down or recuperated by opposing forces, which could even lead to a fundamental waning of belief in the world as capable of creating new forms of life, to reference Deleuze's famous concerns with belief in the 1980s and '90s. This situation, however, forced thought to find new directions and to reconsider previous stances, including on what it means to produce the new. This is the problem space of Sonimage. It is set up in *Numéro deux* (1975) and extended in subsequent Sonimage works like *Six fois deux* and *France tour détour* that also contain embryonic cinecepts.[2] This chapter begins with a close examination of *Numéro deux*'s articulation of this problem space. This is followed by descriptions of two embryonic cinecepts in *Six fois deux* (1976) and four in *France tour détour* (1977–78), with a brief section in between on further aspects of the problem space with a focus on *Comment ça va* (1976).

A note on this chapter's delimitation
Sonimage is approached here with a twofold focus: 1) as a general problem space concerned with novelty in blocked circumstances, and 2) as containing sections that determine aspects of this problem space in ways that approach the cineceptual—that is, cinecepts that are "embryonic" in the sense that they are intriguing indications of but not full cinecepts.[3] Some things therefore fall outside the delimitation. "The complexity of material in these programmes is astounding", as Colin MacCabe says about *France tour détour* (1980: 149); or as Drabinksi writes: "Godard's [and Miéville's] work in the seventies has an irreducible polysemic character. There is no single story to be told about [these] works" (2008: 11). Compared to my twofold focus here, which brings out unacknowledged aspects, these works also have more explicit themes (that the previous literature mostly focuses on): for example, family dynamics, women's liberation, media, communication, and advertising. While explicating such themes is not a direct focus below, aspects of them are considered but as folded into the larger problem space concerned with blockage and the production of the new.

Numéro deux: Forming a Problem Space

[A] "mother" type in the grand sense of the term, someone who doesn't hear or know anything but the pregnancies and child-beds of his spirit.

Nietzsche (2001 [1882]: 233 [§369])

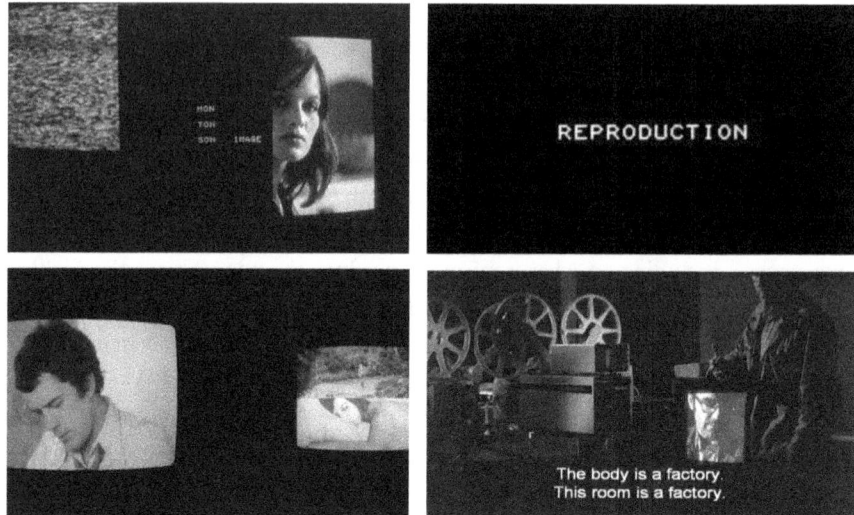

Figures 4.1a–d *Numéro deux*

Numéro deux[4] accords directly with the formal logic developed only hesitantly in *Ici et ailleurs* (see Chapter 2), and it does so in a restrained way that articulates a problem space. This space has—literally and conceptually—a *ground*. Most of the film's images—one or several screens or green text—appear within a dark meta-background. Serge Daney refers to this background—in passing, without elaboration—as a "fetal blackness" (*le noir fœtal*) (1976). The term fetal generally refers to a human or animal organism in stages of development prior to birth. *Numéro deux*'s black ground is like a general creative plane, which not only includes the biological, as Godard establishes in the film's preface, but also creativity in thought (Daney himself also described previous black screens in Godard as a blackboard for theory and pedagogy). In Chapter 2 I discussed the black background as it first appeared in Godard's *2 or 3 Things I Know About Her* and more extensively in *Le gai savoir* as a ground of consciousness (in the latter film) and a general plane of creative intensity (in both). I also mentioned that the title of the latter film is taken from a book by Nietzsche, no stranger to conceiving of thought in relation to grounds of intensity. To this we can add that Nietzsche likened creative thought to pregnancy and birth. Derrida even described Nietzsche as "*the* thinker of pregnancy" and as someone who "referred to his thought as a pregnant woman might speak of her unborn child" (Derrida 1979: 65, emphasis mine). As Sigridur Thorgeirsdottir characterizes this aspect in Nietzsche:

> By abstracting from real, physical birth he turns birth into a metaphor for the creative disposition of the Dionysian philosopher […] The creativity of the philosophers

of the future is not restricted to production of works of art. It is rather creativity in the much wider sense of the ability for a creative form of embodied thinking, a thinking that Nietzsche thinks is more in tune with life itself. (2010: 158)

This Nietzschean frame together with the longer discussion of the ground in Chapter 2 provides some more substance to Daney's notion of the "fetal" in *Numéro deux*. As a core part of the general problem space articulated in this film, this ground implicitly extends in subsequent discussions of pregnancy and birth throughout Sonimage.[5] In *Numéro deux*, first, what do we see in this ground?

For Kaja Silverman, *Numéro deux*'s images "swim in a pool of blackness" and are "unlike any we have seen before" (Silverman and Farocki 1998: 141). (Phrasing that reminds me of the lit fetuses floating in dark wombs in Lennart Nilsson's 1965 *A Child Is Born: The Drama of Life Before Birth in Unprecedented Photographs*.) Most images were shot on video and show the domestic life of a three-generation family. Some images are from television (news, sports, films, film analysis programs, pornography, political demonstrations, etc.). A third category of images involves shifting green electronic texts on the black background. Technically, the visual compositions were made simply and concretely: the video images play on monitors placed in a dark studio, mostly two monitors next to each other, which are then captured by a 35mm film camera. The effect, however, is complex and abstract. For Farocki, this setup "adds mystery to the everyday activities which are depicted" and the composition of "fragmentary details of the apartment" elevates them "to the status of ideas" (Silverman and Farocki 1998: 143). At times there are also internal montage formations within a screen (which was more prevalent and unrestrained in *Ici et ailleurs*). Mulvey and MacCabe described this as "rolling superimposition, direct superimposition and vision-mixing" (1980: 96; see also Dubois 1992: 170f). *Numéro deux* also has an intricate audio track that presents, as Jerry White writes, "a series of voices—onscreen, off-screen, and in voice-over—many of which are women's voices (such as Miéville's)" (2013: 19). These images and sounds articulate a problem space also as a set of sub-problems, which I will now examine focusing on key scenes and sections. (To clarify, *Numéro deux* sets up a problem space and follows a logic of formal organization that can extend into cinecepts, but this film does not itself contain embryonic cinecepts. Embryonic cinecepts appear in *Six fois deux* (1976) and *France tour détour*, which I analyze later.)

Godard's Preface: A Set of Machines Placed Directly in the Black Background

Two minutes into the film an almost eight-minute-long preface appears (after an initial double-screen section introducing the characters who live together in a small flat: the main couple Sandrine and Pierre, their children Vanessa and Nicolas, and two grandparents). The preface is basically a long static shot of Godard in the dark studio, leaning against a monitor that screens his face with a blue tint shot from a different angle by another camera (see figure 4.1d). The dark background is present: Godard with some video machinery is seen faintly lit against an otherwise pitch-black room. Yet, this shot is in one sense an exception to the film's main template: instead of one or several images played on monitors placed within a meta-blackness, we now see Godard and gadgets placed directly in the blackness (except for the doubling of his face in the monitor). He speaks seemingly randomly about various things: anecdotes, governmental subjectivation, global politics, local school politics, his move from Paris, DNA, language, wordplay, literature, film financing, and the printing of books and money. But there is a larger theme: the politics of factory production and machines, as connected to and including—with evident inspiration from Deleuze and Guattari's *Anti-Oedipus*[6]—human bodies: "Man, machines. Me and machines. Men, women, machines", Godard says while physically attached to a monitor whose screen doubles his face—being both the producer and the product— and with the monitor connected to a noisy apparatus running reels of video tape. Godard: "In biology, this room is a factory. You could say it's a factory. The body is a factory. This room is a factory." And the film we are about to see, he adds, is about (also comes from? is?) ass/sex [*un film du cul*].[7] The last part of the preface speaks about production while giving way to green electronic text spelling "there will be" (*Il y aura la*) and double screens of the grandparents. The preface ends as the grandparents shout at each other "Always"/Never again!", followed by the same green text which then changes into "Reproduction". This leads to shots of domestic life, green electronic text that morphs into a different word—impossible → possible; work → shit; equality → liberty—and television clips (of films, political protest, etc.) screened on two monitors with sound in the studio (and barely visible under the lower monitor is Godard's hand pushing buttons). The main takeaways so far: production and reproduction are connected to the black background, they concern equality as well as what is possible/impossible, and span the biological body, the technological, the social, and the political.

Sandrine's Introduction[8]

As the visual track remains the same (with Godard continuing to zap between partly audible television programs shown on two screens in the studio—film, drama, pornography, war), a new section starts (14:24–19:49) in which the main character Sandrine introduces the film with prose-poetic declarations in voice-over. She begins by saying that *Numéro deux* "shows all of this. Unbelievable things. Things in close-up.

Ordinary things. Shitty things and pleasurable things." And as she continues we see the word "Cinema" in green electronic text change to "possible". The image then shifts to an unsettling sex scene, which will recur throughout the film. It consists of a single-screen video superimposition of two shots: 1) Pierre taking Sandrine in the "ass"—which here means, or partly means, in that general bodily area, and not, or not necessarily only, a specified part of that area—and with the clear implication that it is rape (with certain conceptual complications, most clearly that this is done to her by a social system). 2) Their daughter Vanessa's face appearing as a negative cutout silhouette over the act (on a narrative level we are later told that she saw the act). Sandrine continues: "[*Numéro deux* is not left or right] but before and behind. In front are children. Behind is government." She goes on to talk about how also cinema and television are factories that produce images, and how *Numéro deux* is "a film produced by Anne-Marie Miéville and Jean-Luc Godard" which is "coming to this screen soon. And this screen is on a wall. What do you think this wall is between?"

A second part of the introduction starts a moment later (16:49–19:49). Sandrine now explains that *Numéro deux* is a film about both politics and ass/sex [*cul*]. There is a cut back to the studio with one monitor screen blank and the other with static/white noise (no signal coming through)—and there are variations of blank and static/white noise mixed with television clips throughout the rest of the introduction. A third monitor is also turned on which shows an image of a girl writing on a blackboard. Sandrine continues to imply that the spectator should not just expect this film to spell things out in talk, that it is important to sometimes listen and watch, and that this is difficult like a revolution is difficult: "et c'est difficile" ("and it is difficult") spelled in green electronic text gradually changes letter by letter to "comme la revolution" ("like revolution"). As Sandrine adds: "there is quite a lot to see".

Sandrine goes on to speak about work, whether dad and mom respectively are factories or landscapes, looking at one's own sex, charging and discharging, as the green letters *comme la revolution* change to *dans un pays riche* ("in a rich country"), and the monitors show a mix of programs, blank screens, and one that keeps showing the girl writing on a blackboard. As a program about jazz is heard, Sandrine says: "So you play music. What's the music for? To see the unbelievable [*incroyable*]. What is the unbelievable?" There is now a shift to the main visual template: the shot of the writing girl appears alone in the black background (that is, the image seems to float in the black instead of being shown on a visible monitor among others in the studio.) We also hear bird sounds. Sandrine says: "The unbelievable is what you don't see." We now see more clearly what the girl writes on the blackboard: "before being born I was dead" (*avant d'être née j'etais mort*).[9] Prior to birth, however, she did exist as a fetus. And to tie this with the "unbelievable" in Sandrine's voice-over: we do not always clearly see what precedes birth, the virtual potential that can lead to actual change, and it may seem like an obscure black background. This is followed by a black screen and green electronic text spelling "reproduction" and gradually changing to "adjustment" (reglage)—differently put: that which is birthed tends to be immediately coopted into regulated systems and thereby function as reproduction of the same rather than production. Or as Deleuze writes in *Cinema 2* (in a discussion of Nietzschean themes in Orson Welles): "There is only a slim chance, so great is the capacity […] for exhausted life to get control of the New from its birth […] (C2 147).

A General Downstairs, Cyclical Reproduction, and Blockage

In a shot with just Vanessa, intermixed with this shot being superimposed over the recurring forced sex scene, she says the following: "Sometimes I think it's pretty, mom and dad, sometimes I think its poop [*caca*]." Vanessa's perception of her parents and their act—as beauty *and* waste—resonates with *how* this is a film about ass/sex [*un film du cul*]: the film conceives of this area as a general re/production machinery. Sandrine refers to her (constipated) behind as "mon cul" and to Pierre's sex as "ton queue". They sound similar when spoken here—*cul* and *queue*—and the latter word can also mean tail or bottom, so they sort of phonetically / linguistically / thematically merge into a downstairs area that re/produces things. Sandrine even describes giving birth to her son as doing number two, so to speak (ca. 1:19:07).[10] In the world of this film, however, the downstairs cyclically reproduces the same, as regulated by a socioeconomic framework, rather than produces the new (i.e. creation that isn't immediately recaptured by the framework). Mulvey and MacCabe see in *Numéro deux* a portrayal of "the basic unit for production and reproduction of labour power" (1980: 96).[11] Amie Siegel sees in it a depiction of "a production line manufacturing of familial narratives, female subjugation, domestic and sexual labor" in which "[r]eproduction is an act of repetition" (2014: 362). Yet the film's portrayal is complex: its depictions of even the most routine and ordinary household or bodily activities are, as Farocki says, "semantically dense" (he goes so far as to call them "explosion[s] of meaning") (Silverman and Farocki 1998: 141). Much of the density, however, includes the larger sociopolitical system as determining the other themes. Morrey notes how "the family is bordered on all sides by society and these borders are repeatedly permeated and crossed by flows of desire which invest society as easily as they do the family" (2005: 117). Mulvey and MacCabe see the film as Godard's "most thorough and self-conscious attempt to depict the problem of sexuality under capitalism" (1980: 95). And MacCabe—more to the point—ties this to the barring of change: *Numéro deux* reflects how the "economic determinants that circumscribe […] our lives now begin to appear as immutable; unchangeable by even the most radical politicization" (1980: 75).

Numéro deux portrays cycles of reproduction as well as blockage of the new, and the latter is mainly thematized (part of an overall conscious commitment to metaphorical bluntness) as constipation. "*Numéro deux*, in the end, is a long story about Sandrine's constipation", Drabinski writes. "That's the literal story, also the figurative. And, finally, it is the drama of Godard's tightly packed—so to speak—aesthetic space" (2008: 106). While Jerry White reads the constipation as "a transparent metaphor for the ravages that consumer capitalism visits on the body" (2013: 74), Mulvey and MacCabe find it to stand—more in line with my reading—"for the blockage in the social system as a whole" (1980: 99). The metaphor (and the bluntness) also extends to the apartment and to Pierre's body. In one scene (32:00–33:34) we peak into the bathroom through the doorway. We hear Pierre: "Shit, it's blocked again! The plumbing in social housing is terrible!" He approaches the bathroom sink: "Can I piss here?" Sandrine: "Yes, go ahead." We see parts of Sandrine's hand at the side of the image. Sandrine: "Do you want to do it tonight?" Pierre: "I don't know. We'll see." Sandrine: "Thanks, boss." Pierre: "What is it now?" Sandrine: "You heard me." Pierre finishes up, as Sandrine grabs his *queue* and tries to instigate sex. He remains soft.[12] Pierre: "It's shit. I can't even get a hard-on when I want to."[13] "You're so full of shit!", Sandrine retorts, connecting his physical state to waste and being full of it—as if he was also constipated. At the end of the scene Sandrine says: "Things have to change. But where does it happen?"

Behind Is Memory, In Front Is the Future

Why ask *where* rather than how? The film plays with pseudo-spatiotemporal coordinates for re/production and for how real change can happen. The theme of producing children—as we will see—recurs throughout Sonimage. One aspect is to portray this as a matter of before/after and behind/in front. *Numéro deux*'s primal scene even functions this way. Vanessa is "in front" on a literal visual level (in the superimposition) and in con-fronting the act. But she is also positioned in front as an *after*, as a product of the behind/before of her parent's activities. In the introduction Sandrine says "*Numéro deux* is not left or right but before and behind. In front are children." We also learn that the *behind* equals the social context more broadly, including the government and work. As a potential for creation, the behind is blocked from producing sociopolitical difference and organized to reproduce a state of things.[14]

"Behind" here also means *memory*. Memory can serve as preservation, as reproduction of the same, but it can also serve as potential for the new, and as such it can be blocked from connecting with the present. The two grandparents, who live in the same apartment, have a large presence in the film overall, as well as their own scenes. There is a five-minute section (starting 51:06) with double screens showing the grandmother variously sitting, doing domestic work, intimately washing herself, while also talking in voice-over, (critically) paraphrasing Germaine Greer on the patriarchy and conditions for female liberation, with a focus on sexual organs.[15] In this section, memory—represented by someone with most of life behind her—appears like past oppression charged with new potential (mixed with sadness and regret). With the grandfather it is the opposite: political potential stuck in the past. Immediately following (56:12), there is a four-minute section in which he sits alone by the stove stirring a pot. He talks about his previous life as a union man, albeit also his work in a weapons factory that indirectly led to the killing of women and children. About ten minutes later (ca. 1:11:40–1:12:25) he sits alone drinking whiskey at a table, showing his *queue* underneath (sort of mirroring a previous shot of the grandmother sitting with an open robe while rubbing her temples). He shares more stories about his political work from his youth. He then says: "She [his wife] always says I jerk off with my memories. I don't jerk off. But I sometimes look at my cock."

In the grandfather's discourse, potential appears as that which can no longer productively connect with the present. It appears as masturbatory or as being "obliged to listen to an 'oral history' program on the radio", as Farocki describes a scene where the family listens to him talk. For Silverman his stories seem "definitively in the past" in the sense that "he no longer has access either to narrative or affect" (Silverman and Farocki 1998: 151). Farocki adds that they represent "a form of political action which no longer seems possible within the present tense of the film" (150).

Memory is the *behind*, the ass if you will, seen as a general downstairs. As such it can be masturbatory, cyclically reproductive, or potential (blocked or not) for the new. Memory is also the landscape, and the content of the black background, connected through the reproductive organs. In a scene with Vanessa taking a bath she asks her mother (21:18): "Do all little girls have a hole?" Sandrine: "Yes." Vanessa: "Is that where memories come out?" Sandrine: "Of course." Vanessa: "Where does it go? "Sandrine: "It goes away. Into the landscape. And there's a factory now in the landscape." The landscape/factory metaphor is a multifarious leitmotif in this film, but in one sense the landscape can be seen as social territory—as Godard says in episode 2A of *Six fois deux*: "society supplies a landscape" (ca. 50:50)—that contains conditions for production more broadly, and the factory as a more determined territorial machinery that ties things up into reproduction. From this perspective, Sandrine's constipation can also be seen as healthy resistance to certain reproduction cycles that forcibly take her from behind for the purpose of reproducing the same.

Epilogue: Is It Over?

How (if at all) can the memory landscape be rejuvenated to produce the new (beyond cycles of reproduction)? This question is explored from many angles throughout Sonimage. The epilogue of *Numéro deux* (1:20:12–1:24:49), however, appears ambivalent as to whether this is possible—as Jerry White writes: "It is this sense of idealism that has been lost, but what remains is a sense of engagement, despite an awareness of futility" (2013: 77). Godard sits with head in arms leaning over a table with editing equipment. The black background is gone: the light is switched on. We hear Sandrine: "All of a sudden, it's over. Something else is happening. My role is over. What the fuck are we playing at?" She goes on to talk—now both as the character and as the namesake actor playing the character—about her experience of patriarchal structures in the personal and everyday (with implicit references to the narrative). Sandrine then appears on one of the two monitors behind Godard. It is a recurring shot (it was also the last one before the epilogue): she sits semi-leaned over her kitchen table in a white robe (echoing Godard's physical position). This is also how and where we have seen her talk about constipation and blockage.

Sandrine's voice-over continues—now seemingly addressing Godard who looks up at the monitor but who is still silent and with his head in one hand—to talk about gendered aspects of telling other's stories in film and television and the "crime" of letting others talk for you. After a while Godard seems to push a button and an image appears on a second monitor to the right showing Vanessa in her bath. Godard, with his head graphically positioned between the two monitors, twists a nob on the one showing Vanessa. Sandrine: "Still and already. Already me. And yesterday. Today. Children and parents." Godard twists a nob on the left monitor. Sandrine continues: "Today and tomorrow. Now and later. Number one and number two. And me. Finally in my place. [Where she is unblocked or just further subjugated?] Number three." The monitor with Vanessa is now turned off. Sandrine: "I am present. Between my past and my future. Between youth and old age. Me who invents the grammar." The monitor with Sandrine is turned off. Godard remains bent over the table. Sandrine continues to talk about music and of wanting a kind of power, as a Léo Ferré song about the old days and things being too late comes on the soundtrack. After a moment the image cuts away from Godard's lit up room to a single screen against the black background again showing Vanessa bathing. We also hear Pierre (and see parts of him in front of the bath) reading a book to Vanessa about the need for a good father to comply with social arrangements.

With the third and final part of the epilogue (1:24:50–1:26:50), we are back in the studio—*now dark again*—with a closer shot of a small audio mixer board and rolling tape and with Godard's hands moving volume levers. We hear the family speaking to each other about what a landscape is, and whether dad is a factory or a landscape. Godard pulls down the volume and raises the lever with Ferré's song. Being asked by Sandrine what he is doing, her son Nicolas answers: "I'm examining my plan carefully." Sandrine: "And?" Nicolas: "I can see that it's 'unrealizable'" (Nicholas quotes Brecht here, a quote that is repeated in *Six fois deux* and *Histoire(s) du cinéma*). We now hear bird sounds that were also heard at the beginning of the film and during Sandrine's talk about seeing the unbelievable. We also hear Vanessa outside: "There was that. There was a factory, and, all of a sudden, there was a landscape." Ferré repeats previous lines. Godard pulls down levers and closes the lid of the mixer board. The lights go out completely in the studio. Black screen. Short string swell. Film ends.

This reading of *Numéro deux* serves to introduce the more general problem space for Sonimage. This film lays out this problem space poetically more than through explicit theoretical systematicity. Regardless, this problem space serves as a plane of immanence for the embryonic cinecepts in *Six fois deux* and *France tour détour* to which I will now turn.

Six fois deux—Two Embryonic Cinecepts

Six fois deux (1976) is overall even more experimental in form and in its essayistic mix of genres, modes, and approaches. It was produced for television with six pairs of episodes:

1A: Nobody's There (*Y'a personne*) (57:21 min).
1B: Louison (41:45.)
2A: Lessons about Things (*Leçons de choses*) (51:33 min).
2B: Jean-Luc (47:48 min)
3A: Photos and Co (*Photos et cie*) (45:39min).
3B: Marcel (55:07 min)
4A: No History (*Pas d'histoire*) (56:45 min).
4B: Chicks (*Nanas*) (42:42 min)
5A: Us Three (*Nous trois*) (52:12 min).
5B: René(e)s (52:55 min)
6A: Before and After (*Avant et après*) (44:32 min).
6B: Jacqueline et Ludovic (49:48 min)

The first of each episode pair, as Witt writes, "raises a loose set of concerns, which are then picked up and reworked through reference to an individual or group of individuals in the second" (2014: 329). MacCabe—although the division between the episode pairs is not always fully divided in this way—describes the first episode as examining "a problem theoretically and conceptually" while the second "holds some of the concerns in the first half in tension" through an interview or conversation with someone who has a particular life experience (1980: 142). However, while the conversations—mostly with "ordinary" people[16] with a focus on their personal lives or work—are openly explorative, most are of low cineceptual interest. Although some of the "same logic of superimposition and the displacement of boundaries is detectable even in the purely verbal exchanges that dominate *Six fois deux*", as Michael Cramer writes (2017: 166), the medium is still mainly used there to document the dialogue. The main template: a static long shot showing the person in focus and audio of talk between the person and the interviewer (and the interviewer is always Godard, except in episode 2B in which he is the interviewee). These conversations are therefore left to the side.[17]

Six fois deux's formal inventiveness is well acknowledged in the literature. Jerry White describes the series as a "didactic visual essay" that "uses a great deal of visual effects [...] to make its arguments" (2013: 84), or in subjecting things, as Michael Witt writes, "to analysis and criticism" (2014: 329f). White, more specifically, notes how "Godard and Miéville use drawing and writing directly onto the video images and similar effects, such as wipes or superimpositions, to isolate various parts of the image, focus the viewer's attention", as well as using "arrows that delineate directions" or a grid "superimposed on the image" (2013: 86). And Deleuze already talked about *Six fois deux* turning "writing into a new televisual resource, a sort of expressive material with its own particular current in relation to the other currents on the screen" (N 43).

Six fois deux hereby also contains resources for cinecepts, in two ways: 1) Even when its ideas—its arguments, analyses, critiques, and essayistic explorations—are *more* poetically than philosophically determined, which is most of the time, its palette of forms for doing this can be reutilized for more distinctly cineceptual ends (I will come back to this idea in the next chapter with a focus on *Histoire(s) du cinéma*). 2) On two occasions, the explicitly philosophical takes charge enough for *Six fois deux* to coalesce into embryonic cinecepts.

First Embryonic Cinecept: Borders Are Where Revolutions Happen

This embryonic cinecept appears towards the end of episode 2A, called "Lessons about Things" (*Leçons de choses*). Godard talks through most of the episode, by himself and in the beginning (and briefly towards the end) with a character called Paolo. This is mixed with various imagery, electronic texts and video pen handwriting/drawing, and some light montage. While talking with Paolo about editing at first, Godard suddenly says (ca. 2:25): "Here, a baby now." Paolo responds with some generic Althusser/Foucault inspired discourse about the social confinements that the baby will later be forced to go through as part of growing up. But this quickly turns into a more complex and varied flow of ideas. It is about how things can change with a focus on *things*: how things are represented and communicated, the production of things, machines, work, speed, money, media, global inequality, why an egg changes when fried, the possibility of change when capitalism eats everything while ensuring that things fundamentally stay the same, and change as a matter of *when* and *where* in the sense of circulations over the border between what is behind (*derrière*) and in front (*devant*).

Between ca. 27:30–32:12 things crystalize into an embryonic cinecept—although this one can be seen as a kind of setup for the second embryonic cinecept which is also about borders but more explicit and extensive in its philosophical exposition. This section *condenses*—as all philosophical concepts do—a larger set of ideas into a smaller set of signs. But it also sticks out like a cascade in an essayistic flow rather than through clear signs of delineation towards what precedes and follows. Yet, it has a structure made up of five parts, with varying degrees of explicit philosophical reasoning about borders (which is further developed and deepened in the second embryonic cinecept). Godard talks, writes, and draws[18] on

1. a black screen
2. a color photo close-up of two mating ladybugs
3. a color photo of a couple embraced in a sixty-nine
4. a color photo of two mating crickets
5. the couple again interspersed with the black screen

The first part starts in the midst of an ongoing elaboration on the black screen.

Part 1

Godard: "The revolution, yes, but ..."

[*Godard-Miéville draw an arrow with a white video pen, which starts mid left of center pointing horizontally to the center. They then write "rêve", the French word for dream, at the arrow's base.*]

Godard: "... who will come to meet it?"

[*They draw another arrow pointing into the middle from the opposite side, and at the arrow's tail, which bends upwards, they write the word "évolution". So that we see something like this: "rêve → ← évolution, but with 'évolution' higher up due to the curved arrow. That is, a splicing of the word revolution into two parts, dream and evolution, and arrows emphasizing the space between the two.*]

Godard talks about how some occasionally succeed in going outside, with outside indicated to mean a place for revolutionary action.

[*An arrow is drawn from left to right above "rêve" that points towards "évolution". Under the curved evolution arrow, they draw an arrow pointing in the opposite direction. Graphics erased. Black screen.*]

Godard raises a question that implies no one or too few will be there to meet them. That those succeeding in going outside will be or have been too alone.

[*On the empty black screen they draw a horizontal arrow pointing from the middle of the upper part of the frame towards the left. They add an arrow underneath pointing in the opposite direction with its head in the middle of the frame. To the left of both arrows, they draw an equals sign. On the right side of the frame, sort of pointed to by the lower arrow, they write "égal", the French word for equal.*]

Godard now asks about spatiotemporal coordinates …

[*Graphics erased, black screen.*]

… he repeats and expands: "Where and when will it happen?"

[*They draw a horizontal arrow pointing from the middle of the upper part of the frame towards the left, and at the arrowhead they write "òu", the French word for "where". Then an arrow underneath which points in the opposite direction, and at the head of that arrow they write "quand", the French word for "when".*]

Godard: "We do not know. But where and when it happens …"

[*Cut to a shot, recurring in other parts of the episode, of hands with a cigarette on a table, a coffee cup in the middle, and a pack of cigarettes and parts of an ashtray.*]

Godard: "… it is possible to show it".

[*Cut to a black image.*]

Part 2

Godard: "Seeing, then, is not what people think it is."

[*Cut from the black image to the photo of two mating ladybugs, one mounting the other on the left side. This photo remains for the rest of this part.*]

After adding that newspapers are misleading in this regard, Godard now refers to the image on display.

[*They draw a white line with the video pen along the curved profile of the female ladybug, and under the from-behind-mounting male ladybug, marking a border between the two.*]

He isolates what there is to see in it: "That which is *between* the two. Between the two, that is what is to be seen here."

[*They draw vertical lines to mark out the space above the border line, first over the male ladybug to the right in the image then on the left side where we see a black background.*]

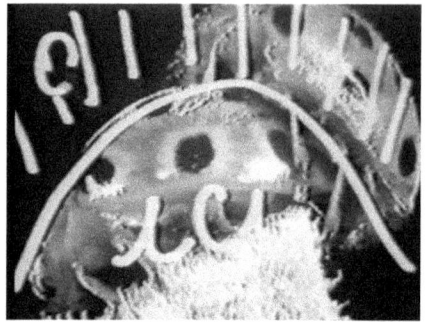 

Figures 4.2a–b *Six fois deux*, ep. 2A

Godard: "If you don't see it, things end up bristling with difficulty."

[*They write "ici" (here) underneath the border (see figure 4.2a), and "ailleur" (elsewhere) above the border and across the vertical lines.*]

Godard now addresses a "you" that remains "here" while desiring to go "elsewhere", and how this "you" fails to "see the connection between here and elsewhere".

Part 3

[*Cut to the photo of a couple embraced in a sixty-nine on a beach, and with the white video-pen graphics from the previous image remaining. As we can see in figure 4.2b, the photo shows a woman's legs framing the head of a man sticking out between them in the direction of the camera. The man's arms partly frame the woman's legs. One of the man's legs sticks out further back on the left side of the frame. They both lie on flat almost white sand.*]

With this image as an example, Godard adds that "people" evidently still go elsewhere, and that this is interesting.

[*They begin to slowly erase the border line and the graphics on top of it.*]

He claims that seeing "this"—i.e. what's in between—can sometimes require erasing.

[*The slow erasing of the video graphics continues but leaves "ici" at the bottom. After a few seconds "ici" starts to blink.*]

Godard: "But when you erase one part …"

Part 4

[*Cut to the photo of two mating crickets. The crickets are reddish/orange and beige with black dots and lie in green grass. The one on the left mounts the other who is in the middle of the frame. The blinking "ici" remains.*]

Godard: "… well, you are forced to see the other. You erase in front of the others."

[*"ici" stops blinking. They start drawing a curved border line between the mating pair.*]

Godard: "In fact, if you don't see this …"

[*They zigzag along the line for emphasis.*]

Godard: "… well, then you don't move. This is what you must see."

[*They begin to erase the borderline.*]

Godard: "If you don't move, then precisely you want to go elsewhere. Love should erase many things but that's …"

[*Borderline erased*]

Godard: "… what's wrong with it".

Part 5

[*Cut back to the photo of a couple embraced in a sixty-nine on a beach. They draw a borderline across the couple with a thick black video pen.*]

Godard argues, as a contrast to the common wisdom that love lacks borders, that borders are the interesting part.

[*The black border starts from the low left side following the leg of the man, up to the knee of the woman, then down through the woman's thigh, and round below the man's head, then up through the woman's other leg to that knee, after which it swerves towards the upper right side of the frame.*]

Godard points to this border but adds that there are many more.

[*They mark out a different border as a dotted line made by a thinner black video pen. It starts from bottom right, first following the man's arm then the woman's foot and lower leg, crossing her other foot and down through the man's arm on the other side, passing his hand before going diagonally across the sand back towards the right.*]

Godard refers to what we see as another border.

[*The two borders now shift color to white.*]

He points to the border between these colors, having just shifted from one to the other, but also implies that there is a limitless amount of borders to see in this image.

[*They draw a thick white border line along the horizon in the background, which crosses the top of the other two border lines, and goes to about a third or fourth from the upper limit of the frame.*]

Godard describes this as yet another border.

[*They erase all graphics and draw a new border with a thick white video pen. Starting from the bottom right it goes over the man's arm, the woman's foot and lower leg, her other foot, and a bit down through her thigh before shifting 90 degrees to the left, following the horizon to the end of the frame.*]

After mentioning a border also coming *from* the horizon, Godard suddenly adds: "Your horizon is blocked, you know that."

[*They draw a thinner white border line starting from the man's hand to the left, going up through his arm around his shoulder, following the woman's foot and whole leg, around her buttocks, and then diverging diagonally towards the right bottom corner.*]

A blocked horizon calls for the following, Godard says: "you have to learn to see the borders".

[*They draw a circle about the size of a head just next to the man's head, partly overlapping with it to its left.*]

Godard speaks about there being many different "kinds" of borders and adds: "here is another one that closes".

[*They draw the circle once more and then fill it.*]

He refers to this as a "country" and as "your" country.

[*Cut to a black image with the video graphics remaining.*]

He adds that one needs passports to cross borders, and that "[u]ltimately, this is an image of a passport".

[*Cut back to the sixty-nine image with the graphics remaining. The graphics change color from white to black.*]

Godard: "Here is another passport."

[*Cut to black.*]

To tie things back to Deleuze's concept of concepts (see Chapter 1 above)—and abstracting for a moment from the level of audiovisual form—this embryonic cinecept "orders" the following "intensive components" in "zones of neighborhood" with partly overlapping areas:

- Black Background
- Revolution
- Evolution
- Dream
- Mating/Sex
- Borders/Frontiers/In Between
- Movement
- Borders as either Multiple Frontiers of Potential or as Closed
- Passports for Crossing Closed Borders
- Seeing/Not Seeing

This embryonic cinecept begins to conceive of borders as possible frontier areas of revolutionary force, which can also circle back on themselves and close (and require passports to cross). It states that we must first learn to see such borders/frontiers and then even help draw them up ourselves based on what we see. As such it is in tandem with the more developed second embryonic cinecept described below, which takes us from looking at such borders in conception (mating organisms) to explorations of their function in the relation between mother and baby. Before looking at the second of these tandem embryonic cinecepts, a point about how Deleuze's reading of *Six fois deux* relates to them: Already the first spells out how borders/the in-between are where revolutions happen, and with the second, as we will see, a string of adjacent philosophical points are made concerning the nature of the in-between as a "third"—the third as suppressed in Western, Aristotelian logic—and the complex interrelation between the two sides of the border. Some of this is of course precisely what Deleuze picks up on in his 1976 piece on *Six fois deux* (the details of what is said in that text were examined in Chapter 2). What is noteworthy here is that Deleuze does not really add philosophically in that piece to what is already said in these two embryonic cinecepts. It may rather be the case that the second of them is even more philosophically (and not just artistically) developed and explicit than Deleuze's explanation. As Witt says about Deleuze's more general take on Godard's focus on the in-between (to reiterate a quote from the Introduction): "it is unclear that Deleuze is doing very much more than stating the obvious: his formulae are extremely close to those proposed by Godard himself" and "could equally well have been taken from one of Godard and Miéville's films or television series of the 1970s" (1999: 111). And Deleuze himself credits Godard, with direct reference to *Six fois deux*, for "thinking and presenting [the conjunction] AND in a very novel way" (N 44f).

Second Embryonic Cinecept: The River Between Mother and Baby

The second embryonic cinecept, which appears in the second half of episode 4A, develops the ideas about borders (and rivers, also discussed in 2A) in some other directions. The episode at large revolves around a situation: Godard-Miéville have put a writer in a room with a pad and a pen with the purpose of showing how a story is created. Godard interviews the author and tries to get him to reveal the creative process. The author talks about his process and about writing more generally but does not produce much text. This is interspersed with a set of sections titled like the episode but with a number added: "No History Zero" (*Pas d'histoire zero*), "No History One", "No History Two", and so on: 0) A section with the writer not writing. 1) A close-up of a boy, with a man in voice-over reading a story that seems like an example of Althusserian interpellation. 2) A set of television extracts on politicians. 3) The writer again. 4) A young girl new to reading spelling her way through a text. 5.) A man drawing a four-framed comic illustrating how capitalist appropriation and devaluation of both people and the natural elements leads to alienation. 6) The writer again. 7) Shot of tanks and military vehicles driving on a (contemporaneous) Paris street. 8) The reading girl again. 9) A little story reimagining Till Eulenspiegel as coming to Paris in 1968 to be part of the revolution. 10) The writer again, talking about where stories come from.

11) The second embryonic cinecept appears here, in the twenty-minute-long concluding eleventh *pas d'histoire* (35:10–54:44). The whole section is a condensed essay in which a series of cineceptual crystallizations occur that all make up the same embryonic cinecept (in the rest of this chapter I will at times abbreviate embryonic cinecepts to "EC"). While the longest, this EC is also the most philosophically developed, explicit, and even clear. Let us look closely at key parts of what we see and hear in this section.

The section starts with a prelude. We see a black-and-white photograph of a two–four-year-old kid with a black background. A male voice-over talks about opening, discovering, or instead appearing to close. Godard-Miéville draw two curved arrows with the video pen, so that each makes up one half in a circle, with their arrowheads meeting at the bottom. Cut to a color photo that will be one of two main photos in this EC (and which was previously shown in episode 3A as part of the cover of a brochure or the like—it also flashes by already in *Ici et ailleurs*, at 27:50): In the upper left side, taking up a little more than a third of the frame, we see a woman's face in profile. She looks down on and kisses a baby who is lying down. The background is white with a yellow-blue tint. The baby's face is shown in profile at the bottom of the frame with its forehead towards the left and mouth towards the right. The baby's arms are stretched up towards the mother's forehead in an angle on the right side of the frame (see figures 4.3a–b and 4.4a–b). The arms thereby also outline parts where circles are later drawn across the mother and baby. And the point at which the baby's hand touches the mother's forehead is later referred to as the key connecting point along with the mother's lips touching the baby's forehead towards the bottom of the frame. The mother as a left vertical and the baby as a low horizontal also recall the following voice-over from an earlier episode: "You must be two to become three. The two sides of the angle: The mom side and the baby side. The mom space, and the baby time" (3A: 32:34–32:58).

After this prelude there are a few minutes of a build-up, which uses the same basic audiovisual parameters as the ensuing EC: voice-over, video-pen writing, drawing, diagramming, and photographs of babies—the one just described, another where a breast instead of a face is pointed towards the baby, and a third with a baby bottle close to a baby's open mouth. In this build-up, the philosophical ideas start out as variations on what strikes me as fairly familiar psychoanalytic/Lacanian notions of mother–child unity and the child's separation and development into a split subject, through, as presented here, circulations between self and outside/other. But this is also mixed with slightly more idiosyncratic charts of circulations of love and nourishment, ideas about the child as open and closed towards society, as well as more Deleuze-and-Guattari influenced conceptions of machinic connection with a focus on *breast/baby mouth*.[19]

This build-up leads into a more cineceptual section. It starts with a shot of a newspaper page over which they talk as well as draw and write with a video pen. The page has parts of text columns bordering the right and bottom sides, and a photo taking up a bit more than half the frame and positioned towards the upper left. The photo shows a baby in profile to the left with its mouth open towards a baby bottle to the right held by an adult hand. In the build-up, this image was a key part of the discussion of subjectivity formation in relation to the outside or the other. This image bridges into and remains at the start of the cineceptual part (but it does not reappear after that). The rest of the section focuses on the relation between the mother and the baby in the following sense: the relation itself as a third, as a border that is itself something, which the EC at times likens to a river with its own currents, something both parties have to pass in order to connect and communicate, and which is also something that can, but does not have to be, suppressed, as it is in Aristotelian, Western logic (the law of the excluded middle). This second EC, then, presents a conception of the border as its own positive, third sphere or current between the two.[20] Let us now look at what we see and hear in this regard—given the length and audiovisual density of this section at large and how the cineceptual parts are spread out in it, I will focus on key parts of this EC.

Over the image of the baby from the newspaper page, the entry point to the EC, Godard-Miéville draw a slightly curved arrow from the bottle to mouth, and the male voice-over says this concerns a passage. He rhetorically asks about the location of the passage, if it is indeed there, before saying it is "here" (ca. 39:18): They now outline a border as tight zigzags with the video pen, which follows the baby's profile and the side of its upper body. The voice and video pen further emphasize the separation itself as what is important in the relation between the two: the "third" that is "never shown". After about twenty seconds the section also transitions to the recurring photo of a mother kissing a baby's forehead (with the baby's arms stretched up to touch the mother's forehead), and to borders and passages between them, as a complex three-part relation of insides and outsides and circulating streams of love, nourishment, and communication (rather than a unit that can separate into two halves). Audiovisually, all these points and the points that follow are made through these basic parameters: a talking voice, editing back and forth between two photos and a black screen, as well as a video pen with varying thickness that produces a stream of words, arrows, circles, numbers, curved and straight lines, dots, zigzags, etc. These parameters, regardless of poetic liberties and levels of abstraction, all combine in a fairly clear line of philosophical reasoning. The voice and the pen reference each other and both engage directly with the photos. This is the case in the following bit of the EC centered on the kissing mother photo, and which comes after claims about how communication requires distance of varying kinds and degrees (starting at 42:42):

> A male voice speaks about one sense in which the "distance" is "thinner" …
> [*They draw a thin border line between the mother/baby that mostly follows the mother's profile.*]
> … how "*this* touches *that* …"
> [*The video pen marks out the area where the baby's hand touches the mother's forehead.*]
> … and how this "reduces the distance".
> [*The pen marks out the area where the mother's upper chin/lower lip area connects with the baby's forehead (see figure 4.3a).*]
> Shifting to what is both more "difficult" and "important" to see, the voice asks "if there is a separation between the two that in the end is a little wider".
> [*They draw a parallel border line.*]
> He suggests we call this space between the two "a river, for instance".
> [*They write "fleuve" in the "river" created by the parallel lines. Cut for two seconds to the photo of a breast pointed at a baby—further described below—with the video graphics remaining, then back to the photo of the kissing mother.*]
> The voice talks about this river as clearly visible and as containing …
> [*They draw lines throughout the river with a thicker video pen, and then fill the whole river.*]
> … "a current" that can go "in one direction" or "another".
> [*Graphics erased.*]
> It can go "in this direction":
> [*They draw a thick arrow, where the river is, that points downwards.*]
> "Or it can go like this":
> [*They add an arrowhead at the top so that the arrow points in both directions.*]
> The voice says this might clarify how it is a river, before also pointing to the river's shores. First there is "shore 1".
> [*They write "rivage 1" (French for shore 1) with a thinner video pen on the mother's face.*]
> Then, there is "shore 2".
> [*They add "rivage 2" on the baby's face and arm (see figure 4.3b).*]
> The voice says the two shores "want to communicate", that this requires "a current that flows/passes [*un courant qui passe*]", and that "we have seen that it flows/passes". He then says this occurs "here":

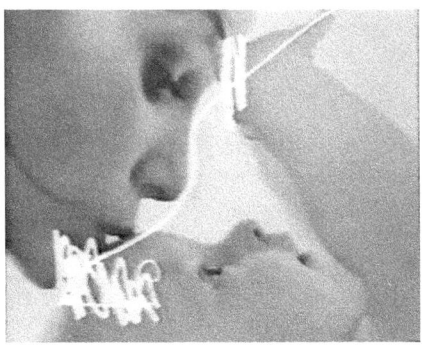 

Figures 4.3a–b *Six fois deux*, ep. 4A

> *[They draw a full circle that passes through both faces and with their foreheads as connecting points.]*

The voice adds that "flows/passes" between the two—or one shore going to the other and vice versa—means going "through the river", and to understand this situation well is to recognize that this is unavoidable and necessary.

> *[Graphics disappear.]*

It is always the case, the voice says, that whenever "there is *this*",

> *[They draw a half circle through the mother's face and continuing through the baby's face, and then start making dots/points on the line.]*

… "at each small point, at each moment, in the form of time and space",

> *[Graphics disappear.]*

… there is a passage "through the river".

> *[They draw a smaller circle over the eye, nose, and upper chin of the woman, and then a line out from the circles, its own half circle going down to the forehead of the baby.]*

… after which the current passes back, and then "continues" …

> *[Graphics disappear.]*

… "on the line". But there is more to see here: the voice talks about the possibility of "enlarging" …

> *[They draw a quarter circle across the woman's face pointing towards the baby, and a slightly larger point on the line.]*

… "each point on the line" and that it is not by chance that "this is done in the form of a circle".

> *[Graphics disappear.]*

The voice explains that enlarging each point would show "this" …

> *[A smaller circle movement, like a tight spiral is drawn on the woman's cheek.]*

… and how whenever this is done, it is part of "continuation of this which advances":

> *[They draw a chain of these circle-spirals towards the baby (see figure 4.4a).]*

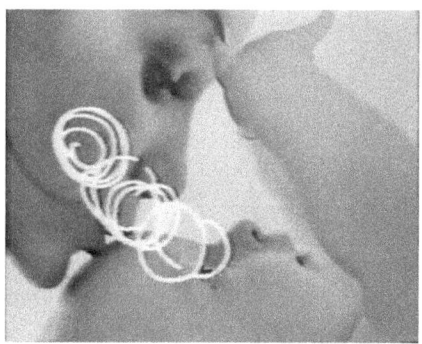 

Figures 4.4a–b *Six fois deux*, ep. 4A

The voice-over likens them to "links in a chain".
[*Graphics disappear.*]
"[A] chain of events from one to the other."
[*They write "1" on the mother and "2" on the baby.*]
Each side "wants to link/chain itself" in this way.
[*They draw two parallel lines where the river or "channel" runs between them.*]
As the graphics now show a river/channel again, the voice-over calls this number "3".
[*They also write "3" in the river/channel (see figure 4.4b).*]

They make further points—with the same audiovisual means—about gender, society and how work and love condition each other. They code the river / channel / border as "work" that love has to pass through in order to exist, and which also changes things. They then diagram the differences in need, complexity, and spatiotemporality between the baby touching his mother's forehead with his hands and the mother kissing the baby's forehead, and the necessity of such differences between the two parties for all this to work. But they also show how love and hate can make the two parties come so close that the in-between is suppressed. After a cut to the recurring breast/baby image they caution that "in this linking [*rapprochement*] one must be careful not to eliminate the third". In this photo, parts of the mother's torso and one breast largely take up the same left-side area within the frame as the mother's baby-kissing face in the other recurring photo, with the nipple directed at—close to but not touching—the baby's open mouth. Compared to the kissed baby, this baby head is a bit more upright, directed the other way towards the left/breast, and positioned further to the right in the frame. The background is white and the mother wears white garments. The river / channel / third is drawn with a fairly thick video pen as two parallel lines between the breast and the baby's face.

The voice-over now explains that even if the two parties get even "closer to each other here" this does not mean the elimination of the third, since "in the movement" …

[*Cut back to the kissing mother photo. They erase the two river lines.*]

… "within these two lines" …

[*They redraw the two river lines a bit narrower, but more so as to mark out the route between the two points where hand and mouth respectively connect with the other's forehead, i.e. the main nodes in the river and for its currents. The space between the two lines is filled with one stroke with a thicker pen.*]

… (in which "they approach becoming one") there is also "this":

[*They draw a large circle-formed arrow from the baby's forehead round to his hands crossing the river over to the mother's forehead and then round over her cheeks to her mouth where the arrowhead points to the river between them.*]

The voice cautions us to "pay attention precisely so the third" …

[*Cut to breast/baby image, with graphics remaining.*]

… "has not been eliminated".

[*Graphics erased.*]

And it starts to critique a logic that specifically performs such eliminations of thirds, a "Western way of reasoning" that forbids "contradiction".

They go on to express a series of other points about how work, needs, and synchronizations/contradictions of movements can influence the suppression or preservation of the third/in-between in this mother–baby relation. After another cut back to the breast/baby image an embryonically cineceptual bit follows. In ways too audiovisually intricate to detail here (although continuing with the same means: the two photos, a black screen, video pen, voice), it covers the river as an in-between "surface" that is also made up of two individual surfaces: the surface of the mother/breast and the surface of the baby. Both seek not so much to go to the other as to "get out of its own surface", and thereby reach their *own* "three"—sort of like their own entry into the river—which differs from the three / surface / river-entry of the other, so that when they are "together", when each has come to their respective surface, it is their respective threes that are together. (We can pause here to note how this EC conceives of the breast/baby relation not in psychoanalytical terms, that is, as a matter of *lack*, but as something more machinic and as containing border-zones that are positive in their potential productivity.)

At one point they produce these graphics over the breast/baby image: a thin line following the contour of the breast; "milk" [*lait*] on the breast; an arrow pointing from that word down alongside the nipple; a line just above the contour of the baby; "drowned" [*noyé*] written on the baby; an arrow pointing up from the baby's nose towards the surface. They go on to use more words and graphics to underline the river in between and its currents, and the importance of not forgetting it. *Suddenly*—as they go on to express similar points about the relation and what happens when the river/current is removed, in practice or through "this reasoning that comes from Aristotle"—the EC opens up to world politics, through another photo underneath the breast image and some graphics and video erasings:

> The voice-over says that "this" is eliminated.
> [*They fill the river with one line of a very thick pen, but halfway through, the white-marked river area turns into an erased area showing parts of a black-and-white photo below, but in the river so to speak, or where the river is. This erasing begins to reveal an archetypically famished "African" mother whose one breast we can see, subtly extending, on a graphical level, the original breast, and in whose lap lies a baby positioned next to the baby in the original image (see figure 4.5).*]
> The voice talks about what the elimination of this would actually entail, but then shifts to describe the two people in the first image as an example of how Western people can be happy, well-nourished, and—it is implied—thereby have the opportunity to interact with love.
> [*They "erase" more of the breast/baby image to reveal more of the black-and-white photo underneath.*]
> The voice says "they eliminate a third".
> [*We now see the face and whole naked upper body of the "African" mother and legs of people in the upper background. This image now takes over the part of the frame where the mother is in the first image but with the baby still visible underneath.*]

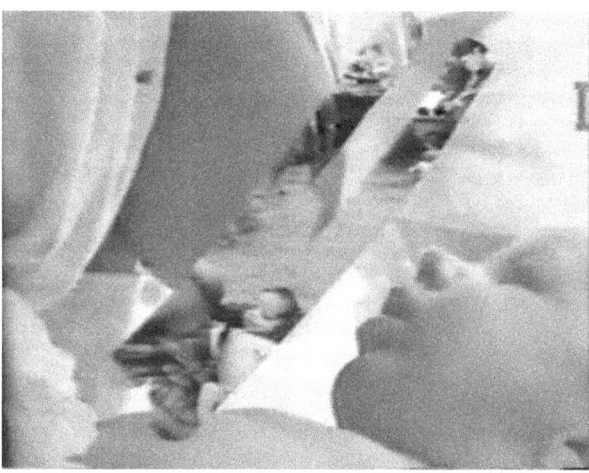

Figure 4.5 *Six fois deux*, ep. 4A

He adds that it is no coincidence that we call this particular third "the third world".

[*Cut to a black image.*]

"The one-third of the world" [*le un tiers du monde*—which also sounds here like *le entiers du monde*], the voice-over argues, "is excluded" [*le un tier exclu*].

[*Cut to the preceding image in which the black-and-white, "third-world" image is revealed more fully with only parts of the border showing from the original breast image.*]

The voice-over goes on to talk about how the third-excluding Aristotelian logic dominates education and all our thinking.

To again tie things back to Deleuze's concept of concepts (and abstracting from the level of audiovisual form), this second embryonic cinecept (albeit being spread out over a long section) mainly orders "intensive components" in "zones of neighborhood" with partly overlapping areas, which can be short-handed as follows:

- The Relation between Two Parties as Autonomous Third
- The Third as a River with Currents
- Desire to Communicate
- The In-Between seen as a Channel
- The River/Channel Being Thin or Wide
- The Two Relating Parties as River Shores
- The Need for the Relating Parties to Differ
- Crossing / Passing / Linking across the River
- A Chain of Points Passing through the River, Which When Enlarged are Revealed as Circling or Spiraling Movements or Events
- The Two Parties as Individual Surfaces to be Penetrated to Reach Their Respective Aspects of the River/Channel
- Seeing vs. Suppressing/Eliminating the River / Channel / Third
- The Third as also the Third World and its Material Relation to the West
- Work
- Love/Hate
- Learning
- Nourishment

Comment ça va: A Note on the New as Communication Matter

Before examining four more embryonic cinecepts, a brief return to the problem space: Much of the literature on Sonimage focuses on its treatment of communication, such as its "quest", as Witt writes, "to isolate and magnify the presence of capital in information flows, and to examine its potentially corrupting impact on the nature and quality of any messages they might contain" (2014: 335). Godard-Miéville's use of a model from Claude Shannon's information theory is often raised. In an article on *Comment ça va* (1976), Kevin J. Hayes describes the basics of Shannon's model as follows: "An information source selects a message to communicate, and a transmitter then encodes the message into a signal, which is sent over a channel to the receiver, which, in turn, decodes the transmitted signal into a message and hands it to its destination." And the key aspect: the signal can be "affected by noise, defined broadly as anything that distorts, deforms, or otherwise affects the signal during the transmission process" (2002: 73f). This offered Godard-Miéville, Witt writes,

> a relatively simple communications model with apparently almost limitless potential applicability in different fields, from television and the media to language, genetics, and cybernetics. Based on the premise that the transmission and reception of all information is governed by universal laws, Shannon had set out to explore the accuracy with which symbols are transmitted, how these symbols convey the desired meaning, and how efficiently this meaning affects behaviour. (2014: 323)

While the model may be reductive to the point of emptiness at least in its simplest form—see René Thom's critique of its idea of information in *Six fois deux* episode 5B, a critique that clearly impacted Godard-Miéville's take on the model—it is Godard-Miéville's expansive application and philosophically abstracting use of the model that is interesting, especially in relation to biological re/production as connected to the problem of the new. Witt argues that information theory "enabled [Godard-Miéville] to isolate and analyse points of blockage" (2014: 324). He also notes how "relations between the sexes are frequently presented as being blocked" and that some Sonimage works "examine sex in terms of communication" (337f).

In contrast to blockage, however, noise as distortion or deformation can also be what is needed to break with the cyclical reproduction of the same. This is indicated in a scene in *Comment ça va* that explicitly ties the communications model to biological reproduction. It builds on aspects of Godard's conversation about communication channels with René Thom, Thoms's critical dismissal of Shannon in light of his own theories of morphology and heritage, and Godard-Miéville's reimagining of the whole thing. A newspaperman called Marot, one of two main characters, reads a letter to his son in voice-over:

> One day you entered a corridor, your mother's cunt, and several months later you came out of the corridor, of the tunnel, of the channel. There was an "in" and

"out" socket, and your mother received a signal. How does she communicate it? How does it go from the entrance to the exit of the machine? The reproductive machine. The machine for making copies. You, a copy of me.[21]

The letter goes on to worry that the mother will distort the signal and deform his image. From this perspective, the signal appears as a narcissistic desire for the reproduction of the same. But implied is also that the creation of the new is a kind of distortion. Of course, what is biologically created by such distortion tends to be immediately recaptured in sociopolitical cycles of repetition (socialization, subjectivation, etc.). Which means other kinds of productive distortion are needed on that level. Witt similarly connects the letter to another part of *Comment ça va* which "touch[es] on the topic of the transmission of genetic information via DNA [...] and by extension the tension between attempts to bring about political change and the influence of heredity" (2014: 338).

France / tour / détour / deux / enfants—Four Embryonic Cinecepts

Godard-Miéville produced *France tour détour* (1977–78) as a series for television. It follows *Six fois deux* in having twelve episodes (although each is shorter, ca. 26 minutes), in examining an idea or a set of terms in each episode or pair of episodes, and in mixing formal invention with more straightforward dialogues/interviews. In *France tour détour*, however, the dialogues/interviews focus exclusively on two children, a girl called Camille (Virolleaud) and a boy called Arnaud (Martin). The two children echo the similarly aged siblings Vanessa and Nicolas in *Numéro deux*, but Camille and Arnaud are ethnographical rather than fictional subjects (although Godard, who interviews the children, is formally referred to as a "reporter" called Robert Linard). Camille and Arnaud are interviewed, observed, and their daily movements are "decomposed" through slow-motion. Why are they examined in this way? In terms of the general problem space, this is part of a study of how the biologically new—children—are recuperated into cycles of reproduction of the same. Differently put, it is "part of a broader analysis of the socialization process", as Witt writes, the "conditioning of the human infant as a docile subject of capitalism" (2014: 333). "Informed by Foucauldian theory, and armed with video and the power of altered motion, they set out", Witt continues, "to 'slow down the machinery of the State,' and to study a variety of instances of manipulation, copying, reproduction, dictation, and repetition in Camille's and Arnaud's daily lives" in order to "cast in relief the regulatory constraints, privations, and obligations involved in producing human docility-utility" (334).[22] A central part of this is the "ideological charge" of the everyday language "through which the children perceive, make sense of and inhabit the world", which Witt also refers to as "blocked information flow" (338f).

However, Godard's conversations with the children are far from reducible to analytical revelations of ideological language or disciplinary techniques. His questions also proactively interfere with the children's relation to language and reality. Not just by "involving them", as Witt writes, "in the imaginative work of metaphor-making" (2014: 339), but more primarily through a deconstruction of language and reality in line with the concern with returning to zero, as discussed in Chapter 2. Godard's questions are deliberately naive about the most obvious aspects of the everyday and even the fundamentals of reality—not only about what we are socialized into not questioning, then, but also that which everyone takes for granted for what seems like self-evidently good reasons. Some of the questions are Cartesian in their existential reduction—"How do you know that you exist?" he asks both children (see for instance movement 5)—but here the "I think" poses no ground.[23]

These conversations with the children, which take up a lot of running time, are of concern here only indirectly as connected with other parts of *France tour détour*. In Brenez's description of this work as a "masterpiece of real dialogue, all the more so because each dialogue is reprised, commented upon, and given a broader perspective" (2007 [2004]): 170), I find things of direct cineceptual interest only in the latter aspects. That is, in its larger essayistic-poetical-theoretical discussions and experimental thought-forms, which at times coalesce into embryonic cinecepts.

The General Content Structure

The episodes are called "Movements", and each movement is named after the abstract themes it explores:

- Obscure/Chemistry (*Obscur/Chimie*)
- Light/Physics (*Lumière/Physique*)
- Known / Geometry / Geography (*Connu/Géométrie/Géographie*)
- Unknown/Technique (*Inconnu/Technique*)
- Printing/Dictation (*Impression/Dictée*)
- Expression/French (*Expression/Français*)
- Violence/Grammar (*Violence/Grammaire*)
- Disorder/Calculation (*Désordre/Calcul*)
- Power/Music (*Pouvoir/Musique*)
- Novel/Economy (*Roman/Économie*)
- Reality/Logic (*Réalité/Logique*)
- Dream/Morality (*Rêve/Morale*)

In most of them Godard speaks to one of the children about things that concern the themes of that movement.[24] Throughout each movement there are shots of traffic or of adults on the streets, entering or moving inside subway passages, and implicitly referred to in voice-over as "the monsters".[25] The conversation and/or the general theme is also commented on by one or both of two fictional television hosts called Albert Dray and Betty Berr—whom Jerry White considers to be "obvious stand-ins for Godard and Miéville" (2013: 93). Albert and Betty sometimes interrupt the conversations with the children with a critical comment on how the interview is going or could have been conducted differently. They can also interrupt with a more abstract reflection, sometimes along with elaborate montage, especially at the end section of each episode. These end sections are always framed by a sort of spoof of prime-time television modes of address. First, either Albert or Betty makes (basically) the same speech while looking into the camera, which ends with shifting their gaze to the side while announcing a "hi/story" [*histoire*]. These hi/stories sections, also presented by Albert or Betty, often contain more extensive essayistic reflections and montage forms with clear cineceptual tendencies—and recalling the above-analyzed problem space, we can note that Godard later described the purpose of these stories as showing "why there's no change" (quoted in MacCabe 1980: 157).

Third Embryonic Cinecept: The Pregnancy Scene

> [T]here are those who inherit the [...] problem of pregnancy and the secret task of forming, ripening, and bringing to completion [...] and others who need to impregnate and be the cause of new orders of life [...] These two types of genius look for each other like men and women; but they also misunderstand each other.
>
> Nietzsche (2002 [1886]: 149 [§248])

This embryonic cinecept stretches out across three other hubs throughout the series, but its main center is at the end of movement 1A: Obscure/Chemistry (this is the EC initially described at the start of the Introduction above).[26] For some context, let us begin at the end of the preceding section. We see one of the two children, Camille, in medium shot in her room being interviewed by Godard/Linard off screen, and this is mixed with some of Betty Berr's commentary. Godard/Linard presents Camille with a question—to which she answers yes—about whether she closes her eyes when sleeping and if this makes everything "black" and "dark". He then invites her to shut her eyes now for a moment and asks: "is it the same black as the dark when the light is out? Or is it different?" Cut to the television studio introduced with a black screen with blue letters spelling "TELEVISION". Betty Berr speaks about what it would be like if people could take time to ask the television reporter questions instead. In the background we can hear Godard/Linard continue to pose questions to Camille about blackness/darkness and existence. After a moment the black screen with "TELEVISION" returns as a transition back to the interview. Godard/Linard now asks Camille if her existence "stays lit" despite her closed eyes and the darkness in the room where she sleeps. Camille thinks it does stay lit because "mom knows I exist, even when I sleep". Godard/Linard starts asking if she does not "think it's unclear/dark [*obscure*] when…"

The film then cuts to a black screen with large white letters forming the word "*HISTOIRE*", as a transition to the television studio where we meet Albert Dray, who looks into the camera and makes the speech that is repeated by either him or Betty Berr at the beginning of each movement's concluding section, with slight variations such as changing pronouns. He thanks Robert Linard and says it is "time for a story". This story, he specifies, is not Hers, or something that comes from Her. Rather, it is

> Her coming from a story. And both. But both before. Her before and the Story after. The Story before and Her after. Or superimposed. The (hi)story of…

To the left of Dray's face, we now see "IL ETAIS UN FOIS" (once upon a time) spelled out in white digital letters. This concludes the speech that introduces all the stories, and Dray continues to introduce the story specific to this movement. We learn that this is not the usual story of a girl in the sense of "there once was"—"*IL*" *in the digital text starts to move to the right in the frame.* It is rather like "Once there was a time"—"*IL*" *now starts to shift to "ELLE" across Dray's eyes*. "It/he" [*il*] not "she", Dray reasons, or perhaps "the story of '*she/it* was once/one time'" [*Elle etait un fois*]—"*ELLE*" *is now moved back above the other digital words.* Or rather, Dray adds, "a story of a beginning".

There is then a cut to the black screen with "HISTOIRE" in white letters, as the story section begins more properly: Dray's voice-over continues but with a different tone/sound. He says that when following a story—*as the image shifts to a shot of hands crocheting a yarn, while the HISTOIRE text remains*—"we mustn't lose the thread". But he also wonders "where" the story "begins" as well as what is in the other direction of the thread: "How can you tell, before you speak of it, that the future exists? That it will still be light when the lights are out?" Shift to the black screen and the word HISTOIRE. The letters change to "ISTOIRE" then to "STOIRE". Dray continues to wonder how Camille could "know" light would still exist in the darkness. The text changes to "TOIRE" then "TOI E" then "TOI". TOI remains on the black for a moment, then over the shot of the crocheting hands for a few seconds, followed by a very brief return of the black image.

What follows is an embryonic cinecept (starting at ca. 23:40): The digital TOI disappears for a second as we cut to an image of a fully pregnant naked woman standing in a bathroom combing her hair. We hear sounds from the scene, including what appears to be a man speaking in the same or an adjacent room. The top of the frame goes along the woman's chin and the bottom of the frame along her knees. She is turned slightly to the side. After a second, Handel's aria *Lascia ch'io pianga* enters the soundtrack, and the word TOI returns, now positioned on her belly, almost directly shifting to MOI before disappearing after a couple of seconds. Dray's voice-over continues as the montage formation becomes more complex:

Dray: "The truth. It is unable to imagine tomorrow, but it can remember yesterday."
  [*A slow zoom in towards the belly.*]
Dray: "And it is able to remember it inside and …"
  [*A round separate shot of the face of a sleeping baby grows out from the middle of the image, through video montage, as if emanating from the womb (see figure I.1a).*]
Dray: "… project it outside".
  [*The separate round shot of the baby now reaches the borders of the main frame on top and bottom, while still revealing some of the image behind on the sides, only to immediately contract …*]
And because of this projection outside, Dray continues …
  [*… and then rapidly expand back again. The aria stops.*]
Dray: "… it becomes an image".
  [*The round shot of the baby is now contracted again. Then it rapidly expands and takes over the whole image.*]
Dray describes such an image as "the trace of what it will be after", but he adds that "[y]ou cannot see what it will be after".
  [*The shot of the pregnant woman begins to grow as a round shape from the middle of the baby's face, expanding like the previous shot of the baby projected from the womb.*]
Yet the projected image allows you to "see the form it had before".
  [*The growth stops before reaching the boarders of the frame. It remains basically the same size for a couple of seconds, then contracts just a little. The aria returns.*]
This, however, is also "where there is darkness/obscurity".
  [*Both images shift: the round image is now of the baby, and the surrounding background image is black (see figure I.1b).*]
Dray further specifies that this dark/obscure trace is not …
  [*The round image contracts a bit.*]
… "the trace of one, but of two".

> [*Both images shift again: the shot of the woman is now the surrounding image, and the small round image becomes a black image, which also begins to contract over the belly (see figure I.1c).*]

Dray specifies this as the "memory of two people's desires".

> [*The small black image has now contracted to the point of disappearing.*]

Which is to say: "Before and after. Father and mother."

> [*Cut to the shot of the baby. Aria stops*]

But it is also "[a] sickly and inevitably fatal desire",

> [*The round image of the woman starts to grow in the middle, on the left side of the mouth of the baby, and it expands fairly rapidly to take over the image.*]

... this desire "to be more than one", since it entails an "*other* than the self who announces your death."

> [*The round image of the baby now grows from the belly and takes over the frame, accompanied by swelling coda-like string music.*]

End of embryonic cinecept.[27] To again tie things back to Deleuze's concept of concepts (and abstracting from the level of audiovisual form), this embryonic cinecept mainly orders the following "intensive components" in "zones of neighborhood" with partly overlapping areas:

- Pregnancy
- Memory/History
- Beginnings
- Desire
- Parents (The Need to Be Two to Create a Third)
- Stories
- Expansion/Contraction
- Projection
- Image
- Imagination
- A Black Image
- Dark/Obscure
- Obscure / Dark Form / Trace of What Will Be
- Light/Clear
- Before/After
- Baby
- Self/Other
- Existence
- Death

We can recognize a certain clear—albeit quite poetic—extension of the problem space, such as the production of the new as a matter of memory as a behind which is projected forwards and the black background as connected to pregnancy. Pregnancy is presented here as movements of the "dark/obscure" and "clear/light", as memory/behind and "the trace of what it will be after," and in the context of doubt about whether the future—as the most fundamental mode or aspect of the new—can exist at all in dark times. Now, this EC may itself seem like a mix of bits that are clear and bits that are more obscure and thereby require further interpretation (which, we should also bear in mind, is the case with much philosophy, not just art): We start by seeing *you* and *me*, TOI and MOI, in electronic text over the pregnant belly—the two parts required to make a new human body; two parts in a memory that can be projected forwards; two aspects in a machinery for producing/reproducing. TOI and MOI also appear along with Handel's *Lascia ch'io pianga*. Later on in the series, in the middle of movement 9 (ca. 13:58), this music is connected to the question of what it means to take power. At the end of movement 4 it is connected to a story about socialism, slowing down the machine of the state, and women's bodies as machines. The pregnancy EC in movement 1 focuses on the aspect of the female body as a machine that is literally re/productive. This can of course mean reproducing the machinery of our current state, but here it seems rather like an effort to slow down and reconceive this machinery as *also* a potential for producing the new, and in a broadly ontological rather than just sociopolitical sense. Dray begins by connecting "The truth" to an inability to "imagine tomorrow" and an ability to "remember yesterday" within itself, as the camera zooms towards the belly, which contains this remembrance within. We then see this memory "projected outside": a separate image of a baby grows from the womb.[28] While the new image threatens to cover the old generating image, it expands and contracts in doing so. It "becomes an image", it is stated, "because it is projected outside", but it contracts after each expansion, as if emulating breath or a beating heart. And the image of the pregnant woman expands as a round shape from the middle of the baby's face, so that these contractions/expansions appear to mirror the continued coexistence of memory and expansion into the future in ways that can break with the past (cf. the coexistence and interrelation between what Deleuze calls the second and third syntheses of time, as discussed in the previous chapter).

As an "image" the pregnancy is "the trace of what it will be after"—an embryo, a fetus—which means that its full new form cannot be foreseen: "You cannot see what it will be after", only "the form it had before". Put differently: the production of the new is primarily a concern with potential, not the actual new itself. And the form it had before is equated with "darkness/obscurity", which connects the fetal to darkness (that key component of Sonimage's problem space: the black background.).

At this point, darkness enters also on the visual track. When the round image shifts to the baby, the surrounding image behind is black. The surrounding image then shifts to the woman, and the small round image is now black and starts to contract towards the belly. This blackness has a double meaning: fetal/potential and death. Albert speaks about the "trace" of "two", the "memory" of two people's desires, father and mother, and "before and after". But he also speaks about this as an "inevitably fatal desire" which produces what also "announces your death", just as the baby image finally takes over the frame. In this EC, however, the darkness/obscurity is *more* connected to memory as potential, and the aspect of death is developed in another EC (the sixth one described below). Back in the studio, Dray and Berr connect clarity/light to a current state of consciousness and socialization. They say the girl Camille could only think of school and the like when asked to exemplify what is "clear/light". They themselves describe the pregnancy scene as "an example of 'dark/obscure'". Dray concludes that what we saw was therefore "not a story, but the hi/story [*histoire*] of this story [*histoire*], even the prehistory [*pre-histoire*] of this prehistory [*pre-histoire*]". Put differently: the contours of potential *of* a potential for the new.

This embryonic cinecept is extended, varied, or developed in three other ECs that appear in movements 5, 7, and 11 respectively. All four thereby belong in some regards to the same *set* of ECs, with the first as base or center. But all four are also separate ECs and the next three are examined as such below.

Fourth Embryonic Cinecept: Typewriting and the Birth of the Letter A

The fourth EC appears in the fifth movement, called Printing/Dictation. The movement at large covers things like leftist political struggle and disciplinary machines that "dictate orders", as Betty Berr says in an early section titled "Dictée" (04:36–07:09). And it contains the quote in the second epigraph at the top of this chapter, on how everything has been tried leading to a political desert and a need to regroup (06:18–06:42). This is the episode context.

The EC itself appears as part of a "story" at the end (21:32–25:45). It starts with the recurring electronic "HISTOIRE" text, now in see-through white letters, over two images that are partly superimposed or interchange: 1) a black-and-white image showing the top of the pregnant woman, seen from breasts to hair, and 2) an image of the front of a white cabin. Betty Barr speaks over these images on whether there were "paper or a pencil" and "squares or circles" in "the beginning" At 21:42 a black screen appears with the "HISTOIRE" text remaining but with each of its letters now gradually replaced: "SISTOIRE → SASTOIRE → SAMTOIRE → SAMEOIRE → SAMEDIRE. Just as the word is almost changed into "SATURDAY" (*SAMEDI*), or a mix of the words for Saturday and saying (*dire*), Berr verbalizes this weekday word: "On Saturday I accompanied Arnaud to the Museum of Mankind." In one section they notice "a huge old wooden compass". A complex montage follows (21:50): In the background a moving image of a huge old wooden compass—the kind that looks like an upside-down V with an arm in between that is used to draw circles—which straddles a typewriter, slowly on its way to make a circle around the typewriter. Superimposed over this is an image from a page in a book that analyzes ancient Greek writing consisting of syllabic signs, ideograms and numbers. The page disappears and comes back in, then disappears again. After a few seconds this white digital text appears: "Once upon a time there was A."

Berr says that Arnaud was struck by the realization "that the shape of the letter A came from the compass and the invention of the circle", a means still for regaining "a point of departure" if the "right direction" is lost.[29] Towards the end of this account there is a cut to a black image that is quickly supplemented with "ABC" in white see-through letters, which goes away for a brief moment and then comes back, going back-and-forth two more times. Berr continues to speak about language as "a material means for fabricating memory"—as we see language on or in the black background—and how "the body, like paper, is a recording surface". The letters ABC continue for seventeen more seconds as the image changes to the pregnant woman now sitting in an office at a typewriter talking to a female colleague. Berr adds that the body—echoing *Numéro deux* and more so Deleuze and Guattari—is also a machine that "fabricates" itself as a "surface". This EC, then, extends aspects of the previous EC: it connects its notion of the black background and pregnancy to the invention of language and letters, but also presents language and letters as means for creation in and through memory and with the material means of the body and/or paper as recording surfaces.

This EC also sort of extends into a semi-narrative part (starting ca. 22:20) that isn't strictly part of the EC in form but is directly attached in content, and it connects things also with other aspects of the problem space: blockage and the difference between reproduction and production. The same pregnant woman—still

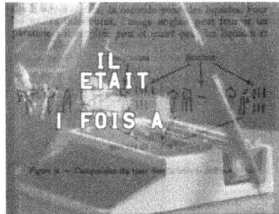

Figures 4.6a–c *France tour détour*, movement 5

fully naked—is now in an office having just started working as a "secretary of the director" or "secretary of directions" [*secrétaire du directions*]. She converses with the female colleague about typing, learning to type, and worries that they are strict about time management at this place. The phone rings and the pregnant woman is called into the boss's office. She stands up and takes a pen and a pad and walks out. Over a shot of her going through a fairly dark greenish corridor, Berr asks about the direction of this now moving secretary of directions. Cut to a man sitting at a desk in an office. Berr talks about how women could change the direction of the world, and how men, "who by nature" are deficient when it comes to imagination, tend to "condemn the majority of the women to dictation, copy-typing and reproduction". This is bluntly illustrated by the scene: the woman takes notes about some secretarial tasks she is asked to do, and she is visibly near the end of fulfilling her biological role as reproducer. She then walks back through the corridor and ends up at her desk, as Berr repeats how most women are condemned by most men to this kind of work. She adds that the reproduction included there is precisely *not* production, and that this is what is available for women as "sensitive surface[s]". The camera now zooms in towards the pregnant woman as she types. Berr reads a dictionary definition of the main word in the woman's work title: "'Secretaire': = secretary, office desk, a desk drawer, a school desk." The zoom lands on the pregnant belly while we still also see the woman's typing hands. The following white electronic text appears: JE T'AIME. 123456789. Half the text is positioned over the belly. After a few seconds a round black image starts to grow from the middle of the image, sort of from behind the text and from the belly. It swallows the image but with the white electronic text remaining. After a few more seconds a round image grows which is the preceding image of the woman at her typewriter. But it can only grow halfway until the whole section ends.

From the perspective of Deleuze's concept of concepts, this embryonic cinecept orders the following "intensive components" in "zones of neighborhood" with partly overlapping areas:

- History of Linguistics and Mankind
- Wooden Compass
- Circle
- Typewriter
- Inversion of the Letter A
- Finding the Right Direction When Lost
- Language as Means to Fabricate Memory
- The Body as Recording Surface That Also Produces This Surface
- Black Image

- Pregnancy
- Female vs. Male Imagination
- Production vs. Reproduction / Copying / Dictation

Fifth Embryonic Cinecept: Dark Justice Piercing through the Postcard/Landscape

This EC appears in the end story of movement 7 (Violence/Grammar). The focus in the movement at large is social re/territorialization, and this is treated in the EC specifically through reflections on frames of postcards and landscapes, property, justice/injustice, and the dark background. Albert Dray begins presenting a story:

> [*Superimposed over Dray is an image of handwriting on the back of a postcard, and then also a photo from a street likely in the US, with a Texaco gas station in the middle, as the postcard fades out.*]

Dray's voice-over speaks about having one time visited Bernard …

> [*We see the street with the gas station, without superimpositions.*]

… "Bernard Lambert".

> [*We see the postcard superimposed over Dray and then by itself.*]

We get a more precise location for the visit: Lambert's "farm in Nantes".

> [*We see the street with the gas station, with no superimposition.*]

At the time the place had unusual weather: "There was snow", which was last seen in this place in "the Middle Ages".

> [*Back to a straight shot of Dray in the studio. Then cut to a shot of a wintery mountain village landscape with "HISTOIRE" in electronic letters in the middle. The sound is now different, as if Dray is out in the field.*]

Dray asks if we "see". He says he wavers between a story about "postcards" and one about "landscapes", but that his wavering may stem from both being stories that concern framing.

> [*A smaller rectangular frame now grows from the middle of the image gradually revealed to be of a postcard of a small castle by a lake in a valley with autumn leaves in the foreground.*[30] *The postcard takes over the whole frame.*]

Dray describes the postcard as "a sign that property exists", a "territory" that "is outlined and demarcated" so that "free space" can be invaded by "writing".

> [*A new frame starts to grow in the middle of the image, a black-and-white photo of a man staring seriously to the side—perhaps a law-enforcement agent given what is said next. The image at first only takes over half the image, so the postcard is seen in the background.*]

Dray talks about how "laws" can be "recorded within order" and how all that we see here is order but also "beauty".

[*The black-and-white image now starts to grow further.*]

Dray repeats how he one time visited Bernard Lambert but adds that it was on a "fact-finding" mission,

[*The black-and-white image has taken over the frame.*]

… and that this mission was itself part of writing a story on enforced buyouts of "farmers' land".

[*A new frame grows in the middle.*]

Lambert, we learn, had told Dray something that Dray had wanted to speak to the girl Camille about.

[*We can now see that the image growing is the previous image of the wintery mountain village landscape, which soon covers the frame.*]

We also learn that it concerned "justice" and was said to him on "an icy morning".

[*The "HISTOIRE" in white letters reappears.*]

Dray continues with how they had wine while waiting for the law enforcement agents.

[*A black image grows from the middle and within a second fills the screen, with "HIS-TOI-RE" broken up into three sections in separate rows forming a diagonal, but with TOI suddenly enlarged and gradually moving to the right, and then changed to LOI, the French word for law.*]

Lambert, however, had friends with weapons …

[*Back to the image of the wintery mountain village landscape. The following sentence appears in white electronic letters: "Quand la loi n'est pas juste, la justice passe avant la loi."*]

Dray verbalizes this sentence [*When the law is unjust, justice comes before the law.*]

[*We now hear a song with lyrics concerning winter visiting "my" country, sharp critiques of this country, of it even being a country, a sense of a song as one's own, comparable to one's own life, and wanting to let go for someone else, and not doing that.*]

Back in the studio, Dray asks if Berr thinks that "memory" "resembles a landscape or a factory", to which Berr answers "[a] bit of both". Seen through the lens of Deleuze's concept of concepts (and abstracting from the level of audiovisual form), this embryonic cinecept orders these "intensive components" in "zones of neighborhood" with partly overlapping areas:

- Postcards
- Landscapes
- Framings

- Writing
- Property
- Territory
- Farmers' Land
- Beauty
- Order
- Law
- Law Enforcement
- Weapons
- Implied Resistance
- The Unjust
- Justice
- History
- Memory
- A Black Image

So this EC—while perhaps verging on being too poetic/narrative even for an *embryonic* cinecept—concerns various stakes on land, and how law and writing can create unjust framings of the land and the implied existence of resistance. But a slightly more abstract point may be summarized as follows: Memory is that which exists. It can be framed to reproduce the given in ways that maintain an order that is unjust. But memory is also a black background that could recreate or produce justice beyond the given.

Sixth Embryonic Cinecept: Evolution and Death

The final EC comes early in movement 11 (Reality/Logic). It consists of a section on the "logic" of reproduction, sexuality, change, evolution, and death (04:09–06:15).[31] This section begins with a black screen with "Logique" in blue letters, followed by a few seconds of a (proto-*Histoire(s) du cinéma*-like) flickering (i.e. very rapid shifts) between two images. The first shows a woman screaming with her hand close to her mouth, naked shoulders, and a man positioned behind her. The second image shows the teeth-filled grin of what looks like a hyena in close-up. The latter image in the flicker is then replaced with an image of a man and a woman carrying a child with closed eyes and blood on his/her face. Cut to a close-up of a hand throwing dice in a dark room. Betty Berr begins to speak, and most of what she says in this section, as Witt explains, consists of "lightly adapted passages" from the conclusion of a history of biology book called *The Logic of Life: A History of Heredity* (*La logique du vivant*), by François Jacob (Witt 2013: 48). In the following descriptions of what Berr says I use quotations taken directly from the translation of Jacob's book, chosen from among the passages Berr herself quotes rather than paraphrases.[32] The idea that man evolved from "a succession of micro-events, from mutations, each occurring" purely by chance, she relays, is contradicted by "time" and "arithmetic". For chance alone to produce the immense complexity of the human body would take "far more time than the span generally attributed to the solar system". Berr skips a few lines in Jacob to get to the topics of sexuality and change: As the organisms "become more complicated" so did "their reproduction", and a "whole series of mechanisms appears" that helps "to [rearrange] the programmes and compel them to change". And "the most important inventions are sex and death" (Jacob 1973 [1970]: 308f).

As Berr utters the last sentence a new flickering between two images appears: the first a black-and-white image of two naked women kissing; the second of a man in a yellowish-beige-off-white mask and black clothing, which signals death, carrying a stick over his shoulder from which hangs a read garment, a bag or a flag. After this emerges a series of shifting flickerings between the various images of sex, a bloody child, death, etc., as Berr continues through Jacob: "Sexuality seems to have arisen early in evolution. At first it was a kind of auxiliary of reproduction", something "superfluous", as no organism, including man, fundamentally needs "sexuality in order to multiply". When Berr says "multiply" there is a cut back to the shot of a hand throwing dice. "It is the necessity of resorting to sex as a reproductive device", Berr continues to quote, which, however, "radically transforms the genetic system and the possibilities of variations" (Jacob 1973 [1970]: 309).

New flickerings appear. First between an image of a man with a shaved head and a white shirt, leaning against the grill of a big white car, with a big machine gun (graphically emphasized as an erect phallus) and carrying a band of large bullets around his neck. The other image: a woman standing with a cigarette and a sitting naked man embracing her leg. Rapid shifts between these images, which after a moment include the one with a child with a bloody face. Appearing in the flickering a few times, starting when Berr says the word "family", is a small image of a man and a woman holding a baby. After a moment we see it more clearly as inserted in a collage with the family in between two large faces with open mouths. In the left part of the image there is a large male face (indicated by a moustache). His tongue pierces out from his open mouth to form a background to the head of the man in the family. In the right part of the image, the large face is female (indicated by red lipstick); she leans back a bit and also has an open mouth. The flicker now returns to the other images. During this passage Berr continues to quote Jacob (with the odd word missing or added), who writes:

As soon as sexuality becomes obligatory, each genetic programme is no longer formed by exactly copying a single programme, but by [rearranging] two different programmes. The genetic programme is then no longer the exclusive property of one line of descent [or family]. It belongs to the collectivity, the group of individuals who communicate with each other by means of sex. (Jacob 1973 [1970]: 309)

Back to the hand throwing dice. Berr continues to relay Jacob, now this part: "The other necessary condition for the very possibility of evolution is death"—as Berr says "death" we see an image of Marilyn Monroe flickering with what looks like a gun ad and the image of the man and woman carrying a bloody child. "Not death from without, as the result of some accident; but death imposed from within, as a necessity prescribed from" the very beginning of "the genetic programme itself" (Jacob 1973 [1970]: 309). This is followed by a few seconds of the hand throwing dice.

This embryonic cinecept orders these "intensive components" in "zones of neighborhood" with partly overlapping areas:

- Evolution
- Probability and Chance
- Biological Complexity
- Genetic Systems
- Heredity
- Sexuality as a Condition for Change
- Systemic Variation
- Sociobiological Collectivity
- Children
- Death

The body as re/production and as a locus of sexuality is connected to questions of biological variation and evolution. And the thread in the fourth EC, on the birth of a child as not only a figure of the new but also an announcement of the parents' death, is picked up and extended to a kind of sociobiological, collective level. A more abstract and independent point, however, is that while the child—as novelty—means the coming inexistence of the old, this may also entail the death—or at least the cooption—of the child. Again: "There is only a slim chance, so great is the capacity […] for exhausted life to get control of the New from its birth […]" (C2 147).

I have now described six embryonic cinecepts. Their forms as well as their contents are poetic-essayistic crystallizations but also semi-philosophical determinations of aspects in Sonimage's general problem space. But to be clear: They are all *embryonic* cineconcepts, not the full philosophical determination of problems that we can call cineconcepts (and some may verge on relying a little *too* much on my interpretations to even appear as embryonic—notwithstanding that interpretation is an unavoidable part of dealing with also the most realized philosophy). They are embryonic, to repeat, not because they fail to live up to the likes of Anglo-American notions of clarity, but because they do not really live up to Deleuzian notions of philosophical rigor, determination, and systematicity either, as they lean too much into theoretically inclined poetic imagination. From the investigations above we can add that they are embryonic also from tending to lack somewhat in structural economy and condensation. Cineconcepts—given their formal heterogeneity—cannot be expected to do what word-only concepts do in this regard: crystalize aspects of a larger text into a very brief form. But most of the embryonic cineconcepts examined above could be more condensed. They also tend to lack a standout "intensive component" that serves as a "main point" around which the cineconcept condenses, which for Deleuze is part of what characterizes the concept's internal organization and helps give it a determined consistency. Furthermore, these embryonic cineconcepts determine aspects in a problem space that, however intricate, is not itself laid out with enough explicit philosophical systematicity, which makes cineconceptual determination more difficult to achieve. Still, they clearly point—not least formally—in a cineconceptual direction that can be taken further. Sonimage makes up a rich but not fully realized potential or starting point for how to think and develop a cineconceptual practice.

Much potential can also be found in some of Godard's *ideas* about how to use filmic montage for thinking. In the next chapter I will expand on the theory of cineconcepts through a look at Godard's ideas about montage as *rapprochement* and juxtapose them with Deleuze's concept of concepts. I will also briefly reflect on *Histoire(s) du cinéma* (1989–98)—while less cineconceptual than Sonimage—as a resource for the *formal* articulation of full cineconcepts.

Notes

1 This is said in voice-over by the character Betty Barr in a section between 06:18–06:42, in "Movement 5: Impression/Dictée" (Printing/Dictation).
2 While less cineconceptual after Sonimage, Godard and Godard-Miéville continue to grapple with the problem of the new. Not least through a more explicit turn to nature imagery in the 1980s. Daniel Morgan partly explores this turn in Godard's *Soigne ta droite* (1987), *Nouvelle vague* (1990), and *Allemagne 90 neuf zero* (1991), mostly through Adornian and Benjaminian frames. Morgan shows how these

films explore nature, natural history, and natural beauty as complexly intertwined with or caught up in the sociohistorical, while also being a resource, beyond the sociohistorical, of potential for political change and emancipation (see specifically 2012: 72, 97ff, 105, 114–20, 139f, 147–50). Morgan also notices a simultaneous dissatisfaction with such strategies: an implication in these films that while "we're back [to] the same questions and anxieties that prompted Benjamin's and Adorno's turn toward natural history"—however original Godard's own such turn—their "gamble did not provide the solution" and has "already failed" (149f). We should add, however, that an ambivalent attitude towards the possibility of producing the new—a continued political work combined with a certain lack of belief—is congruent with the problem space of Sonimage. (See also Morrey for an intriguing overview of the role of nature and the cosmos in Godard's slightly earlier work (late 1970s and early 1980s) [2005: 137f, 149–52, and especially 158–62].)

3 The word combination "embryonic cinecept" is established from the beginning of this book and refers to *quasi*-cineceptual forms in Godard-Miéville: promising, or nascent, but not yet fully developed cinecepts. The use of the term embryonic here must therefore not be confused—despite connections—with the thematic discussion of pregnancy in the rest of this chapter, that is, with the problem of the new as conceived through the figures of the fetal, pregnancy, and birth in Sonimage.

4 The "two" [*deux*] in the title refers to a web of things. An inexhaustive list: The human body doing number two. Woman as the "second" sex. Pregnancy/birth: the body producing another. Parents come first (behind) and children second (in front). Politics and ass/sex [*cul*]: these are stated as the two main themes in the beginning of the film. Their second completed film as Sonimage. Film and video: most of the film's images were shot on video and replayed on monitors in a studio and then filmed in 35mm. Showing two different scenes simultaneously on two screens within the same screen. The two sides in each of the oppositions that make up language systems (Godard 1985 [1980]: 408). The two "producers" of the film: Anne-Marie Miéville and Jean Luc Godard. Another direction for making films (Godard 1985 [1975]: 386). The film as a "second" debut film (while Godard's 1980s *Sauve qui peut (la vie)* is more well-known as such, *Numéro deux* was also playfully—and for financial reasons—conceived in such light; and as MacCabe adds, it not only had the same producer as *À bout de souffle*, it even had the same budget [1980: 24]).

5 Drabinski offers, on the one hand, a sort of opposite reading: "The blank, black screen—like the hole of abjection—swallows up the monitors while offering nothing (even nothingness) in their place" (2008: 107, see also 108, 136). On the other hand, his reading is complex and includes the notion that this "empty space" is also "fecund, productive", a "space of the feminine in itself" seen as a "countersignature", with "the possibility of another memory, another speech, another thinking and relation" (112). But this latter aspect is not much developed in his

reading, which seems attributable to limitations in his philosophical frameworks, as discussed in Chapter 2, note 28 above.

6 For more on this aspect see Morrey (2005: 115).

7 Godard-Miéville, as they often do with terms, pack the word *cul* with various meanings. It literally means ass, and ass has several senses here, as we will see, which includes sex. Emmelhainz also explains that the phrase "*[u]ne histoire du cul* means a story about sex which is shared privately among women" (2019: 131, note 14). *Un film du cul* may furthermore imply a connection to pornographic film, which flashes by in *Numéro deux* on occasion.

8 Silverman calls this a "second prologue" instead of an introduction (Silverman and Farocki 1998: 146f).

9 This shot of the writing girl returns in a later section (1:13:17–1:14:27) along with another image: the girl writing in the top left of the image and in a slightly bigger screen at the bottom left we see Pierre sitting on the toilet fully dressed and shaving. He and his daughter Vanessa, who is outside the frame, have a conversation about the meaning of the word impossible, with a basis in the concrete situation of their domestic life.

10 Yosefa Loshitzky connects this to how children, according to Freud, conceive of how birth happens (1995: 166).

11 Such reproduction is not only the most central labor in the literal sense of producing workers—as Marx duly noted—it is also historically central: the "original proletariat" were made up of "women in ancient society" who "were too poor to serve the state with anything but their wombs", as Terry Eagleton writes, adding that even the "word 'proletariat' comes to us from the Latin word for 'offspring'" (Eagleton 2018 [2011]: 169).

12 Sandrine makes several such efforts throughout the film. While Farocki is correct to see Sandrine as a "solitary machine" that does not plug "into other machines", this is not, then, as he claims, because she is "onanistic"—although she does have such a moment in one scene—rather she constantly tries to connect with Pierre's body which is not properly responding (Silverman and Farocki 1998: 160).

13 Even on the literal narrative level, the impotence is said to be an effect of Pierre's work, rather than about individual psychology or physiology. See also Silverman and Farocki (1998: 154) and Morrey (2005: 117).

14 Sandrine later on (1:18:11–1:18:44) says: "I thought I was producing. But my goods had already been sold. Basically, I was producing at a loss. And who was profiting. Who? No, not [Pierre]. Someone behind him. Something between us. Work." This is followed by a long discourse on her constipation in which she says that "now everything's blocked."

15 Kaja Silverman identifies the voice-over as rooted in Greer's *The Female Eunuch*, and Farocki later adds that the film also "problematizes [the Greer text] in important ways" (Silverman and Farocki 1998: 144, 153). See also Godard (1985 [1975]: 386).

16 The enquiring dialogues or open interviews with people purported, as Emmelhainz writes, "to give visibility and voice to those who did not usually have the chance on television", such as "a worker, a cleaning lady, a prostitute, a painter, a photojournalist" (2019: 132).
17 Episode 5B, which revolves around a conversation with the French mathematician (later turned philosopher) René Thom, is a bit of an exception. The present study included a detailed description, analysis, and reinterpretation of this episode, which in the end did not find a place in this chapter. A few key things to note: This episode has not yet been explored, or has been described only sweepingly, although it is quite rich in ideas, and despite the fact that Thom appears (not least from statements made by Deleuze) to have been an important influence on Godard. The episode also provides interesting alternative perspectives on some basic tenets in the Sonimage problem space (and it is unusually, for one of the conversation episodes, interspersed with light touches of cineceptually interesting form). The interaction between Thom and Godard/Godard-Miéville is also subtly complex as regarding the critical and affirmative (MacCabe sees *only* a critical rejection of Thom in Godard [1980: 143]). Not just in what transpires in the dialogue, but through writings, drawings, and visual montage, of which most are illustrations, independent connections, extensions, reframings, or conclusions drawn from what Thom says. While some are confirmatory and some more critical or opposing, most are rather like nuanced explorations within a space in-between Thom and Godard as explored by Godard-Miéville. In episode 6A, which looks back at the whole series, episode 5B is referenced as an exploration of the limits of mathematics. But 5B clearly also conducts an open-minded investigation. It could be seen as a probe into whether mathematics can help think and realize impossible dreams of the new, or instead just help dream of the possible in existing reality. And while the episode leans towards concluding the latter, intriguing ideas are explored along the way that are directly relevant for the problem space. They speak about the richness of possibility in birth and the generation of new forms more generally—biologically, ontologically, socially, politically—albeit seen from the perspective of a mathematical/morphological model.
18 Although I will say "they"/"Godard-Miéville" draw through this chapter, since I do not know who draws what, it is likely Godard who draws at least most of the time. Godard took drawing lessons and in the 1970s often expressed his keen interest in drawing as a means of expression beyond words. See Witt (2013: 192).
19 The Deleuze-Guattari aspects aside, given the Lacanian part of this build-up, as well as some of what follows later, a reader versed in Julia Kristeva and Luce Irigaray may perceive certain echoes of concerns with the maternal body, birth, children, but also change and even the in-between as discussed in the approaching EC. However, most of Kristeva's and Irigaray's respective publications on such matters I believe came *after* the release of *Six fois deux*. One may point to passages in Kristeva's doctoral dissertation (1974) on the mother—child relation, which did

come out two years earlier, but those passages are—as far as I can see—focused on pre-/oedipal semiotic and symbolic language, so they hardly just say the same thing as what follows in the EC. There may have been some influence in the early parts of the section, but as with all or most of Godard-Miéville's references, this is likely best described as one of several frames for independent explorations and/or points of departure. And to the extent that some bits have a straighter line of influence, no philosophy, however original, as established in Chapter 1, is created *ex nihilo*. Kristeva herself certainly builds quite a lot on others, be it Arendt, Bakhtin, Freud, Lacan, Nietzsche, or her *Tel Quel* colleagues (as each of them built on others). Godard-Miéville should perhaps most reasonably be seen as independent fellow travelers, in a partly different form, of, for instance, Kristeva or Irigaray, along with others who, due to shared social-political contexts and certain similar influences, sometimes develop similar themes in different directions. (See also the Introduction above for a discission of Godard and that generation of French philosophers.) Nevertheless, the relations between Sonimage (and especially Miéville) and Kristeva and Irigaray—and let us add the concern with natality in Hannah Arendt—deserve their own studies, which, despite the preliminary speculations in this note, fall outside the delimitation of this study.

20 The French word for border, *frontiére*, contains meanings that are a bit lost with the English word. The French *frontiére* covers not only given borders as delimitations, but also, similarly to the English word frontier, something remaining to be discovered, zones between the known/unknown or existing/not yet existing in which there is implied movement or expansion, instead of an already made delimitation. However, while the border / river / third here is clearly about an in-between with a frontier-like autonomy rather than just a line between two given things, the latter meaning must also be retained and for two reasons: 1) The line is required also as a marker of *difference* between two things, and if the in-between does not have this differential function it will be eliminated. 2) The line can also close and demand a passport, as stated in the preceding embryonic cinecept, and thereby move closer in meaning to a border. (As stated in a note in Chapter 2, the English translation of *Cinema 2*, in contrast to Deleuze's text on *Six fois deux*, translates Deleuze's discussions of the *frontiére* in Godard with the English word frontier [C2 180f].)

21 As translated by Witt (2014: 338). For other discussions of this letter see ibid.; Hayes 2002: 80f; Drabinski 2008: 81f.

22 For a more extensive examination of slow-motion in *France tour détour* see Witt (2007 [2004]).

23 In a comment from 1980, Godard described his questions to the children with reference to Descartes and Aristotle (Godard 1985 [1980]: 404). For more on the philosophical roots of Godard's ways of posing questions more generally, see Brenez (2007 [2004]).

24 Godard later (1980) described other aspects of how he conceived of the general structure that each movement follows (1985 [1980]: 410f).
25 What does "monsters" mean here? According to Godard's later statements this is an attention-grabbing synonym for human beings (*"les être humaine"*) (Godard 1985 [1980]: 410), which is echoed by Jacques Aumont saying it refers to "the monstrous character of humanity as a whole" (2011: 136, translation mine). This reading is supported most clearly in sections of movement 5 which talk about the evolution of the monsters (described as part of the sixth embryonic cinecept below). Yet, the term clearly also holds more specific meanings in the series. First, as MacCabe writes, the monsters are the grownups as opposed to the children (1980: 151). Second, the skeleton script and other parts of the series itself imply that the monsters are workers caught in a social machinery (script in Godard 1985: 401ff). And the larger thematic context implies that they are the repetitious end point of socialization (also when fighting against this system). Constance Penley even argues that the main point of the series is to examine how the monsters reproduce themselves in such ways (1989 [1982]: 114).
26 The skeleton script for *France tour détour*, which consists of a few lines about each movement, only says the following about the whole section: Albert "tells the story of a beginning" (*"raconte l'histoire d'un debut"*) (Godard 1985: 401).
27 Despite this pregnancy scene having a prominent place in the first episode and being one of *France tour détour's* most conceptually and formally intricate parts, it is little acknowledged in the Godard literature. Witt refers to the scene in passing as "the reflection in the first movement on the image and the mystery of origins" (2013: 47). Jerry White mentions it only as containing an example of visual connections between Sonimage and Brakhage: "a recurring shot in the first episode […] of a naked, pregnant woman with a circular, iris-image close-up of a baby's face, which startlingly recalls the layered image of a baby's face in Brakhage's *Dog Star Man* (1964)" (2013: 31). MacCabe is a bit more generous with his attention in describing the scene as "a consideration of the most obscure chemistry, the most mysterious beginning of all: the birth of a child. The process by which two becomes three and how this generation also spells death is examined in an image of quite extraordinary force: a pregnant woman has superimposed on her stomach an ever-growing image of a baby, one that finally blots her out altogether" (1980: 149f.)
28 On late Godard's ideas about projection as also connected to birth, see Witt (2013: 63–6, specifically 64).
29 Godard has described this as a philosophical or scientific discovery made in *France tour détour* (Godard 1985 [1980]: 411).
30 This postcard with a castle and autumn leaves is the same image, although cropped, as one shown in *2 or 3 Things I Know About Her* (ca. 36:30). When it appears in that previous film a voice says "so art is what gives humanity to forms", which is quite a contrast to what is now said when it is shown cropped in *France tour détour*.

31 Witt describes this section as "a two-minute montage on the subject of the impact of the twin concepts of sex and death on human behavior" (2013: 48).
32 I quote François Jacob directly here so that the number of words I quote from *France tour détour* in total can align with "fair dealing". As an aside we can note that Jacob's work—which won him a Nobel Prize with two colleagues in 1965 and helped establish the field of molecular biology (and take it in nonlinear directions)—was also referenced by Deleuze and Guattari in *A Thousand Plateaus* (ATP 10f, 62). They reference the same book and, like Godard-Miéville, they focus on its (sort of or potentially vitalist) take on genetic mutation or variation, while of course also subjecting it to philosophical interpretation and weaving it into their own larger system (which itself built on Deleuze's previous work on such issues in *Difference and Repetition*). For more on Deleuze and Guattari and Jacob see Marks (2006).

5 *Rapprochement*, Concepts, and Cineceptual Form

IN PARTS OF Chapters 1 and 2, I juxtaposed the following two things: A) Deleuze's descriptions of how concepts are constructed, and B) Deleuze's descriptions of how Godard's film thought is constructed. We saw how remarkably similar they were. We also saw how Deleuze evaded the natural extension of the similarity—cinecepts—by sticking to a clear differentiation between philosophical conceptualization and (however advanced or analytic) cinematic thinking. This chapter returns to this Deleuze-Godard juxtaposition but from another angle. Instead of comparing Deleuze's descriptions of concepts with *his* descriptions of Godard's cinematic thinking, I will compare Deleuze's concept of concepts with Godard's *own* conception of his filmic thought—more specifically, with Godard's notion of montage or the image as *rapprochement*. We will again see remarkable similarities with Deleuze's concept of concepts, similarities that could easily be pushed in a cineceptual direction in audiovisual practice. This chapter will also reflect on *Histoire(s) du cinéma* (1989–98)—the work perhaps most attached to Godard's notion of *rapprochement* (certainly so in the Godard literature)—not as a work that contains embryonic concepts, but as a resource, due to its advancement of montage techniques, for the *concrete formal* articulation of cinecepts.

Rapprochement and Concepts

For Godard *rapprochement* means a certain unexpected juxtaposition of different elements (images, sounds, texts, people, things, events, etc.) that together form what he calls an *image*. This is an idea of montage that also develops an already "fundamental operation of thought", as Morrey writes: that of "combining discrete elements in new and productive ways" (2005: 221). This idea was developing in Godard long before it was referred to as *rapprochement* in and leading up to *Histoire(s) du cinéma*. Michael Witt's work helps us to overview its history and some key influences, as well as to examine its meaning:

> A true image, Godard has long argued, is always the result of the combination, tension, and dynamic interplay among a number of component elements. He has rehearsed this idea repeatedly in his work and in interviews, and related it [to] a number of models. He explored it in particular in his video work through the use of superimposition as a means of bringing together two or more visual sources within the same frame. (Witt 2013: 180)

Witt mentions Shannon's information theory as a "particularly important early source of inspiration" for Godard-Miéville's use of superimpositions in *Comment ça va*. He also points to a poem by Raymond Queneau from which Godard read the following passage in a 1983 television interview:

> The image is a relationship. It's either two distant things that we bring together, or two things that are close together that we separate. "As thin as a hair, as vast as the dawn." A hair is not an image; dawn is not an image; it's their relationship that creates the image. (Quoted in Witt 2013: 180)

Notice the likeness to how Deleuze describes the work of classification in forming concepts: "In any classification scheme, some things which seem very different are brought closer together, and others which seem very close are separated. This is how concepts are formed" (TRM [1986]: 285).

Yet, the "principal reference [...] through which Godard has elaborated his theory of the image since the beginning of the 1980s", and continuously subjected to an "obsessive reworking", Witt argues, is Pierre Reverdy's poetic text *L'image* from 1918 (2013: 180; 2000: 49).[1] Witt quotes the English translation of its twenty-nine opening lines as recited by Godard in *King Lear* (1987)—here slightly abbreviated and presented as two separated block paragraphs (instead of shorter verse lines):

> The image [...] cannot be born of a comparison, but of a reconciliation of two realities that are more or less far apart. The more the connections between these two realities are distant and true, the stronger the image will be, and the more it will have emotive power. Two realities that have no connection cannot be drawn together usefully. There is no creation of an image. Two contrary realities will not be drawn together. They oppose one another. One rarely obtains forces and power

from this opposition. An image is not strong because it is brutal or fantastic—but because the association of ideas is distant and true. The result that is obtained immediately controls the truth of the association.

Also here we can notice key connections to Deleuze's concept of concepts. The linking of previously unlinked more or less distant realities in a way that is true—or as Godard says in an interview, "the articulation of unknown yet sudden convincing relationships" (quoted in Witt 2000: 40)—pairs well with Deleuze's already mentioned idea of forming concepts through bringing closer together "things which seem very different" or separating "others which seem very close", as well as his claim that the "primary feature of a concept is its novel redistribution of things" (TRM 285, 381). Witt describes *rapprochement* as a "power of revelation rooted in a unique facility for bringing disparate ideas into the same orbit as one another and holding them in dynamic tension" (2000: 49).

This dynamic tension is *not* a dialectics of contradictions (or rather: if dialectics equals negative dialectics, this dynamic is *a*-dialectical). Reverdy's poem contrasts the image's organization of differences to such dialectics: "Two contrary realities will not be drawn together. They oppose one another. One rarely obtains forces and power from this opposition." And as explored in Chapter 1, Deleuze's concept of concepts is an organization of differential components according to a logic beyond negative dialectics.[2] There is also a shared emphasis on how the strength and truth of the image/concept are a matter of creation—even if requiring certain pre-existing connections—rather than representation. As Morgan writes, "[t]hrough Reverdy, Godard treats the image not as something self-evident or given but as an achievement, a creation" (2012: 233).

In the remaining part of Reverdy's poem, however, there are also some important points of differentiation—aspects important for Godard that are conceptually/cineceptually limiting:

> the power or virtue of the created image depends on the nature of these connections. What is great is not the image—but the emotion it provokes; if the latter is great, one esteems the image at its measure. The emotion thus provoked is true because it is born outside of all imitation, all evocation, and all resemblance. (Quoted in Witt 2013: 180f)

What is limiting in this part of the poem is the centrality of provoking emotions for determining the nature of the connections, which makes them appear more as a matter of art than philosophy. This is reflected in Godard's practice from the 1980s and onwards (as discussed in the Introduction above). Witt provides examples from especially *Histoire(s) du cinéma* of actual motifs in Godard that elaborate or work in accordance with Reverdy's ideas, and what stands out in these examples is their *poetic* nature. Witt describes a section full of these motifs as offering "a concise evocation of the idea of the successful formation of a poetic image". And he says that in late Godard more generally *rapprochement* often amounts to "productive puzzles or riddles" (Witt 2013: 181, see also 183f). Deleuze, on his part, sees this principal difference—regardless of webs of overlap (see Chapter 1)—between the respective "pedagogies" of art and philosophy: "art must awaken us and teach us to feel" whereas "philosophy must teach us to conceive" (WP 218). The aspect of the second part of Reverdy's poem that holds out provoking emotion as a key criterion for the success of a particular *rapprochement* therefore appears—translated to a Deleuzian frame—as a matter of artistic rather than philosophical pedagogy. But as we have seen, there are a range of other aspects of *rapprochement* that connect directly with a philosophical pedagogy. In Godard's own later moving-image work, as stated, the artistic pedagogy tends to dominate. But Godard's own *mode* of execution of the idea of *rapprochement* does not have to be followed. And the other parts of Godard's *idea* of *rapprochement*—which he also continued to develop[3]—can be directly relevant for bridging a Deleuzian notion of concepts, extended through the idea of cinecepts, to a practical method for audiovisual montage.

Rapprochement is Multimedial

Another key influence on Godard's idea of *rapprochement*—which will also take us further towards concrete audiovisual form—is André Malraux. Malraux, as Witt writes, "pursued a remarkable experiment in iconographic history" in three volumes published in the 1940s and '50s; he talked about "having discovered and demonstrated through the use of visual rapprochements 'an intelligence of images, which is faster than that of ideas.'" This is not just about "images", however, as Malraux's work "combined *writing* with juxtapositions of images", which entailed a "shifting relationship between image and *text*" (Witt 2013: 86f, emphasis mine).[4] As established in the Introduction and Chapter 1, cinecepts are not to be confused with "images" as opposed to text. Cinecepts, rather, are audiovisual compounds of moving images / sounds / voice / texts / graphics / montage. And for several reasons the image/text relation is a central juncture.

The image/text relation is key also for Godard (who is often misread as being anti-text or valuing the image over text in some almost absolute way). The written word, to reuse a previous quotation, "has been no more fully and comprehensively introduced into cinema than by Godard" (Lahey Dronsfield 2010: 93). And Godard's work, as Witt writes, "has consistently accorded onscreen text the same status as the other imagery" (2013: 55f). Godard himself says this about working with photo and text: "In my view they were on a socially equal footing from the start; one may come first at a given moment and the other second, one can be stronger than the other for a moment, but without any inequality at the start or finish…" (Godard and Ishaghpour 2005 [1999]): 47f). For Godard, there is "equivalence or fraternity or equality between the photo and the text", which does not mean they add up in some equilibrium where one merely represents the other. The "real work is done" only "where there's a space" between "the text and the image", in which one can be made to enter into the other, or they can appear to spring from each other, instead of a "simple relationship of illustration" (49f). Such a space, Godard adds, "makes it possible to exercise your capacity to think and reflect and imagine, to create" (11).

Image/voice is the other central juncture in cineceptual audiovisual compounds—and in Chapter 7 I will come back to Godard's careful work with actor voices and compare this to Deleuze's comments on the human voice as a tool for expressing nuances in concepts. And sound more generally is certainly a key multimedia aspect of Godard's *rapprochement*. The audio track is often quite complex and multiple in its internal composition—with stereo being a central "compositional method"[5]—and in its relation to texts and images in larger audiovisual compositions.[6]

Histoire(s) as Resource for Concrete Cineceptual Form

Above I have looked at Godard's notion of *rapprochement*—as a particular idea about making connections and as a method of montage reliant on multimedia—as further means to build a bridge from Deleuze's concept of concepts to a theory of cinecepts as audiovisual practice. I have also established that Godard's most formally intricate practice of *rapprochement*, *Histoire(s) du cinéma*, is more poetical than philosophical in its determination of relations between "distant things". As Witt writes:

> Godard's histories are subjective, imaginative, sensuous, anecdotal, digressive, discontinuous, lacunary, rhythmic, repetitious, humorous, dramatic, and frequently contentious. Brimming with emotion, intuitions, insights, and provocations, they are made up in large part of resonant fables, tall tales, shaggy dog stories, quasi-mathematical riddles, and—above all—poetic images. Their dense texture and serpentine forms are closer to those one more readily associates with poets and musicians rather than historians, and recall in particular the traditions of serial and fugal composition of modernist authors. (2013: 69)

Witt, then, sees this as "*poetic* visual thinking" (2013: 87). *Histoire(s)* presents intricate and thoughtful ideas and even arguments, but they are to a large extent poetically suggestive and in ways that tend to be, as Morrey writes, "mythical and very personal" (2005: 221).[7] Accordingly, it is often stated or implied (by late Godard himself and in the literature[8]) that *Histoire(s)*'s ideas are determined—*philosophically* determined, we can add—*only in the viewer*. Cinecepts, in contrast, are philosophical determinations in themselves *first* (reinterpretations, redeterminations, creative misunderstandings, unexpected applications, personal takes, etc., come *after*).[9] (What "philosophical determination" means here is detailed in Chapter 1 above.) In some contrast to aspects of the Sonimage works examined above, then, *Histoire(s)* is less interesting as containing embryonic cinecepts (albeit some sections could be interpreted through such a lens) than as a resource of intricate, inventive montage forms that can be useful also for the formulation of certain cinecepts.

Now, Sonimage's formal tools go a long way and could be enough for most cinecepts. *Histoire(s)*'s basic forms—especially on the visual track—are furthermore largely the same: complex superimpositions and intricate layers of sounds, voices, images, graphics, and texts.[10] Yet, *Histoire(s)* undoubtedly advances the nuance and sophistication in the use of such basic forms—due to new technology in some regards (perhaps especially for the sound mix) but even more due to formal or aesthetic invention. The advances in *Histoire(s)* of such previously established basic forms can be seen as means for the kind of cinecepts that require further nuance and detail in their audiovisual articulation.

On a more general and structural (and even aesthetic) level, *Histoire(s)* may also serve as inspiration for how to compose such cineceptual bits together with sections that are less condensed. Zsuzsa Baross describes *Histoire(s)*'s general logic of organization as following "two principal lines of movement": the first, a "'prismatic' dispersion" of elements from a "latent theme" with "associations forming multiple series" (of course, from a conceptual perspective, this line of movement must be translated from a poetic associative dispersion to philosophical argumentation and explorations of problems); the second, a "contrary movement of condensation, as in dream-work", which "contracts distant, heterogeneous elements into dense and opaque image-signs". Here "different series (image and sound series, voice and text series, music and writing series, image and image series, etc.) intersect in the contracted space of […] complex montage, knotting together multiple strands" (Baross 2017: 329). *Histoire(s)*'s ways of formally coalescing at times into such dense units of complexity, then, might be useful as a template for positioning certain formally complex cinecepts within larger works. And while this can also be an aesthetic consideration to some extent, the cinecepts themselves must always have a primarily philosophical determination of their components.

Notes

1. For more discussion of this Reverdy poem's influence on Godard, see e.g. Morrey (2005: 171); Morgan (2012: 232f).
2. Chapter 1 also provides a larger explanation for why such a "beyond" is not itself a negation, and addresses this most explicitly in note 14.
3. This includes how the idea develops after *Histoire(s)*, not least as connected to Walter Benjamin's notion of poetic "constellations." Godard: "to cite Benjamin who says that stars, at a given moment, form constellations and there is resonance between the present and the past" (Godard and Ishaghpour 2005 [1999]): 7). Godard spells this out further in his and Miéville's *The Old Place* (2000). For more on this particular connection to Benjamin, see Witt (2013: 183f); Morrey (2005: 203f); Morgan (2012: 232); Emmelhainz (2019: 9).
4. Morgan connects Malraux's influence on Godard in this regard also to the importance of similar ideas in Aby Warburg and a larger context of related modernist practices, and to Élie Faure's having brought such ideas to cinema (2012: 218ff). For more on Malraux and Faure as forerunners to and influences on *Histoire(s) du cinéma*, see Temple (2000).
5. For more on the importance of stereo see Witt (2013: 206f). For more on Godard's use of sound and music and his general work as a multimedia "sound artist", see Witt (2013: 198–208).
6. For a more detailed, book-length study of sound in late Godard see Fox (2018).
7. I should add that *Histoire(s)* is not thereby reducible to the personal or the poetic, since it aims towards saying general things about the world. Some of what it says, however grand, idiosyncratic, or lyrical, is actually quite developed and even clear, as well as general and un-subjective—or rather: the subjective is an entry point into larger universes and ideas about how they work (or, relatedly, as Godard says in chapter 3B of *Histoire(s)*: "finally, the inner world has rejoined the cosmos" through a "form that thinks"). Brenez therefore offers a perhaps more productive way to regard some of the argumentation: "the first two episodes of *Histoire(s)* are organized according to a scenography of the lesson—but it is a lesson whose didacticism is nourished by the speculative virtues of fundamental research rather than by classical argumentation" (2007 [2004]: 165).
8. E.g. Morgan (2012: 234f); Morrey (2005: 227f); Pantenburg (2015 [2006]: 204, 44, 27, 151f); Witt (2013: 18, 184).
9. This is an underacknowledged Deleuzian position on both philosophy and art, but expressed more emphatically about art. Art, Deleuze writes in *What is Philosophy?*, is "independent of the viewer or hearer, who only experience it after" and only—regardless, again, of the unpredictability and variety of their reactions—"if they have the strength for it" [*s'ils en ont la force*] (WP 164). Accordingly, Deleuze's cinema books hardly mention spectators, and when they do, it is to say things like

"Nothing happens in the viewer's head which does not derive from the character of the image" (C2 104). See also Introduction, notes 2A, 6, 8, Chapter 3, note 20 above (and Preface, note 10).

10 "The early experiments with superimposition in *Comment ça va*", for instance, as Witt writes, "provide[d] the blueprint for the wide variety of forms of vision-mixed imagery used throughout *Histoire(s) du cinéma*, including those that are technically more sophisticated or conceptually denser" (2013: 52f). And among the "range of techniques" that Godard uses in *Histoire(s)*, Morgan considers superimposition to be "most important"—"two- and three-layer superimpositions out of clips, stills, photographs, printed words, and paintings" (2012: 229).

6 Scholarly Video Essays: A Critical Examination and a Cineceptual Alternative

A THEORY OF cinecepts was developed in previous chapters with the work of Deleuze and Godard-Miéville as the main terrains. In this chapter cineceptual theory is placed on a different—less philosophical—terrain and has a more indirect function. While a few further clarifications about the cinecept are made along the way, it serves here mainly as a frame for an evaluation of contemporary debates within film and media studies about this question: how can video essays be scholarly? I will critically examine key arguments, conceptions, and presumptions in these debates, spanning artistic research, the essayistic, ideals of clarity, medium specificity, and differences between images and language. This gradually leads to a few condensed suggestions for an alternative cineceptual path for scholarly video essays (suggestions that should be read with the preceding chapters in mind). This look at scholarly video essays is *one* way to start relating cineceptual theory to efforts in the actual present to do scholarly work in audiovisual form (followed by connections to existing video philosophy—and a more direct focus on cinecepts—in the next chapter).

What are scholarly video essays? The last fifteen years or so have seen a proliferation of online-published video essays on film, and the term scholarly video essays indicates some kind of scholarly version of such essays. They are sometimes referred to as videographic essays (or videographic "criticism": analysis and discussion of individual films). Such works, as Jason Mittell writes, express "scholarly ideas via moving images and sound in audiovisual form" (2019). Scholarship in video essay form, as is often pointed out, solves the classic Bellourian problem of the "unattainability of the text": moving-image material can now be directly quoted, instead of having to be laboriously and incompletely described in text. This form also comes with new digital tools for analysis, as pointed to by Laura Mulvey in a book that was an early influence for the field (2006). Potentially, scholarly video essays "can explore a wide range of topics, theoretical approaches, or objects of study", Mittell adds, but most of them "are focused on discussing formal features and interpretations of films" (2019). The majority of such essays, furthermore, appear less as finished scholarship in a traditional sense and are often closer to so-called artistic research, journalistic criticism, or—when least scholarly—even fan-culture videos. So what makes them scholarly? There is a growing debate about how and when video essays that are said to be scholarly really are scholarly, and about the meaning of the latter term in this context.

Two Kinds of Preferences

Two generalized sets of preferences have framed much of these debates: 1) experimental and poetic exploration, and 2) explicit linear argument. In a 2016 article, Ian Garwood points to two books published that year that partly represent these two preferences. The first is Christian Keathley, Jason Mittell, and Catherine Grant's anthology *The Videographic Essay: Criticism in Sound & Image* (published as a book in 2016 and as an online, partly multimedia book in 2019). Scholarly virtue here leans more towards poetic, experimental, and unfinished modes of research. The second is Miklós Kiss and Thomas van den Berg's online book *Film Studies in Motion: From Audiovisual Essay to Academic Research Video*, which argues for more traditional forms of rigor, clarity, and structural coherence, and what they call the "autonomous and explanatorily argumentative research video" (2016: Intro). These books contain arguments reflected and extended also in other texts by these authors and by other videography scholars, which I will look at below.

This division is related to an influential distinction previously made by Keathley between poetical and explanatory modes of video essaying. In their purest form these modes are "two ends of a continuum", but most video essays are closer to one of them (Keathley 2011: 183). While Keathley's own preferences lie closer to the poetical end, he sees advantages and disadvantages with both. The explanatory mode entails "interpretation, analysis, explication" of films combined with a "guiding critical language" that "illuminate[s]" (179). This means increased lucidity, Keathley argues, but also the domination of sound and image by explanatory language. The "rich audio-visual possibilities" offered by "multi-media technologies" thereby remain underutilized (183). The poetical mode instead subordinates explanatory language and explores images and sounds in ways that use the multimedia form "to its fullest", but this can make the work opaque to the point that it goes "unrecognised as [scholarly] criticism" or requires "deciphering" in that regard. Keathley therefore finds that the poetical mode should be balanced with explanatory aspects so as to not "totally abando[n] the knowledge effect that we associate with the essay form" (182f, 190). What does "knowledge effect" mean here?

Knowledge Effects, New Knowledge, Scholarly Knowledge

In a later text, Keathley and Jason Mittell argue that combinations of explanatory and poetical modes tend to produce "the most potent knowledge effect", and they do so while rooting the term in Roland Barthes's notion of a "third form". This third form (starting in Proust) has elements of both "Essay [and] Novel", and as they quote Barthes saying, it "subject[s] the objects of knowledge and discussion—as in any art—no longer to an instance of truth, but to a consideration of *effects*". Barthes himself, Keathley and Mittell add, "produced extraordinary examples of this writing" (although "few other scholars took up such a model"). They do not here, however, go further into this Barthian distinction between truth and effects, or how they read these terms.[1] Their focus is on the mix of modes—"imposing a poetic form on scholarly writing"—rather than the terms' fuller meanings (Keathley and Mittell 2019 [2016]).

Catherine Grant is also a proponent of such a mix—which is quite established as an ideal in videographic film studies—but she leans further towards the more openly explorative poetic side. Not unlike Keathley and Mittell, Grant (2019 [2016]) speaks of "new knowledge" generated through "material thinking", a kind of direct open handling of the filmic material through the editing software. With reference to Barbara Bolt's Heideggerian notion of hands-on practical knowledge, Grant argues that material thinking "occurs [in] the joining of hand, eye and mind" rather "than through [talk]". While "words may allow us to articulate and communicate the realisations that happen through material thinking", the latter "involves a particular responsiveness to or conjunction with the intelligence of materials and processes in practice" (Grant 2014: 49). This entails "perform[ing]" the film "affectively, as videographical thinking-feeling 'with rhythm and timing' […] that is to say, poetically", and handling the material in "a relation of care and concernful dealings" rather than, further echoing Heidegger, "a relation where the world is set before us (knowing subjects) as an object" (54f, 50). This also means "a coming to knowledge" through research that "knows not what it thinks before it begins" (Grant 2019 [2016]).[2] The more such a conduct was followed in her own videographic work, she adds, "the more new knowledge about the film[s] [she] seemed to produce" (Grant 2014: 53).

Keathley and Mittell (2019 [2016]) argue similarly for the mantra "Make First, Think Later" and for adhering to the pedagogical principle "that one learns by doing". Elsewhere Mittell also emphasizes how working with editing software provides a "methodological shift" in which "[a]ny strong work of videographic criticism builds on something learned through the editing process itself, not merely expressing ideas that were fully formed before" (2019). What is the epistemological, scholarly status of what is learned that way? Differently put: what scholarly notion of knowledge is implied? Rarely if ever is this question substantially addressed in videographic discourse.

The question can, however, be actualized in interesting ways. As when Grant speaks of new knowledge in a 2021 online discussion:

> As an academic, I have been employed to try to generate new knowledge. And I have turned to the video essay form, because it is a way of generating new knowledge in a different way from writing. For me a very compelling, immediate way, where I *can* make an argument, but not in a conventional, verbal way, but maybe just by joining two pieces of film together to see, to show how similar they are or how different they are. […] I am also interested in making forms that, for me, create new knowledge but for someone else may be a creative experience, an experience of watching any kind of film. (Grant 2021a: ca. 24:50–25:55)

New knowledge seems to mean here that the scholar makes an analytical discovery, something at least new to the scholar, but Grant does not say much about how to differentiate *scholarly* new knowledge from personal or poetic discoveries. Given the variations in disciplines, schools, epistemological preferences, etc., there are of course no fully universal criteria or procedures for evaluating the newness and significance of a scholarly work. If we take a tiny step from artistic research ideals towards more traditional notions of the scholarly, however, this could reasonably be deemed a universal scholarly procedure: the findings are explained as new knowledge in relation to previous research and recognized as such by other scholars. I could also suggest more detailed, but still fairly universal criteria (which even if they are not fully universal, at least provide an example of *having* criteria): 1) The study revolves around a research problem which is implicitly or explicitly shown to be significant in relation to relevant areas of existing research or theory. 2) There is a purpose and an aim that show, in relation to previous research, why the study is relevant and how it is a contribution. 3) The "new knowledge" is discussed also on a theoretical level, and thereby clarified as a contribution in relation to the existing literature. 4) There is a scholarly peer review process that evaluates the validity of the claims to new knowledge and significance in at least some of these senses.

If these or similar criteria are not at least partly met, the new research finding—if new in *some* other sense (rather than simply illustrating existing knowledge)—may more accurately be described as a discovery, idea, or insight which *could be further subjected to* scholarly treatment. If it holds up to such a treatment and is woven into a larger scholarly argument (which doesn't have to be linear or boil down to a proposition), it may *become* part of new knowledge in a scholarly sense.

On the one hand, Grant, as a seasoned scholar, briefly states that academic "originality only comes if you know what *is* original" and that "scholarship is building up a body of experience with existing areas of knowledge"—which, while insufficient, at least touches on the type of criteria I list above. On the other hand, she directly adds that she "[doesn't] always want to subject [herself] to those processes" (2021a: ca. 55:30–55:57). Grant makes video essays, rather, to get away from the strictures that she associates with the textual academic essay. Interestingly, she still maintains that her video essays are scholarly. On what grounds? Her argument is basically that her video essays are scholarly because she is a scholar, which is not a useful way of distinguishing scholarly video essays themselves from other kinds of video essays.[3]

While Grant does point beyond the scholar as an individual by mentioning how "peer review can improve work" (2021a), she is unclear about whether peer reviews are meant to improve *scholarly* aspects, rather than artistic or communicative ones. In the current standard for videographic peer reviews, which Grant has been part of developing, it is even unclear whether peer reviews should entail any suggestions for improvements or serve as a critical assessment prior to publication. The leading videography journal *[in]Transition*, of which Grant is a co-founding editor, publishes what they call peer reviews alongside the video essays, but they mostly appear as explanatory complements to the videos rather than critical examinations with suggestions for changes that are worked on by the video maker prior to publication.[4] Mittell, another co-founding editor, says that their primary function is to help explain the scholarly value of the video essays (2017). On the one hand, I see the usefulness of such explanatory accompanying texts. Not because many video essays are more artistic than scholarly, and therefore in need of explanatory texts like artworks can be, but because even the most scholarly video essays are not yet established as scholarly expression; that is, their scholarly aspects may need translation for those not yet used to seeing such aspects come in this form. On the other hand, redefining *peer review* to primarily have this function also helps to undercut the scholarly nature of the whole procedure.

Kiss and van den Berg's Critique and Conflicting Scholarly Standards

For Kiss and van den Berg (2016) most video essays made by film scholars (up until that point at least) aren't very scholarly, and are "almost indistinguishable from [those made by] non-scholars" (ch. 3). They find them too personally driven, satisfied with being artistically explorative, and, at their analytically best, charting patterns or themes in films or groups of films, rather than offering clear and substantiated argumentation informed by theory. Videographic essays tend also to be short, only reference other films, "and base themselves on either small or vaguely demarcated topics", which circumvents the possibility of doing the "extensive contextualization or in-depth exploration" one can expect from "an average length research paper" (ch. 3). Most instead manifest a "relatively uninhibited (or, willfully naive) conduct that neglects their chosen medium's potential, and consequently does not really innovate the study of films, but occasionally even threatens to loosen the academic integrity that characterizes Film Studies as a scholarly practice" (Intro). Kiss and van den Berg call for video essays that are "autonomous and self-sufficient" and that "both *maintain* and *refine* traditional academic values", instead of just offering "an appropriation of traditional video artistry, or a mere audiovisually upgraded extension of our analytical practice" (Intro). They also find that too many are "actively and openly" opposing the establishing of such scholarly principles for videography, and that Grant's statements are particularly "undercutting" (ch. 3).

Kiss and van den Berg's own criteria for distinguishing the scholarly center around autonomy, clarity, and structure (and as we will see they are useful but also limited). I will start with autonomy (and circle back to critical examinations of their notions of clarity and structure below): A scholarly video essay, they argue, must add new information or a new approach to a subject, but it must also contain all of its scholarly argumentation within itself. The video must itself "introduce a thesis, place this within a broader context, develop a theoretical notion and argument with an array of both aural as well as visual means", and "represent the analytical findings" in a "a full-bodied and standalone" work (ch. 3).

The Method/Process vs. Finished Work Divide

With this criterion Kiss and van den Berg takes a clear side in a larger debate we can call Method/Process vs. Finished Work. The Method/Process side focuses on new technical possibilities for an openly explorative and even poetical analysis of film. The Finished Work side acknowledges that such analysis can be productive for parts of the research process, and even function as elements of a finished work, but it also argues that they are not enough on their own to make up and be published as a scholarly work. The Method/Process side, in contrast, sees *scholarly* virtues in publishing non-finished research. Mittell argues that the humanities are too concerned with finished research, at the expense of methodology:

> Too often, the humanities frames 'research' as the finished products of scholarship: the book, the essay, the lecture. But research and its associated methodologies are not limited to the final product of scholarship: rather, the processes of discovery and experimentation are often the more exciting and insightful parts of scholarly endeavors, and it is in such processes where methodologies are used and developed. (Mittell 2019)

There are two clear issues with Mittell's argument: 1) There has been a clear tendency for scholarly video essays—as Kiss and van den Berg also point out—to overcompensate and focus too exclusively on method and process. 2) More misleadingly, such video essays are generally—not least by Mittell's own journal—published implicitly *as if* they were works of finished research, or there is at least insufficient clarity about their status in this regard (see also Kiss 2020). I should note here that a *cinecept* is precisely a *product* of research rather than a method to get there or an unfinished or unconceptualized idea.

Implied Medium Specificity[5] vs. Conventions of Use

Does video as a medium—more so than words—have inherent qualities that make it suitable for the unfinished and poetic? This is heavily implied in much of the discourse on scholarly video essays. For instance, there is a common view that video analysis equals *showing* the (unfinished) research *process* because video is a visual medium. But why would the preference for analysis left in process be explained by the visual nature of the medium? A text could be made up of not yet fully processed research notes and ekphratic descriptions. And reversely, a video can leave only the aspects of the analysis that are processed into a whole with a problem, an aim, a theoretical discussion, and a conclusion. Relatedly, it is often said that references do not work well in video. After acknowledging that "reading the work of other scholars and positioning [one's] own thoughts in relation to theirs" is "central to the work of scholarship", Tracy Cox-Stanton adds that this should mostly take place outside the video in a textual "script". Why? The video essay, she explains, is "not well suited" for references because they "distur[b] the work's artful flow" (Cox-Stanton in Cox-Stanton and Gibbs 2020). Granted, the aesthetic aspect of scholarly work can be important. But why would artistic flow necessarily take a new kind of *precedence* just because of a shift from text to video? Chloé Galibert-Laîne claims that references make video essays harder to follow. Even without references, she writes, "the spectator often has hardly enough time to process one concept or concrete example before the editing of the video has moved on to the next point, the next image, the next sound" (2020). But why not just use the pause button, going through the video slowly and carefully and perhaps in several bits, just as one would when reading a scholarly text? Not "well suited", then, seems to mostly imply not well suited for dominant conventions of production and reception, rather than inherent restrictions in media. Video essays *could* be produced differently, and different expectations *can* be established for reading and engaging with scholarship in audiovisual form.

The cinecept is opposed to conflations between conventions of use and inherent qualities in media. While the inclusion of references in a video is not necessarily required (since cinecepts could be part of digital multimedia texts, as discussed in the Introduction and Chapter 7), the cinecept equals a way of use that goes beyond at least certain preconceptions about what video is "well suited" for. Granted, the cinecept rests on the assumption that there are significant formal differences between media, otherwise it would serve no purpose, but this is about audiovisual media offering means to formally develop a particular conduct, and it says nothing about whether audiovisual media inherently lends itself to this conduct over others.

Videographic discourse can also imply medium specificity in subtler or more indirect ways, as in this passage by Mittell:

> Images are typically a less denotative and more expressive communication medium than the written word, especially within the norms of academic writing. Creating scholarship with moving images and sounds forces critics to engage with the aesthetic and affective dimensions of their expression far more than do typical written works; they must draw on artistic practice as well as scholarly analysis. Additionally, expressing ideas with video enables more possibilities to use irony, ambiguity, sensation, and other poetic elements than does academic prose. (2019)

That may be the case, but which aspects here are determined by conventions of use and which are determined by inherent differences in media forms? This is partly unclear due to the following asymmetry: When Mittell speaks of images/video it is as an open media possibility, a way of avoiding the "typical". But when speaking of writing, it is not about the medium of writing so much as a constrained *kind* of writing which *is* typical, and which limits the possibility for aesthetic and affective excursions. Relatedly, what is meant when Tracy Cox-Stanton and John Gibbs argue that "The audiovisual essay as a form is itself 'in between' scholarship and filmmaking" (2020)? This statement makes sense if referring to current conventions of use (a certain idea of the *essay* as form rather than the media itself). It *could* also make sense on the level of media form, but only if pointing to how video-essay making often entails more non-scholarly, technical problem solving than writing does.[6] Saying that the audiovisual media form *itself* is in between scholarship and filmmaking, however, would be comparable to saying that writing is in between scholarship and writing, which more clearly does not make sense.

Images and Words in Audiovisual Compounds

Moreover, if we recognize video/film as a general media category similar to "the written word" (rather than a genre of use)—and this is a precondition for the cinecept, as further explained in the Introduction and Chapter 1—this category must be recognized as a multimedia category that almost always includes—written and/or spoken—words. Do images and words have different generalizable medium-specific characteristics *within* such multimedia? As a form that allows us to "answer images not only with words, but also with other images", Keathley finds video essays to "deman[d] a mode of 'writing' that supplements analysis and explanation with a more expressive, poetical discourse" and "features that resemble art production" (2011: 179). Is this to equate words with "analysis and explanation" and images with "expressive, poetical discourse"? Keathley's argument is not that simple. At one point, he notes how Godard's *Histoire(s) du cinéma* is more poetic than explanatory (cf. discussions of this work from cineceptual perspectives in the Introduction and Chapter 5), but he seems to clearly recognize that this is not through a simple distribution of the poetic in the images and the explanatory in the words. He quotes Adrian Martin saying that there is "a lot of vocalising in Godard" which is "always displaced, decentred, at war with all the other elements of the work" rather than something that "dominates" or "closes down meaning". And in Keathley's own words: "Explanation vies with poetics in a collage of images and sounds, words and music, sometimes gaining the upper hand, sometimes losing it." Yet, two sentences down he describes video essays "composed in a poetical register" as "resist[ing] a commitment to the explanatory mode" by "employ[ing] language sparingly" (2011: 181).

So while Keathley himself may agree that the explanatory/poetic can be expressed in both images and words and through how they are combined, and that worded language itself is not necessarily equated with the explanatory, he also finds in existing poetic video essays the implicit view that worded language can have other-than explanatory functions only when used scarcely. Godard, of course, uses language profusely: "All of Godard's films", Jean-Louis Leutrat reminds us, "accord an important place to the written and spoken word, to language in all its forms" (2000: 179), and, to reuse a quotation from above, "the written word has been no more fully and comprehensively introduced into cinema than by Godard" (Lahey Dronsfield 2010: 93). For Godard there is no given way to use language, regardless of it being used sparingly or lavishly. As Godard responds to philosopher Youssef Ishaghpour's claim that "[t]o you words are enemies": "No, only when they're taken as orders, or thoughtless, or used malevolently as weapons" (Godard and Ishaghpour 2005 [1999]): 103). Godard did regard the talkies to have disrupted the development of montage, but only because *a certain kind* of talking, which was "conspiring" with certain social forces, took control over the image (Witt 2000: 47). And as examined in Godard-Miéville's *Ici et ailleurs*, the quintessential example of language dominating the image in a destructive way is the voice of Hitler taking power through being represented at a given moment by an image which only reinforced the voice. Furthermore, an overabundance of words, even words that attempt to dominate the meaning of a relatively sparce number of images, can instead diminish the analytical and explanatory and increase the poetical, such as the semi-tautological, *nouveau-roman* parodying, voice-over descriptions in Eric M. Nilsson's *Passageraren* (1966). Images, reversely, can be explanatory and relate to words in ways that clarify or even dominate their meaning.

In audiovisual compounds that contain images and words, therefore, nothing is necessarily given as to which parameter is more poetic/explanatory, or rather—to shift the frame a little—how analytic clarity (or the lack thereof) is distributed. And again: this is not just because words can have different functions in audiovisual compounds, but because this also goes for images. Speaking of Godard there is the playful dictum in *La Chinoise* (1967) that "one must confront vague ideas with clear images". This isn't explicitly about image-*word* relations, but it implies that images are not always inherently more vague than other signs such as words: clarity and vagueness *can* be variously distributed across both images and words. Sometimes images are clearer than words and sometimes not, and sometimes they clarify each other in image/word combinations (as evident in certain memes). (Or de-clarify each other as in Magritte.) And sometimes the clearest communication of meaning is a combination of images (e.g. the Kuleshov effect). On a basic formal level, the theory of cinecepts rests on such a notion of an—at least to *some* extent—un-predetermined distribution of something like clarity between images and words (cf. the discussion in Chapter 1 of both images and words as possible forms for the main point around which the cinecept condenses).

What is Clarity?

Additionally, the meaning of terms like clarity and vagueness (not to mention explanatory and poetic) can vary greatly. Godard's aesthetical-political-philosophical conceptions of clarity, which can appear vague, are quite different from the communicational clarity and "streamlin[ed] audiovisual rhetoric" championed by Kiss and van den Berg (2016: Intro). Scholarly video essays, they argue, should provide "information" that is "rhetorically and argumentatively clear, structured and distributed to support explanatory needs" (ch. 3). The methods used in the research process do not have to be lucid, Kiss explains in a later article, but "reason and clarity" is a must when "communicating" the results of the research and its potential value (Kiss 2020, emphases omitted). What is reason and clarity here? They leave terms like this mostly unexplained. But Kiss added later that they built their notion of "academic lucidity" on a "cheeky" article by Steven Pinker about bad academic writing (Kiss 2018b). As they do not much engage explicitly with this article let us look at it directly. Pinker champions a "classical" style which communicates research already done in ways that are "fun" and provide an "unobstructed view"—or as much as possible, since, he admits, we lack direct access—of the truth to a wide audience. But little of the article is explicitly about thinking or research or scholarship per se. Most is (generally good) advice about clarity in sentence structuring and word choice. For instance: cut out unnecessary filler words, don't use the Latin term if there is an English equivalent, and fix syntax that is unnecessarily convoluted. Many scholars who do "groundbreaking work on important subjects" and "reason well about clear ideas" still "stink" at writing in Pinker's estimation (2014). He also sees bad syntax, rhetoric, and style in scholarly texts of all kinds (so he isn't just ranting against "postmodern" academese, although he is hedgingly doing that too). So what is good writing again? According to Pinker, good academic writing communicates research/thinking already done. It may have to use scholarly terms, but it is clear also for the layperson. It is fun and engaging, preferably achieved through (tasteful) wit and panache. While there is nothing inherently wrong with any of that, how does this help distinguish a scholarly conduct from, say, a delightful and digestible journalistic column informed by research?

TREE-Structured Arguments and Falsification

Kiss and van den Berg may not theoretically define clarity as a term, but they do explain how to structure a work to make it clear. Their ideas for doing so, however, are mainly taken from two guidebooks.[7] One is Laurie G. Kirszner and Stephen R. Mandell's *The Wadsworth Handbook*. For Kiss and van den Berg this book "could offer clear criteria and practical guidance that can lead to well-rounded academic conduct". There is little direct description or dialogue with the contents of this guidebook, moreover, and what Kiss and van den Berg do pick up on is mostly its practical advice on how to make the explanatory argumentation more economical through graphical organization (ch. 3). More central for Kiss and van den Berg is to present a clear thesis—*not as an answer to, but curiously supplanting, a research problem* (which they do not discuss). This is how a clear thesis should be presented: There is a "thesis sentence [that] preconfigures all that comes after" and that "asserts, controls, and structures the entire argument". A good thesis sentence "makes a claim", "determines the scope of the argument", "provides a structure for the argument", and signals "not only what your argument is but how it will be presented". The thesis should also be "contextualized and developed through a theoretical framework" (ch. 3). The second guidebook is David Bordwell's brief *Film Viewer's Guide* (for undergraduate students), which Kiss and van den Berg find even "more hands-on and concise" in showing how to structure an essay in this way. An argumentative essay follows the acronym TREE: "Thesis supported by Reasons which rest upon Evidence and Examples". It will include an introduction giving "[b]ackground information or a vivid example, leading up to: *Statement of thesis*", followed by reasons to believe the thesis, evidence and examples, and ending with a conclusion consisting of a "[r]estatement of thesis and discussion of its broader implications" (ch. 3). And surely, such rhetorical and dispositional structures can be useful, even as independently utilized clarifying tools for more problem-based ventures and for scholars rather than undergraduate students.

Now, the issue here is that Kiss and van den Berg present their criteria as universal traits of the scholarly to be contrasted only with the non-scholarly, rather than as partly particular ideas about the scholarly. This is extra noticeable due to their lack of discussion of the theoretical underpinnings of their views, beyond the guidebooks and the Pinker article. Some hints are given, however, so let us look at a particularly interesting one. In a passage criticizing more open "audiovisual experiments" they say that "nothing will ever be falsified nor confirmed" (ch. 3). "Falsified" implicitly references Karl Popper's idea that knowledge is scientific if it is falsifiable. "Confirmed" echoes positivistic verification theory (to which Popper contrasted his falsification theory). Of course, neither of these two schools within the heterogeneous history of theories of science are particularly attuned to the modern humanities. Which would make it even more remarkable to imply that they are part of universal scholarly ideals. So, all in all, Kiss and van den Berg's critique is apt as directed at the too open and loosely poetic in current videography, but their own definitions of what is scholarly, while useful to some extent, are also quite limited.

Furthermore, what even remains of the scholarly when Kiss a little later (2018a) lowers the bar (as part of a specific editorial project but also after broadening his views of what scholarly video essays can be) so that it is no longer a requirement to situate the work in relation to previous research or theory, or even to reference any text? The videos are now presented as scholarly only on the grounds of being autonomous, "focused, analytical, exploratory", providing "straightforward explanation", and "thesis-driven explicit reasoning" while not "shy[ing] away from aesthetic embellishments" (Kiss 2018a). How does that distinguish scholarship from journalism? Journalistic texts on average must be even more focused, exploratory, straightforward, layperson-accommodating, and linear in their reasoning. Also, a thesis backed up by reasoning, evidence, and examples is not easy to separate from classic definitions of the documentary. Bill Nichols, for instance, describes the "organizational backbone of the documentary" as formulating an argument "in the sense of placing evidence before others in order to convey a particular viewpoint" (1991: 125).

Clarity, No Problem

Already in their 2016 book, as stated, Kiss and van den Berg avoided consideration of the research problem: in its stead, as the heart of the matter, they put a clear and linear thesis. And if we look at a scholarly video essay that Kiss himself published the same year, *Jacques Tati's* Playtime—*How to Make a [Critical] Joke* (2016), it appears optional to have a scholarly aim, in the sense of specifying an intended scholarly contribution. Let us look a bit closer at this video's scholarly qualities more generally.

The video is brief and well-delineated: it is nine minutes long and focused on the formal composition of a comedic scene in Tati's *Playtime* (1967). The analysis pays attention to details and could work well as educational material on aspects of the formal construction of a Tati film and some of its basic themes (or as an example of a neoformalist method). Scholarly pillars are nevertheless lacking. The video is not situated in relation to previous research in any regard (while the analysis does quote a sentence from a scholarly chapter called "Playtime: Tativille and Paris" by Iain Borden, this is only to get confirmation for a side argument about architecture). There is no research problem, in the sense of an intriguing new point of concern that calls out to be illuminated. There is also no purpose in the sense of conveying the relevance of the video in light of previous research. And neither of the video's insights are substantially new in a scholarly sense. To the extent that there are scholarly significant new insights in some of the details, the video does not say or indicate how they contribute to existing research—which is to say, there is no scholarly aim. The video starts with a set of aims and questions in other regards: We are told that this "brief audiovisual analysis" wants to "exemplify how the film's playful and comical practice conveys Tati's critical comment [on modern life]" and "How such criticism turns into comedy". Two questions follow, which are of the kind that states how the investigation will proceed rather than help articulate a research problem: "My questions are", Kiss says in voice-over partly doubled by text, "How one could set up and perfect a *direct* physical gag in a movie? [*sic*], and, How are such physical action's comical effects utilized to allow for a more *indirect* criticism?" What could an investigation of these things bring to the scholarly table? What remains to be researched with the comedic social criticism in this film, of all films? The video does not seem to ask itself what is at stake. That is, the kind of "scholarly endeavor" that videographer (and scholar) Allison Fren asks her "students to engage in": "the necessity of answering the question, 'so what?' Why do we care?" (2020). Kiss then presents a more specific aim: "Proving that the film's real protagonists are not the clumsy characters, but the strict and rigid environmental shapes and the cinematic mise-en-scène. And by providing concrete audiovisual evidence about film scholars' general but rarely demonstrated claim concerning Tati's uncompromising and perfectionist filmmaking approach." Why do we need formal confirmation of something so established among critics and scholars? It would be different, of course, if it was the other way around—if Kiss wanted to problematize previous knowledge, find some holes, present some other way of looking at what goes on here, point to some unexplored complexities, or something to that effect. The aim is basically to provide formal evidence for established knowledge. And is it not easier to be "clear" when that is the aim?

When Clarity Conceals

For Pinker—who Kiss references for his notion of clarity—clarity is part of a style preference in which language is enjoyable, includes "handy idioms and tropes", and is as understandable as it can be for the layperson. Pinker often implies that the impetus for this style preference boils down to broadening the appeal: "a writer who explains technical terms can multiply his readership" (2014). Certainly, this rhymes with the increased pressure for scholarly life to adapt to a consumer logic. More subtly, however, easily digestible language *can* also work to uphold established wisdom, including prevailing ideologies, such as those that implicitly maintain said consumer logic. Pinker himself multiplies his readership with the help of this style, while his content tends to explicitly endorse the global capitalist order. Of course, this style can also be used to critique that order, but it is generally harder to do so in scholarly rigorous ways while maintaining the same *accessibility* in the clarifications.[8] The critical examination and conceptualization of complexities beyond dominant ways of understanding the world can sometimes require a partly new language or new ways of using existing language, which from the perspective of established understanding may appear difficult, strange, or vexing.[9] But such language can also provide tools for critical insight or hold potentials for new modes of thought (for examinations of the problem of the new from Deleuzian and cineceptual perspectives as well as in Godard-Miéville's Sonimage work, see Chapters 3 and 4 above). Established orders of things, of whatever kind, tend to protect themselves against such language either through cooption or by labeling it meaningless or deceiving. It might be said that such language is only a style used to make banalities appear profound. Granted, that can sometimes be the case. But is not the opposite both more prevalent and more important? Like when the scholar sort of mimics the politician saying "Let me be clear": there may be significant webs of complexity that this helps to hide rather than acknowledge or illuminate. A cineceptual videography would articulate its insights and arguments as clearly as possible but mainly on its own terms and in relation to relevant existing work. It would thereby allow itself to perhaps appear unamusing or hard to follow for the layperson—whose abilities to understand or creatively engage with complexity should not thereby be underestimated—or at first even for other scholars unfamiliar with the area or the problem.

The Essayistic

In some contrast to Kiss's *Playtime* video, Ian Garwood's video essay from the same year, *The Place of Voiceover in Academic Audiovisual Film and Television Criticism* (2016), while perhaps not all that scholarly in other regards, is one of the few scholarly video essays I have come across that contains an explicit research problem in the sense of a *complex*. What is particularly interesting here is that its main concern—the use of the voice-over in academic video essays—isn't reduced to a linear argument that lays out evidence for a clear and given thesis. Instead, the essay subjects this topic to a problematization from several perspectives that articulates and illuminates some of its complexities. It is in this sense *essayistic*. Essayistic, that is, in a more continental and critical sense of the term. In an early section of Kiss and van den Berg's book, the history of the essay film is covered as one of the precursors to the contemporary video essay. Their brief overview mostly repeats a reductive notion of the essay film as "personal" or "subjective" reflection—a view most extensively conveyed in Laura Rascaroli's *The Personal Camera* (2009). As shown by scholars like Christa Blümlinger (2004 [1992]) and Nora Alter in her recent comprehensive book on the essay film (2018), the essay is just as much a form for theory, sociopolitical critique, and thinking layered or even nonlinear problems, beyond the merely personal or subjective on the one hand, and beyond journalistic or documentary arguments and theses on the other.

There is an increasing number of videographic scholars who connect with such aspects of the essay film tradition. Tracy Cox-Stanton, for instance, argues that "editing software can easily layer images to convey a density and complexity that would be difficult to achieve in writing", in order to make "polysemous arguments" and subject issues to, as she says with John Gibbs, "multiple lines of inquiry". To do this in *scholarly* ways, they add, video essays must "raise questions about a topic, then reconsider those questions within the context of additional scholarly works and new ideas" (Cox-Stanton and Gibbs 2020).

What is important here is not the connection to the essay film tradition per se, but rather that we are starting to move past the frameworks not only of TREE structures and the like but also of mere mixtures of the poetic and the explanatory. That is, the view that the following two poles make up *the* spectrum: 1) artistic research of the kind where everything theoretically or argumentatively explicit is left to the spectator to work out, and 2) clear linear argumentation selling a thesis. In contrast to both, there could be a larger focus on problems and theoretically rooted aims and purposes, and a structure and logic of analysis and discussion that allows for more essayistic forms in the sense of exploring things from different angles, and where the key thing is to articulate and illuminate interesting complexities, rather than to boil everything down to an unambiguous ARGUMENT. That would be one *precondition* for there to be anything like cineceptual videography.

Approaching Cineceptual Videography

Opening a door beyond the artistic research vs. TREE frame of things, and reductive ideas about medium specificity (at least on the side of text), Cox-Stanton writes: "While it's indisputable that the traditional academic essay has evolved into a notably exegetic use of writing, there is nonetheless a solid history of scholars challenging that tradition"; she goes on to reference "Roland Barthes, Jacques Derrida, Hélène Cixous and others" (Cox-Stanton in Cox-Stanton and Gibbs 2020)—and we can recall Keathley and Mittell also referencing Barthes. Still, it is important to be specific about what is gained in *scholarly* senses by going beyond the so-called "traditional" essay in such ways. As is especially obvious from Deleuzian and cineceptual perspectives, the added scholarly value must be understood as providing further philosophical sophistication or scope, rather than merely mixing in poetic ambiguity or pulling down the lever of the explanatory. That is, what the above-named scholars did—however much they differed from each other—is substantially understood as some version of (what is still often referred to as) continental philosophy. How could video essays themselves *do that* (rather than merely sprinkle in references to such writings)? How could we conceive of the philosophical video essay? Or the video essay as philosophy? Or, in more specialized terms: how could the video essay be cineceptual? As the cineceptual itself was defined in the preceding chapters (with some extensions in the next), the question for this chapter is rather: How could contemporary scholarly videography become a terrain also for cinecepts? This is not, then, to ask how the scholarly video essay could become cineceptual *instead* of what it is now or instead of other possibilities (and reversely: cinecepts could develop in a variety of *other* scholarly milieus than the one discussed in this chapter). There are many relevant and interesting works being made in all the modes mentioned above, and they serve different purposes. There have also been recent leaps in the use of this form for conducting and presenting mainstream film studies: while more are sure to follow, I am thinking primarily of Max Tohline's three-years in the making, over two-hour-long *A Supercut of Supercuts: Aesthetics, Histories, Databases* (2021). Instead, the question here—how could the scholarly video essay become a terrain for cinecepts?—concerns one alternative path and not just for film and media studies but for scholars and theorists more broadly. Some answers:

1) Scholarly video essays continue to develop in *problem*-based directions. This is perhaps the most important precondition. From a Deleuzian perspective, there cannot be a concept without a properly posed problem to which it responds:

in philosophy, there are two things at once: the creation of a concept, and the creation of a concept always occurs as a function of a problem. If one has not found the problem, one cannot understand philosophy, philosophy remains abstract. […] Some people talk, but we never know what problems they're talking about. […] I mean, at most, one knows the questions, but not the problems behind certain questions […] What counts is […] to what problem asking that question corresponds and what concept [s/he] is going to fabricate […] If you have neither a concept nor a problem […] you aren't doing philosophy. (ABC Letter H)

And problems are themselves posed rather than merely found: "doing philosophy is to constitute problems that make sense and create concepts that cause us to advance toward the understanding […] of problems" (ABC Letter H). Deleuze also talks about a "pedagogy" of concepts in the sense of allowing us to see and grasp problems previously posed but posed badly or in ways that have not kept up with how problems necessarily change (WP 16, 28). (For more on this, and how Deleuze conceives other scholarly aspects, such as purpose, aim, relating to previous research, etc., see Chapter 1 above).

2) Scholarly video essays continue to move beyond the restriction to formal film analysis or even to studying film or visual culture more broadly. As I quoted Mittell saying above, scholarly video essays *can* "explore a wide range of topics, theoretical approaches, or objects of study" (2019). Kiss and van den Berg already talked about how this type of essaying "could also be adopted by studies and faculties not directly engaged with cinema" and that it "can serve practically *all* study trajectories that now end with a written essay" (2016: Intro).

3) Scholarly video essays continue to develop new ways to use experimental or artistic form in scholarly ways. And this is of course already quite central to what is going on (even Kiss and van den Berg talk favorably about using experimental or poetic methods as "building blocks" for finished scholarly works [2016 ch. 3]). Current video essays, scholarly or not, have created valuable concrete forms of editing and postproduction that could be used also for more cineceptual work.[10]

4) The scholarly video essay opens even more towards philosophy or theory actually being done in and through this form—not as pedagogical illustration of already existing theories or concepts, or merely by including philosophical references, but as original creation.

Notes

1 Some of what *could* be said about these terms: A) TRUTH: If one were to look directly into this and go back to Barthes's own reading of Proust, one could start

by comparing it—first just to show how varied in meaning these terms can be—with Deleuze's reading in which truth is instead found to be at the heart of the Proustian venture, albeit a more profound "truth of time" (PS 4, 26; see also ATP 186, 306; DR 149, 153; WP 167f). B) EFFECTS: Even if this concerns some kind of real knowledge for Barthes himself, "knowledge effect", when used without further definition, implies knowledge seen as appearance—almost like a matter of style similar to Barthes's "reality effect"—rather than producing knowledge itself or entailing more substantial epistemological complexities. If we remain within videographic discourse, we can also note how the scholar and video essayist Allison de Fren signals a clear difference between a knowledge effect and knowledge production. In her own videos she "attempt[s] to take the insights gleaned from audiovisual analysis further" and strives "beyond a 'knowledge effect,' in which interpretation is left open, toward knowledge production and the articulation of an original point of view or argument" (de Fren 2020). Furthermore, one could also draw comparisons with other definitions of the term "knowledge effect", contemporaneous with Barthes's, such as Althusser's (for a brief discussion of this term from a film theoretical perspective, see Baumbach 2019: 3).

2 Cf. Harun Farocki in *Interface* [*Schnittstelle*, 1995]: "For over a year I collected film sequences with the motif 'workers leaving the factory' and studied them at the editing table. What could be the aim of this study? Must the study have an aim?", (12:09–12:24).

3 To look a bit closer at what she is saying, how it boils down to this basic argument, and in what sense this is a problem—Grant: "I had already worked through the complete body of scholarship on Andrea Arnold's film work as well as on British social realist cinema. […] [T]hat's a vast amount of work. I've been a film scholar for a long, long time, so even though I didn't necessarily read it all again before working on this video, it was there. And this is what makes the work that I do always scholarly, whether […] it feels scholarly or not. I am a scholar, and this makes a difference in the form of essayism that I engage with" (Grant 2021b: 19:59–20:32). What is said here? This is clear: Grant is a film scholar, and her expertise informs her videos. Less clear is how her line of argumentation can be used for determining the scholarliness of videos essays more generally. At least if we boil down her argument to the following: 1) if a scholar 2) makes a video about 3) a topic on which the scholar is well read, then 4) the video is scholarly. 1 and 3 can condition and *can* lead to 4, but they do not have to lead to 4. Many scholars produce intellectual outputs alongside their scholarly work that, however informed by the latter, aren't necessarily scholarly themselves (comparable to how artists and writers can read up extensively on scholarly works and then produce artworks or novels that are not works of scholarship). For instance, a film scholar writing a regular review, a column about a favorite film, or a fictional short story about the movie industry. Based on expertise, sure, but *scholarly* only if that is evident somehow *in* the works.

(Cf. Kevin B. Lee: "I have seen examples of what the Wellesley College website might describe as 'a fan tribute or a simple mash-up of favorite clips' being positioned as videographic scholarship for no apparent reason other than that its maker had scholarly credentials" [2020].)

4   In an assessment based on reading "a great many of" these peer reviews, media scholar Steve F. Anderson says they "often provide a critical reframing as opposed to requiring an author to perform extensive re-editing or re-writing", and that their "real value" is "additive and contextual rather than strictly editorial" (Anderson 2020). See also Garwood's analysis of *[in]Transition's* creator statements (2020).

5   I use this term here mostly in the broad sense of differences between written or spoken language and moving images with sound. For a more precise definition of how "media" is understood in this book see the Introduction.

6   Patrick Keating: "When I encourage colleagues to try videographic criticism, I always warn them that a surprisingly large portion of the work is just technical problem-solving. When I write a traditional essay, I can fix a typo in a few seconds. When I make a video, a minor mistake on the voice track might take hours to fix (going back to the sound booth, re-recording a few words, cutting them back in smoothly). This is just one example. Really, video work is filled with these maddening fixes" (Keating 2019 [2018]).

7   They more generally rely also on a third guidebook: a short one for undergraduate students new to film studies and academic writing called *Writing about Movies* (2013) by Karen Gocsik, Richard Barsam, and Dave Monahan. Here Kiss and van den Berg find a clear "overview of the basic principles and strategies of writing about film." Among its general points also relevant for non-undergraduates: the argument should be critical and "analytical rather than personal"; the work must be placed "within the lineage of [the] field" and the "argument within the ongoing critical conversation" (ch. 3).

8   Eager to show how complex language can be simplified, Pinker can appear obtuse about differences in meaning even in the simplest of cases. For instance, he claims that a "prejudice-reduction model" can be clarified as "Reducing prejudice": while I am not familiar with the first term, it is not hard to imagine that it references something more specific than reducing prejudice in general. He also claims that "approaching this subject from a law-enforcement perspective" can be reduced to "calling the police" (Pinker 2014). Is it not obvious that these two things can be completely different on all levels?

9   While Pinker acknowledges the need for "[d]ifficult writing" when this is "unavoidable because of the abstractness and complexity of [certain] subject matter", this is only in the sense of technical terms for the already well-known, which is to say, "insider-shorthand" between professionals, similar to specialty terms in other areas like sailing or skateboarding (2014). Such jargon, of course, is a sort of opposite of opening up new thought.

10 These forms, which to a large extent are an effect of technological developments, also build on previous formal inventions by the likes of Godard and Godard-Miéville (examined in Chapters 2, 4, and 5 above). Not only *Histoire(s) du cinéma* but even aspects of Godard-Miéville's Sonimage period may be said to belong to the genealogy of videographic film and media studies. The inspiration may not always be direct—it might be filtered through, say, Harun Farocki in turn filtered through Kevin B. Lee or through certain forms consolidating as convention. Sonimage is echoed most explicitly, perhaps, in the manner of placing two or several moving images next to each other on a black background (although now appearing more like a flat software chalkboard than the Godardian "fetal" blackness explored in Chapters 2 and 4).

7   Notes on Cinecepts as Multimedia Practice

This brief chapter contains notes on cinecepts that are partly open and forward pointing. They address concrete conditions for the production and reception of cinecepts, further relate cinecepts to a contemporary world of audiovisual media, and offer additional suggestions for how they can function practically as multimedia. This chapter is thereby neither a conclusion to nor a summary of the study. For overviews of the study, see the Preface and the Introduction.

WHY DO FULL cinecepts, as previously established, remain on the horizon? Among many abstract and structural reasons, one is simple and practical: the vast majority of philosophers or theorists are not trained to use film / video / audiovisual media as *means* for forming (and not just documenting or channeling verbal versions of) philosophy or theory. I belong to that majority—although the purpose of this book, I should underline, is to investigate the conditions of possibility for cinecepts and lay a theoretical ground for them, not to simultaneously help establish them in audiovisual practice. Furthermore, there is no tradition for forming cinecepts—the odd examples of embryonic cinecepts aside—to learn from and fall back on (as is the case with words-only concepts). There are also no proper academic infrastructures for their production or dissemination. Equally lacking are the preconditions for their reception: we still tend to learn, at least in higher education, how to read complex theoretical texts; we do not to the same extent learn how to read material that uses the potentials of the audiovisual form to express complex theory. The latter does not mean learning to read theory in a form that is categorically different from theoretical text. The difference between words/text only and audiovisual media is not categorical: audiovisual media, as hammered home in this book, tend to include words and texts. Cinecepts, furthermore, can be part of complex formations of multimedia along with text.

Cinecepts as Multimedia

The term cinecept, as established in the Introduction, conceptualizes the following idea: philosophical concepts (as Deleuze defines concepts) formed as *compounds of moving images / sounds / voice / texts / graphics / montage*. I have become increasingly convinced, over the course of this study, that this is not just a matter of video including sounds / voice / texts / graphics / montage, but rather that cinecepts can be formulated through multimedia more broadly, as long as moving images are somehow included. Cinecepts could just as well come as part of digital multimedia texts that incorporate video. I can only speak of this in provisional terms, however, since digital multimedia will likely continue to evolve: there will be new software for intertwining text, moving images, and sounds that I cannot foresee that might further the technological conditions for cinecepts.

What can be said more generally, however, is that cinecepts are always parts in larger wholes. Words-only concepts of course also only appear at *certain points* in a philosophical text. They depend on and crystalize aspects in the rest of the text, but do not themselves stretch over the whole text. Cinecepts are no different: they would appear at certain points in a larger work, and regardless of its multimedia composition. But how can a cinecept be repeated in a different whole, as with a word-concept that stems from one text and is restated in another text?

How to Repeat, Develop, Describe, or Reference Existing Cinecepts

The cinecept, again, is not about supplanting philosophical concepts solely made up of words, and much speaks for the continued need for words-only philosophy, certainly the whole philosophical tradition. Words-only concepts also have a higher degree of efficacy and repeatability. They concentrate the abstract *content* of a concept into a simpler actual form, which can be easily used and reused—formally, one needs only to write or say a word or two. Yet, we should not exaggerate such differences. Cinecepts may expand parameters for philosophical expression, which means more complexity in actual form, but given all we can now do on our laptops, they aren't necessarily that much more technically and logistically difficult to formulate—or to repeat or develop.

It seems to me—at least given current technological conditions—that an existing cinecept can be quoted, developed, described, or referenced in the following basic ways:

- *Direct quotations of cinecepts in audiovisual media*: In videographic film studies (discussed in Chapter 6) it is common to point out that video essays solve the problem of the "unattainability of the text" that Bellour raised in 1975—that is, with the analyzing form now being itself audiovisual media, the works analyzed can be directly quoted. This is basically also how cinecepts can be quoted, although there may be further complications depending on their specific multimedia composition that would have to be worked out in practice.
- *Cineceptual creation based on previous cinecepts*: How can aspects of a previous cinecept be formally repeated when it serves as the basis for cineceptual development, variation, or the creation of a new cinecept?[1] This necessitates repetition only of certain elements from the previous cinecept/s, and enough of a repetition of each element to establish a clear connection. Such elements could either be recreated or directly taken, if possible, from a previous audiovisual compound and woven into a new one.
- *How to describe an existing cinecept in writing-only*: This is a matter of ekphrasis for images and sounds (including visible text) and quotation for speech, such as in the descriptions in Chapter 4 of what we see and hear and read in each embryonic cinecept (although copyright restrictions limited my use of direct quotes). Since the cinecept has audiovisual form by definition, then, this is not to be confused with straight citation or quotation (apart from the speech), which requires multimedia containing moving images with sound.[2]
- *How to reference an existing cinecept in writing-only*: A cinecept, especially when speech and writing are key components, could be given a title so as to be easily referenced through textual shorthand (similar to the titles for each section of embryonic cinecepts described in Chapter 4 above). Or/and one could point to the specific position of the cinecept in the larger work, such as with timestamps.

YouTube Philosophy as Popular Second Orality and Untapped Formal Potential

If cinecepts do not yet exist, this is not due to a lack of philosophy content in contemporary audiovisual media. The amount of philosophy channels on YouTube is steadily growing, but most of them are verbal-centered, akin to visual podcasts, and generally extend what Walter J. Ong called "a new age of secondary orality" brought about by electronic media technologies like radio and television (2012 [1982]: 133ff). The videos that go beyond talking heads tend to still focus on the voice and presence of a personality and use other audiovisual parameters mostly for illustrations to what is said. Furthermore, it is still uncommon to find senior scholarly work of *original* philosophy. Most of these channels put out videos that contain (however competent and sharp) popular science versions of existing philosophy, or blends of commentary and popular education with relatively broad appeal (although some—more common in the different medium of audio-only podcasts—are more comparable to the seminar or reading group). Some do have a certain pedagogical and aesthetic flair in their use of the audiovisual medium, but there is little use of it to formally develop original philosophical thought.

Yet, all these channels are adapted by default to the fact that (especially young) people increasingly read less and get more of their information through audiovisual platforms like YouTube. As such they have value, regardless of their untapped cineceptual potential, in educating the public and helping to further disseminate theoretical perspectives and approaches. The cinecept is mostly a response to a different concern (the particular Deleuzian issues aside): How can original philosophy formally adapt on its own terms in ways that develop instead of dilute philosophical rigor and specificity? The cinecept offers an answer that focuses primarily on an expanded formal palette for philosophy itself: more differentiated, multilayered, and moving formal means with which to potentially take on more registers of reality with more depth and precision.

The Video Essay More Broadly as Dominant Form and the Cinecept as Alternative

Another way to approach the current media landscape is to look at the various kinds of "video essays"—in a much broader sense than what we looked at in Chapter 6—with which a platform like YouTube is now flooded. Many of these are professionally made in form, while also purporting to present informed commentary, which ranges from in-depth critical analysis, to stylistic exercises, to deceptive propaganda. In a general way, they all have *some* connection to the tradition of the essay film (to which much of Godard-Miéville's work also broadly belongs). In her excellent overview of the history and present of the essay film, Nora Alter is certainly correct in saying that "the essay as a mode of critique" has been "translated […] into a variety of media […] on multiple platforms" (2018: 321). But the current ubiquity of "video essays" also manifests how the "essay as form has transformed its historical role", as Hito Steyerl writes, along with asking (and as Alter herself briefly notes): "Has the essay as form been replaced by the essay as conformism? Or to put it more carefully: Has the essay become a dominant form of narrative in times of post-Fordist globalization?" "The essay as form", Steyerl argues, "has adapted rather well to globalization". It "runs parallel to the post-Fordist coercion of difference, mobility, extreme flexibilization, and distracted modes of attention, whose ideal subjectivity is hybrid and supple", while also "mirror[ing] contemporary global forms of production". But she also argues that the essay, with "its discontinuous and heterogeneous form", is "still capable of providing alternative forms of vision, knowledge and grounds for discussion" (Steyerl 2017 [2011]: 276ff). In her own filmmaking, however, Steyerl went from documentary-based essay film (e.g. *November* [2004]) to video works that, while theory-driven and critical, go further towards art that intricately intensifies the "distracted", "flexible", and "supple" aspects of advanced capitalist society (e.g. *How Not to be Seen* [2013], *Liquid Inc.* [2014], and *Factory of the Sun* [2015]). The cinecept instead goes further towards the philosophically explicit and the philosophically determined.

The Voice as Means for Deception as well as Philosophical Nuance and Rigor

Audiovisual media offer expanded means for nuance in such philosophical determinations, but also new ways of being deceptive. Music, editing, and personality are among the obvious means for seducing and bypassing critical faculties. And a central parameter here is the human voice, at least given the amount of talking this form tends to invite. Two different remarks by Deleuze on the human voice in philosophy, the first frivolous and the second more serious, help illustrate the risks and possibilities of using the voice as a tool for philosophical precision. Deleuze's first remark: "Especially since I have stopped teaching […] I realized that talking is a bit dirty […] whereas writing is clean. Writing is clean and talking is dirty. It's dirty because it means being seductive (*faire du charme*)" (ABC Letter C). While Deleuze is a bit playful here, as he is obviously aware of how seductive writing can be, as pertaining to philosophy there is something to this: writing can allow for a more direct concentration on problems whereas teaching more primarily entails a need to entice and bring along as a primary purpose, and with personality more at the forefront. The other reflection is longer and more considered. It is a short text called "What Voice Brings to the Text" and revolves around the voice of actor Alain Cuny. "What does a text, especially a philosophical one, expect from an actor's voice?", Deleuze begins by asking. Concepts, he adds, "have speed and slowness, movements, dynamics that expand and contract throughout the text", they are "characters themselves, rhythmic characters. They fulfill each other or separate, clash or hug like wrestlers or lovers" (TRM 325). He also argues that the voice can help capture such nuances:

> The actor's voice traces these rhythms, these movements of the mind in space and time. The actor is the operator of the text: he or she operates a dramatization of the concept, the most precise, the most sober and the most linear. […] The voice reveals that concepts are not abstract. […] It is up to the actor's voice to bring forth

the new perceptions and new affects that surround the read and spoken concept. (TRM 325f)

Godard's and Godard-Miéville's careful work with actors' voices is compatible with such a view of the relation between voice and thought (and Alain Cuny also happens to do several readings—seen or in voice-over—in *Histoire(s) de cinéma*). Witt:

> This close attention to the expressive possibilities of the voice can be traced to Godard's work with actors, and to his success over the years in producing often remarkable readings and dialogue delivery from them. [...] His exploration of the power of the human voice as an instrument is also strongly in evidence in the attention to accent, intonation, diction, vocal color, and even to the sound of human breath. (Witt 2013: 205; see also Morrey 2005: 175)

Of course, all this may be quite hard to separate from seduction or even means for bypassing critical faculties. However, if we focus on the voice as expressing concepts, in the sense that Deleuze describes above, as long as the concept itself is thorough and has gone through rigorous processes in its creation, the seduction is not necessarily an issue. The voice, along with editing and music, is double in this sense: it can be a tool for deception just as well as for further philosophical nuance. Therefore, philosophy conducted through audiovisual media demands new kinds of care and caution. And it comes with a greater need for scholarly peer review and scholarly editorial examination. Institutions that uphold such scholarly conducts are now more important than ever.

A Challenge

This study provides a theoretical framework for cinecepts—it examines their conditions of possibility, gives them a general philosophical determination, and suggests how they could be developed in concrete audiovisual practice. Of course, how to develop cinecepts in concrete audiovisual practice is not something that can be fully prescribed in a text-only medium. I therefore end this book with a challenge to philosophers or theoreticians inclined to use audiovisual media, as well as to philosophically inclined video and multimedia artists, to look closely at this framework and then experiment.

Notes

1 For Deleuze concepts are "subject to […] renewal, replacement, and mutation" (WP 8). See Chapter 1 for a more developed account of this and related aspects of Deleuze's concept of concepts.
2 I should perhaps add that this has nothing to do, on any level, with Paisley Livingston's idea of paraphrasability in words as a criterion for determining whether a film is philosophical or not. For critiques of this criterion from other perspectives, see for instance Noël Carroll (2017); Stephen Mulhall (2008); Thomas E. Wartenberg (2007).

Abbreviations of Works by Gilles Deleuze

ABC	*L'Abécédaire de Gilles Deleuze, avec Claire Parnet*	Deleuze
ATP	*A Thousand Plateaus: Capitalism and Schizophrenia*	Deleuze & Guattari
B	*Bergsonism*	Deleuze
C1	*Cinema 1: The Movement-Image*	Deleuze
C2	*Cinema 2: The Time-Image*	Deleuze
D	*Dialogues*	Deleuze & Parnet
DI	*Desert Island and Other Texts*	Deleuze
DR	*Difference and Repetition*	Deleuze
ECC	*Essays Critical and Clinical*	Deleuze
F	*Foucault*	Deleuze
FB	*Francis Bacon: The Logic of Sensation*	Deleuze
FLB	*The Fold: Leibniz and the Baroque*	Deleuze
LS	*The Logic of Sense*	Deleuze
LOT	*Letters and Other Texts*	Deleuze
N	*Negotiations*	Deleuze
NP	*Nietzsche and Philosophy*	Deleuze
PS	*Proust and Signs*	Deleuze
TRM	*Two Regimes of Madness*	Deleuze
WP	*What is Philosophy?*	Deleuze (& Guattari)*

* There are many complexities to Deleuze and Guattari's co-authorship of *Capitalism and Schizophrenia* – the zones of indiscernibility between the two, how Guattari supplied much of the raw material in the form of diagrams and what

he called "schizoid-flows", while Deleuze tied things together into more coherent concept-driven works, etc. (see Smith's 2006b review of *Anti-Oedipus Papers* for a comprehensive overview). Still, these complexities do not put Guattari's co-authorship into question. The authorship of *What is Philosophy?*, however, is more unclear in this regard. I formally acknowledge Guattari's co-authorship credit also of this book – in this list of abbreviations, the list of references below, and certain sections above. In large parts of this study I nonetheless refer only to Deleuze as the author. Here is my reasoning for crediting both Deleuze and Guattari while often referring only to Deleuze when discussing *What is Philosophy?* First, a precedent, second a brief discussion of a claim about the authoring of this book made in a biography, and third, my own specific reasons.

1. Daniel W. Smith, while he is not systematic about this, often only mentions Deleuze's name when referencing (even quoting) *What is Philosophy?* (e.g. 2012: 12, 98, 111, 125, 127f, 129, 133, 134, 136, 137, 148, 192, 205, 273, 292, 305, 309f, 317, 325, 346, 382, 385).
2. While contested by some, we should at least note the claims about the authoring of *What is Philosophy?* in François Dosse's biography on Deleuze and Guattari. The aim of this biography is to "help correct [a] few blind spots that have led to minimizing and even eliminating Guattari's role, leaving only Deleuze's name". Within this context of concern with Guattari's legacy, Dosse also argues that *What is Philosophy?* was "manifestly written by Deleuze alone". There are further complexities here, however, as Dosse adds: "Deleuze agreed to a coauthor credit with Guattari" not just "as a tribute to their exceptionally intense friendship" but also because of how "the ideas developed in the book and its language were the fruit of their common endeavors since 1969" and because, more substantially, Deleuze sent the manuscript to Guattari who made "suggestions, corrections" and even helped define some "new directions" (Dosse 2010 [2007]: 519, 456, 14f). To the extent that this is true, how much does the latter concern authorship, more so than feedback from a closely aligned reader or informal co-editor?
3. It seems to have been a long-standing point of irritation to Deleuze that Guattari was not given more credit for *Capitalism and Schizophrenia*, which they more clearly co-wrote (see e.g. LOT [1982]: 82, 84f). And parts of *What is Philosophy?* do extend from their previous work, certainly those that more directly discuss capitalism and contain concepts like deterritorialization. To add Guattari's name on the cover also of *What is Philosophy?* therefore seems reasonable. Yet, from the early 1980s up until close to its publication, Deleuze explicitly talks about *What is Philosophy?* as *his* project (e.g. LOT [1990]: 55, 79, 90, 95). It was written during a period in which, after having worked intensely with Guattari, Deleuze

said he "had to return to [his] own work" (TRM [1984]: 240). Most of *What is Philosophy?* has a different general tone and conceptual apparatus than *Capitalism and Schizophrenia*. It connects more with Deleuze's single-authored works in the 1960s and 1980s. In this study, I generally focus precisely on the aspects of *What is Philosophy?* that connect with Deleuze's own previous work more than his previous work with Guattari – aspects of the last part of Chapter 3 is (in my estimation) the clearest exception – most specifically, the logic of concepts formulated in *What is Philosophy?* is primarily based on a logic spelled out in *Difference and Repetition*. And as Deleuze wrote in a letter in 1984: "[Guattari's] ideas are like drawings, or even diagrams. Concepts are what interests me. […] Félix with his diagrams and me with my articulated concepts" (TRM 238).

References

Adorno, Theodor W. (1991 [1958]), "The Essay as Form", in *Notes to Literature. Volume One*. New York: Columbia University Press, pp. 3–23.

Alter, Nora M. (2018), *The Essay Film after Fact and Fiction*, New York: Columbia University Press.

Anderson, Steve F. (2020), "Videographic Scholarship and/as Digital Humanities", *The Cine-Files* 15. Special issue on the scholarly video essay, ed. Cox-Stanton and de Fren, at <http://www.thecine-files.com/videographic-scholarship-and-as-digital-humanities>

Astruc, Alexandre (2014 [1948]), "The Birth of a New Avant-Garde: *La Caméra-Stylo*", in *Film Manifestos and Global Cinema Cultures: A Critical Anthology*, ed. Scott MacKenzie, Berkeley: University of California Press, pp. 603–6.

Aumont, Jacques (2011), *Les théories des cinéastes*, 2nd edition, Paris: Armand Colin.

Badiou, Alain (2000 [1997]), *Deleuze: The Clamor of Being*, trans. Louise Burchill, Minneapolis: University of Minnesota Press.

Badiou, Alain (2009 [2006]), *Logics of Worlds: Being and Event II*, London: Continuum.

Bal, Mieke (2002), *Travelling Concepts in the Humanities: A Rough Guide*, Toronto: University of Toronto Press.

Baross, Zsuzsa (2009), "Jean-Luc Godard", in *Film, Theory and Philosophy: The Key Thinkers*, ed. Felicity Colman, Montreal: McGill-Queens University Press, pp. 134–44.

Baross, Zsuzsa (2017), "Godard and/with Deleuze: 'C'est comme ça que le monde naît'", in *The Dark Precursor: Deleuze and Artistic Research*, ed. Paulo de Assis and Paolo Giudici, Leuven University Press, pp. 326–37.

Barthes, Roland (1977) [1964]), "Rhetoric of the Image", in *Image, Music, Text*, trans. Stephen Heath, London: Fontana Press, pp. 32–51.

Barthes, Roland (1977 [1970]), "The Third Meaning", in *Image, Music, Text*, trans. Stephen Heath, London: Fontana Press, pp. 52–68.

Baumbach, Nico (2019), *Cinema/Politics/Philosophy*, New York: Columbia University Press.

Beistegui, Miguel de (2004), *Truth and Genesis: Philosophy as Differential Ontology*, Bloomington: Indiana University Press.

Bell, Jeffery (2016), *Deleuze and Guattari's* What is Philosophy? *A Critical Introduction and Guide*, Edinburgh: Edinburgh University Press.

Bellour, Raymond (1990), "Video Writing", in *Illuminating Video: An Essential Guide to Video Art*, ed. Doug Hall and Sally Jo Fifer, New York: Aperture in association with the Bay Area Video Coalition, 1990, pp. 421–43.

Bellour, Raymond (2010), "The Image of Thought", in *Afterimages of Gilles Deleuze's Film Philosophy*, ed. D. N. Rodowick, Minneapolis: University of Minnesota Press, pp. 3–14.

Bergala, Alain (1999 [1978]), "Le cinema retrouvé (*Comment ça va?*)", in *Nul mieux que Godard*, Paris: Editions Cahiers du cinema, pp. 27–31.

Bergala, Alain (1999 [1979]), "Enfants: ralentir (*France tour detour deux enfants*)", in *Nul mieux que Godard*, Paris: Editions Cahiers du cinema, pp. 32–8.

Blümlinger, Christa (2004 [1992]), "Lire entre les images", in *L'essai et le cinema*, ed. Murielle Gagnebin and Suzanne Liandrat-Guigues, Seyssel: Champ Vallon, pp. 49–66.

Bogue, Ronald (2003), *Deleuze on Cinema*, New York: Routledge.

Bogue, Ronald (2010), "To Choose to Choose – to Believe in This World", in *Afterimages of Gilles Deleuze's Film Philosophy*, ed. D. N. Rodowick, Minneapolis: University of Minnesota Press, pp. 115–32.

Boljkovac, Nadine (2013), *Untimely Affects: Gilles Deleuze and an Ethics of Cinema*, Edinburgh: Edinburgh University Press.

Brenez, Nicole (2007 [2004]), "The Forms of the Question", in *For Ever Godard*, ed. M. Temple, J. S. Williams, and M. Witt, London: Black Dog Publishing, pp. 160–77.

Buchanan, Ian (2008), "Five Theses of Actually Existing Schizoanalysis of Cinema", in *Deleuze and the Schizoanalysis of Cinema*, ed. Ian Buchanan and Patricia MacCormack, London: Continuum, pp. 1–14.

Carroll, Noël (2017), "Movie-Made Philosophy", in *Film as Philosophy*, ed. Bernd Herzogenrath, Minneapolis: University of Minnesota Press, pp. 265–85.

Colman, Felicity (2011), *Deleuze & Cinema: The Film Concepts*, New York: Berg.

Cox-Stanton, Tracy and John Gibbs (2020), "Audiovisual Scholarship and Experiments in Non-linear Film History", *The Cine-Files* 15. Special issue on the scholarly video essay, ed. Cox-Stanton and de Fren, at <http://www.thecine-files.com/audiovisual-scholarship-and-experiments-in-non-linear-film-history>

Cramer, Michael (2017), "Radical Communications: Jean-Luc Godard on and around Television", in *Utopian Television: Rossellini, Watkins, and Godard beyond Cinema*, Minneapolis: University of Minnesota Press.

Daney, Serge (1976), "Le thérrorisé (pédagogie godardienne)", *Cahiers du Cinéma* 262/3, January. An English version entitled "The Therrorized (Godardian Pedagogy)", based on translations by Annwyl Williams and Bill Krohn/Charles Cameron Ball, is available online at <https://www.diagonalthoughts.com/?p=1620>

de Fren, Allison (2020), "The Critical Supercut: A Scholarly Approach to a Fannish Practice", *The Cine-Files* 15. Special issue on the scholarly video essay, ed. Cox-Stanton and de Fren, at <http://www.thecine-files.com/the-critical-supercut-a-scholarly-approach-to-a-fannish-practice>

Deamer, David (2014), *Deleuze, Japanese Cinema, and the Atom Bomb: The Spectre of Impossibility*, New York: Bloomsbury.

Deamer, David (2016), *Deleuze's Cinema Books: Three Introductions to the Taxonomy of Images*, Edinburgh: Edinburgh University Press.

Debord, Guy (2005 [1967]), *Society of the Spectacle*, trans. Ken Knabb, London: Rebel Press.

del Rio, Elena (2008), *Deleuze and the Cinemas of Performance: Powers of Affection*. Edinburgh: Edinburgh University Press.

Deleuze, Gilles (1983 [1962]), *Nietzsche and Philosophy*, trans. Hugh Tomlinson, New York: Columbia University Press.

Deleuze, Gilles (2000 [1964]), *Proust and Signs*, trans. Richard Howard, Minneapolis: University of Minnesota Press.

Deleuze, Gilles (1988 [1966]), *Bergsonism*, New York: Urzone, Inc.

Deleuze, Gilles (2004 [1968]), *Difference and Repetition*, trans. Paul Patton, London: Continuum.

Deleuze, Gilles (2003 [1969]), *The Logic of Sense* [1969], trans. C. J. Stivale et al., London: Continuum.

Deleuze, Gilles (2004 [1981]), *Francis Bacon: The Logic of Sensation*, trans. Daniel W. Smith, New York: Continuum.

Deleuze, Gilles (2003 [1983]), *Cinema 1: The Movement-Image*, trans. Hugh Tomlinson and Barbara Habberjam, Minneapolis: University of Minnesota Press.

Deleuze, Gilles (2003 [1985]), *Cinema 2: The Time-Image*, trans. Hugh Tomlinson and Roberta Galeta, Minneapolis: University of Minnesota Press.

Deleuze, Gilles (2006 [1986]), *Foucault*, trans. Seán Hand, Minneapolis: University of Minnesota Press.

Deleuze, Gilles (2006 [1988]), *The Fold: Leibniz and the Baroque*, trans. Tom Conley, London/New York: Continuum.

Deleuze, Gilles (1996 [1988–89]), *L'Abécédaire de Gilles Deleuze, avec Claire Parnet*, directed by Pierre-André Boutang, trans. Charles J. Stivale, at <https://deleuze.cla.purdue.edu>

Deleuze, Gilles (1995 [1990]), *Negotiations: 1972–1990*, trans. Martin Joughin, New York: Columbia University Press.

Deleuze, Gilles (2004 [2002]), *Desert Islands and Other Texts: 1953–1974*, ed. David Lapoujade, trans. Michael Taormina, Los Angeles: Semiotext(e).

Deleuze, Gilles (2007 [2003]), *Two Regimes of Madness: Texts and Interviews 1975–1995*, ed. David Lapoujade, trans. Ames Hodges and Mike Taormina, Los Angeles: Semiotext(e).

Deleuze, Gilles (1997 [1993]), *Essays Critical and Clinical*, trans. Daniel Smith and Michael Greco, Minneapolis: University of Minnesota Press.

Deleuze, Gilles (2020 [2015]), *Letters and Other Texts*, ed. David Lapoujade, trans. Ames Hodges, South Pasadena: Semiotext(e).

Deleuze, Gilles and Claire Parnet (2007 [1977]), *Dialogues II. Revised Edition*, trans. Hugh Tomlinson and Barbara Habberjam, New York: Columbia University Press.

Deleuze, Gilles and Félix Guattari (2004 [1972]), *Anti-Oedipus*, trans. Robert Hurley, Mark Seem, and Helen R. Lane, London: Continuum.

Deleuze, Gilles and Félix Guattari (1987 [1980]), *A Thousand Plateaus*, trans. Brian Massumi, Minneapolis: University of Minnesota Press.

Deleuze, Gilles and Félix Guattari (1994 [1991]), *What is Philosophy?*, trans. Hugh Tomlinson and Graham Burchell, New York: Columbia University Press.

Derrida, Jacques (1979), *Spurs/Eperons: Nietzsche's Styles/Les Styles de Nietzsche*, Chicago: University of Chicago Press.

Didi-Huberman, Georges (2008 [2003]), *Images in Spite of All*, trans. Shane B. Lillis, Chicago: University of Chicago Press.

Dosse, François (2010 [2007]), *Gilles Deleuze and Félix Guattari: Intersecting Lives*, New York: Columbia University Press.

Drabinski, John E. (2008), *Godard Between Identity and Difference*, New York: Continuum.

Drabinski, John E. (2010), "Philosophy as a Kind of Cinema: Introducing Godard and Philosophy", *Journal of French and Francophone Philosophy* 18(2): 1–8.

Dubois, Philippe (1992), "Video Thinks What Cinema Creates: Notes on Jean-Luc Godard's Work in Video and Television", *Jean-Luc Godard: Son + Image 1974–1991*, New York: Museum of Modern Art, pp. 169–85.

Eagleton, Terry (2018 [2011]), *Why Marx Was Right*, New Haven: Yale University Press.

Eisenstein, Sergei (1949), *Film Form: Essays in Film Theory*, trans. Jay Leyda, New York: Harcourt, Brace & World.

Eisenstein, Sergei (1949 [1929]), "The Dramaturgy of Film Form (The Dialectical Approach to Film Form)", in *The Eisenstein Reader*, eds. Richard Taylor, trans. Richard Taylor and William Powell, London: Palgrave Macmillan.

Elsaesser, Thomas (2019), *European Cinema and Continental Philosophy: Film as Thought Experiment*, London: Bloomsbury Academic.

Elsaesser, Thomas and Malte Hagener (2015), *Film Theory: An Introduction Through the Senses*, 2nd edition, New York: Routledge.

Emmelhainz, Irmgard (2019), *Jean-Luc Godard's Political Filmmaking*, Basingstoke: Palgrave Macmillan.

Farocki, Harun (1990 [1981]), "Intelligence without Experience: Interview with Harun Farocki", in Heiner Müller, *Germania*, trans. B. Schütze and C. Schütze, New York: Semiotext(e).

Fisher, Mark (2014), *Ghosts Of My Life: Writings on Depression, Hauntology and Lost Futures*, Winchester: Zero Books.

Flaxman, Gregory (ed.) (2000), *The Brain is the Screen: Deleuze and the Philosophy of Cinema*, Minneapolis: University of Minnesota Press.

Flaxman, Gregory (2011), *Gilles Deleuze and the Fabulation of Philosophy*, Minneapolis: University of Minnesota Press.

Fox, Albertine (2018), *Godard and Sound: Acoustic Innovation in the Late Films of Jean-Luc Godard*, London: I. B. Tauris & Co. Ltd.

Frampton, Daniel (2006), *Filmosophy*, London: Wallflower Press.

Galibert-Laîne, Chloé (2020), "What Scholarly Video Essays Feel Like", *The Cine-Files* 15. Special issue on the scholarly video essay, ed. Cox-Stanton and de Fren, at <http://www.thecine-files.com/what-scholarly-video-essays-feel-like>

Garwood, Ian (2016), "The Place of Voiceover in Academic Audiovisual Film and Television Criticism", *NECSUS: European Journal of Media Studies* 5(2): 271–5, at <https://necsus-ejms.org/the-place-of-voiceover-in-audiovisual-film-and-television-criticism>

Garwood, Ian (2020), "Writing about the Scholarly Video Essay: Lessons from *[in] Transition's* Creator Statements", *The Cine-Files* 15. Special issue on the scholarly video essay, ed. Cox-Stanton and de Fren, at <http://www.thecine-files.com/writing-about-the-scholarly-video-essay-lessons-from-intransitions-creator-statements>

Godard, Jean-Luc (2020 [1967]), "One or Two Things", *Sight & Sound*, Jean-Luc Godard: a Sight & Sound special.

Godard, Jean-Luc (1986 [1968]), *Godard on Godard: Critical Writings by Jean-Luc Godard*, ed. Jean Narboni and Tom Milne, New York: Da Capo Press.

Godard, Jean-Luc (1985), *Jean-Luc Godard par Jean-Luc Godard, vol. 1*, ed. Alain Bergala, Paris: Cahiers du cinéma/éditions de l'étoile.

Godard, Jean-Luc (1992 [1988]), "Godard Makes Historie(s). Interview with Serge Daney", *Jean-Luc Godard: Son + Image 1974–1991*, New York: Museum of Modern Art, pp. 159–68.

Godard, Jean-Luc and Youssef Ishaghpour (2005 [1999]), *Cinema: The Archaeology of Film and the Memory of a Century (Talking Images)*, trans. John Howe, Oxford: Berg.

Grant, Catherine (2014), "The Shudder of a Cinephiliac Idea? Videographic Film Studies Practice as Material Thinking", *ANIKI: Portuguese Journal of the Moving Image* 1(1): 49–62.

Grant, Catherine (2019 [2016]), "Dissolves of Passion", in *The Videographic Essay: Criticism in Sound & Image*, ed. Keathley, Mittell, Grant, Montreal: Caboose, at <http://videographicessay.org/works/videographic-essay/dissolves-of-passion-1>

Grant, Catherine (2021a), "Videoessay-Panel at Solothurner Filmtage Solothurner Filmtage", at <https://blog.hslu.ch/videoessay/soleure/?fbclid=IwAR0e66cZ7VlEtRlcJoa_87cBkQvo6Wo2OMEochfgTw8zN5EIPcQwhdynZmg>

Grant, Catherine (2021b), "Thinking through the Video Essay", Presentation at the TECMERIN Video Essay Webinar, October 1, at <https://vimeo.com/620218461?fbclid=IwAR1X8crvAPw7GtAGZhjdoOMmjIji_hwbtASPbCKW34PDMa2WJ3pQnX01g-g>

Hardt, Michael (1993), *Gilles Deleuze: An Apprenticeship in Philosophy*, London: UCL Press.

Hayes, Kevin J. (2002), "Godard's *Comment Ça Va* (1976): From Information Theory to Genetics", *Cinema Journal* 41(2): 67–83.

Hegel, Georg Wilhelm Friedrich (2018 [1807]), *The Phenomenology of Spirit*, trans. Terry Pinkard, Cambridge: Cambridge University Press.

Hegel, Georg Wilhelm Fredrich (2010 [1812–16]), *The Science of Logic*, trans. George di Giovanni, Cambridge: Cambridge University Press.

Herzogenrath, Bernd (2017), "Introduction. Film and/as Philosophy: An Elective Affinity?", in *Film as Philosophy*, ed. Bernd Herzogenrath, Minneapolis: University of Minnesota Press, pp. vii–xxv.

Houle, Karen and Jim Vernon (eds.) (2013), *Deleuze and Hegel: Together Again for the First Time*, Evanston: Northwestern University Press.

Jacob, François (1973 [1970]), *The Logic of Life: A History of Heredity*, trans. Betty E. Spillmann, New York: Pantheon Books.

Keathley, Christian (2011), "*La Caméra-Stylo*: Notes on Video Criticism and Cinephilia", in *The Language and Style of Film Criticism*, ed. Alex Clayton and Andrew Klevan, New York: Routledge.

Keathley, Christian and Jason Mittell (2019 [2016]), "Scholarship in Sound & Image: A Pedagogical Essay", in *The Videographic Essay: Criticism in Sound & Image*, ed.

Keathley, Mittell, Grant, Montreal: Caboose, at <http://videographicessay.org/works/videographic-essay/scholarship-in-sound--image>

Keathley, Christian, Jason Mittell, and Catherine Grant (eds.) (2019 [2016]), *The Videographic Essay: Criticism in Sound & Image*, ed. Keathley, Mittell, Grant, Montreal: Caboose, at <http://videographicessay.org/works/videographic-essay/index>

Keating, Patrick (2019 [2018]), "Becoming Videographic Critics: A Roundtable Conversation", in *The Videographic Essay: Criticism in Sound & Image*, ed. Keathley, Mittell, Grant, Montreal: Caboose, at <http://videographicessay.org/works/videographic-essay/becoming-videographic-critics-a-roundtable-conversation>

Kennedy, Barbara M. (2000), *Deleuze and Cinema: The Aesthetics of Sensation*, Edinburgh: Edinburgh University Press.

Kiss, Miklós (2018a), "Videographic Scene Analyses, part 1", *NECSUS: European Journal of Media Studies* 7(1): 345–8, at <https://necsus-ejms.org/videographic-scene-analyses-part-1>

Kiss, Miklós (2018b), "Videographic Scene Analyses, part 2", *NECSUS: European Journal of Media Studies* 7(2): 323–30, at <https://necsus-ejms.org/videographic-scene-analyses-part-2>

Kiss, Miklós (2020), "Videographic Criticism in the Classroom: Research Method and Communication Mode in Scholarly Practice", *The Cine-Files* 15. Special issue on the scholarly video essay, ed. Cox-Stanton and de Fren, at <http://www.thecine-files.com/videographic-criticism-in-the-classroom>

Kiss, Miklós and Thomas van den Berg (2016), *Film Studies in Motion: From Audiovisual Essay to Academic Research Video*. Open access. Scalar, at <http://scalar.usc.edu/works/film-studies-in-motion/index>

Kittler, Friedrich A. (1999 [1985]), *Gramophone, Film, Typewriter*, trans. Geoffrey Winthrop-Young and Michael Wutz, Stanford: Stanford University Press.

Kracauer, Siegfried (1960), *Theory of Film: The Redemption of Physical Reality*, New York: Oxford University Press.

Kristeva, Julia (1974), *La révolution du langage poétique: l'avant-garde à la fin du XIXe siècle: Lautréamont et Mallarmé*, Paris: Éditions du Seuil.

Lahey Dronsfield, Jonathan (2010), "Pedagogy of the Written Image", *Journal of French and Francophone Philosophy* 8(2): 87–105.

Lambert, Gregg (2012), *In Search of a New Image of Thought: Gilles Deleuze and Philosophical Expressionism*, Minneapolis: University of Minnesota Press.

Lee, Kevin B. (2020), "New Audiovisual Vernaculars of Scholarship", *The Cine-Files* 15. Special issue on the scholarly video essay, ed. Cox-Stanton and de Fren, at <http://www.thecine-files.com/new-audiovisual-vernaculars-of-scholarship>

Leutrat, Jean-Louis (2000), "The Power of Language: Note on *Puissance de la parole, Le dernier mot* and *On s'est tous defile*", in *The Cinema Alone: Essays on the Work of Jean-Luc Godard 1985–2000*, ed. James S. Williams and Michael Temple, Amsterdam: Amsterdam University Press, pp. 179–88.

Loshitzky, Yosefa (1995), *The Radical Faces of Godard and Bertolucci*, Detroit: Wayne State University Press.

MacCabe, Colin (1980), *Godard: Images, Sounds, Politics*, London: Macmillan.

MacCabe, Colin (1992), "Jean-Luc Godard. Life in Seven Episodes (to Date)", *Jean-Luc Godard: Son + Image 1974–1991*, New York: Museum of Modern Art, pp. 13–22.

Marks, John (2006), "Molecular Biology in the Work of Deleuze and Guattari", *Paragraph* 29(2): 81–97.

Marrati, Paola (2008 [2003]), *Gilles Deleuze: Cinema and Philosophy*, trans. Alisa Hartz, Baltimore: Johns Hopkins University Press.

Martin, Jean-Clet (2013 [2010]), interviewed by Constantin V. Boundas in "A Criminal Intrigue: An Interview with Jean-Clet Martin", in *Deleuze and Hegel: Together Again for the First Time*, ed. Houle and Vernon, Evanston: Northwestern University Press.

Martin-Jones, David (2006), *Deleuze, Cinema and National Identity: Narrative Time in National Contexts*, Edinburgh: Edinburgh University Press.

Martin-Jones, David (2011), *Deleuze and World Cinemas*, London: Continuum.

Martin-Jones, David and William Brown (eds.) (2012), *Deleuze and Film*, Edinburgh: Edinburgh University Press.

Massumi, Brian (1987), "Translator's Foreword: Pleasures of Philosophy", *A Thousand Plateaus*, Minneapolis: University of Minnesota Press.

Massumi, Brian (2010), "What Concepts Do: Preface to the Chinese Translation of *A Thousand Plateaus*", *Deleuze and Guattari Studies* 4(1): 1–15.

Mittell, Jason (2017), "Opening Up *[in]Transition's* Open Peer-Review Process", *Cinema Journal* 56(4): 137–41.

Mittell, Jason (2019), "Videographic Criticism as a Digital Humanities Method", in *Debates in the Digital Humanities 2019*, ed. Matthew Gold and Lauren Klein, Minneapolis: University of Minnesota Press, at <https://dhdebates.gc.cuny.edu/read/untitled-f2acf72c-a469-49d8-be35-67f9ac1e3a60/section/b6dea70a-9940-497e-b7c5-930126fbd180#ch20>

Morgan, Daniel (2012), *Late Godard and the Possibilities of Cinema*, Berkeley: University of California Press.

Morrey, Douglas (2005), *Jean-Luc Godard*, Manchester: Manchester University Press.

Mulhall, Stephen (2008), *On Film: Thinking in Action*, 2nd edition, London: Routledge.

Mulvey, Laura (2006), *Death 24x a Second: Stillness and the Moving Image*, London: Reaktion Books.
Mulvey, Laura and Colin MacCabe (1980), "Images of Woman, Images of Sexuality", in *Godard: Images, Sounds, Politics*, ed. Colin MacCabe, London: Macmillan.
Nevin, Barry (2018), *Cracking Gilles Deleuze's Crystal Narrative Space-time in the Films of Jean Renoir*, Edinburgh: Edinburgh University Press.
Nichols, Bill (1991), *Representing Reality: Issues and Concepts in Documentary*, Bloomington: Indiana University Press.
Nietzsche, Friedrich (2001 [1882]), *The Gay Science*, trans. Josefine Nauckhoff and Adrian Del Caro, Cambridge: Cambridge University Press.
Nietzsche, Friedrich (2002 [1886]), *Beyond Good and Evil: Prelude to a Philosophy of the Future*, trans. Judith Norman, Cambridge: Cambridge University Press.
Nilsson, Jakob (2014), "Thought-Images and the New as a Rarity: A Reevaluation of the Philosophical Implications of Deleuze's Cinema Books", *Cinema: Journal of Philosophy and the Moving Image* 6, ed. Susana Viegas, "Gilles Deleuze and Moving Images", 94–121.
Nilsson, Jakob (2018), "Deleuze, Concepts, and Ideas about Film as Philosophy: A Critical and Speculative Re-Examination", *Journal of French and Francophone Philosophy* 26(2): 127–49.
Nilsson, Jakob (2020), "Notes on Three Phases in Deleuze's Thinking on Novelty", in *Material: Filosofi, Estetik, Arkitektur: Festskrift till Sven-Olov Wallenstein*, ed. Marcia Sá Cavalcante Schuback, Helena Mattsson, Kristina Riegert, and Hans Ruin, Stockholm: Södertörn Philosophical Studies 24, pp. 155–64.
Noys, Benjamin (2010), *The Persistence of the Negative: A Critique of Contemporary Continental Theory*, Edinburgh: Edinburgh University Press.
Ong, Walter (2012 [1982]), *Orality and Literacy*, New York: Routledge.
Pamart, Jean-Michel (2012), *Deleuze et le cinéma: l'armature philosophique des livres sur le cinéma*, Paris: Kimé.
Pantenburg, Volker (2015 [2006]), *Farocki/Godard: Film as Theory*, Amsterdam: Amsterdam University Press.
Pasolini, Pier Paolo (2005 [1965]), "The 'Cinema of Poetry'", in *Heretical Empiricism*, trans. Ben Lawton and Louise K. Barnett, Washington, DC: New Academia Publishing, pp. 167–86.
Pasolini, Pier Paolo (2005 [1969]), "Cinema and Oral Language", in *Heretical Empiricism*, trans. Ben Lawton and Louise K. Barnett, Washington, DC: New Academia Publishing, pp. 264–6.
Penley, Constance (1989 [1982]), "Les Enfants de la Patrie (on *France/Tour/Detour/Two Children*)", in *The Future of an Illusion: Film, Feminism, and Psychoanalysis*,

Minneapolis: University of Minnesota Press, pp. 93–118; "Les Enfants de la Patrie", *Camera Obscura* 8–10: 35.

Pinker, Steven (2014), "Why Academics Stink at Writing", *Chronicle of Higher Education*, September 26, at <https://www.chronicle.com/article/why-academics-stink-at-writing/?cid2=gen_login_refresh&cid=gen_sign_in&cid2=gen_login_refresh>

Pisters, Patricia (2003), *The Matrix of Visual Culture: Working with Deleuze in Film Theory*, Stanford: Stanford University Press.

Pisters, Patricia (2012), *The Neuro-Image: A Deleuzian Film-Philosophy of Digital Screen Culture*, California: Stanford University Press.

Powell, Anna (2007), *Deleuze, Altered States and Film*, Edinburgh: Edinburgh University Press.

Price, Brian (1997), "Plagiarizing the Plagiarist: Godard Meets the Situationists", *Film Comment* 33(6): 66–9.

Rajchman, John (2000), *The Deleuze Connections*, Cambridge, MA: The MIT Press.

Rancière, Jacques (2009 [2003]), *The Future of the Image*, trans. Gregory Elliot, London: Verso.

Rascaroli, Laura (2009), *The Personal Camera: Subjective Cinema and the Essay Film*, London: Wallflower.

Rodowick, D. N. (1994 [1988]), *The Crisis of Political Modernism: Criticism and Ideology in Contemporary Film Theory*, Berkeley: University of California Press.

Rodowick, D. N. (1997), *Gilles Deleuze's Time Machine*, Durham, NC: Duke University Press.

Rodowick, D. N. (2007), *The Virtual Life of Film*, Cambridge, MA: Harvard University Press.

Rodowick, D. N. (ed.) (2010), *Afterimages of Gilles Deleuze's Film Philosophy*, Minneapolis: University of Minnesota Press.

Rodowick, D. N. (2015), *Philosophy's Artful Conversation*, Cambridge, MA: Harvard University Press.

Rodowick, D. N. (2017), *What Philosophy Wants from Images*, Chicago: University of Chicago Press, 2017.

Roffe, Jon (2012), *Badiou's Deleuze*, Montreal: McGill-Queen's University Press.

Rushton, Richard (2009), "Deleuzian Spectatorship", *Screen* 50(1): 45–53.

Rushton, Richard (2011), "A Deleuzian Imaginary: The Films of Jean Renoir", in *Deleuze Studies* 5(2): 241–60.

Rushton, Richard (2012), *Cinema after Deleuze*, London: Continuum.

Sauvagnargues, Anne (2018 [2005]), *Deleuze and Art*, trans. Samantha Bankston, New York: Bloomsbury.
Sauvagnargues, Anne (2013), "Hegel and Deleuze: Difference or Contradiction?", in *Deleuze and Hegel: Together Again for the First Time*, ed. Houle and Vernon, Evanston: Northwestern University Press.
Shaviro, Steven (1993), *The Cinematic Body*, Minneapolis: University of Minnesota Press.
Siegel, Amie (2014), "Factories and the Factory", in *A Companion to Jean-Luc Godard*, ed. Tom Conley and T. Jefferson Kline, Hoboken: John Wiley & Sons, pp. 351–66.
Silverman, Kaja and Harun Farocki (1998), *Speaking about Godard*, New York: New York University Press.
Sinnerbrink, Robert (2011), *New Philosophies of Film: Thinking Images*, London: Continuum.
Smith, Daniel W. (2012 [2001]), "Deleuze, Hegel, and the Post-Kantian Tradition", in *Essays on Deleuze*, Edinburgh: Edinburgh University Press, pp. 59–71.
Smith, Daniel W. (2006a), "The Concept of the Simulacrum: Deleuze and the Overturning of Platonism", *Continental Philosophy Review* 38: 89–123.
Smith, Daniel W. (2006b), "Inside Out: Guattari's Anti-Oedipus Papers", *Radical Philosophy* 140: 35–9.
Smith, Daniel W. (2012), *Essays on Deleuze*, Edinburgh: Edinburgh University Press.
Smith, Daniel W. (2012a), "The Conditions of the New", in *Essays on Deleuze*, Edinburgh: Edinburgh University Press, pp. 235–55.
Smith, Daniel W. (2012b), "On the Nature of Concepts", *Parallax* 18(1): 62–73.
Somers-Hall, Henry (2012), *Hegel, Deleuze, and the Critique of Representation: Dialectics of Negation and Difference*, Albany, NY: State University of New York Press.
Sontag, Susan (2001 [1964]), "Godard's Vivre Sa Vie", in *Against Interpretation and Other Essays*, New York: First Picador, pp. 196–208.
Sorfa, David (2016), "What is Film-Philosophy?", *Film-Philosophy* 20: 1–5.
Sterritt, David (1999), *The Films of Jean-Luc Godard: Seeing the Invisible*, New York: Cambridge University Press.
Steyerl, Hito (2017 [2011]), "The Essay as Conformism? Some Notes on Global Image Economies", in *Essays on the Essay Film*, ed. Nora M. Alter and Timothy Corrigan, New York: Columbia University Press, pp. 276–85.
Steyerl, Hito (2012), *The Wretched of the Screen*, Berlin: Sternberg Press.
Sutton, Damian (2009), *Photography, Cinema, Memory: The Crystal Image of Time*, Minneapolis: University of Minnesota Press.

Temple, Michael (2000), "Big Rhythm and the Power of Metamorphosis: Some Models and Precursors for *Histoire(s) du cinéma*", in *The Cinema Alone: Essays on the Work of Jean-Luc Godard 1985–2000*, ed. Williams and Temple, Amsterdam: Amsterdam University Press, pp. 77–95.

Thomas, Allan James (2018), *Deleuze, Cinema and the Thought of the World*, Edinburgh: Edinburgh University Press.

Thorgeirsdottir, Sigridur (2010), "Nietzsche's Philosophy of Birth", in *Birth, Death, and Femininity: Philosophies of Embodiment*, ed. Robin May Schott, Bloomington: Indiana University Press, pp. 157–85.

Vaugh, Hunter (2013), *Where Film Meets Philosophy: Godard, Resnais, and Experiments in Cinematic Thinking*, New York: Columbia University Press.

Wartenberg, Thomas E. (2007), *Thinking on Screen: Film as Philosophy*, London: Routledge.

White, Jerry (2013), *Two Bicycles: The Work of Jean-Luc Godard and Anne-Marie Miéville*, Waterloo: Wilfrid Laurier University Press.

Widder, Nathan (2012), *Political Theory after Deleuze*, London: Continuum.

Williams, James (2003), *Gilles Deleuze's* Difference and Repetition*: A Critical Introduction and Guide*, Edinburgh: Edinburgh University Press.

Williams, James (2011), *Gilles Deleuze's Philosophy of Time: A Critical Introduction and Guide*, Edinburgh: Edinburgh University Press.

Witt, Michael (1998), "On Communication: The Work of Anne-Marie Miéville and Jean-Luc Godard as 'Sonimage' from 1973 to 1979", Diss., University of Bath.

Witt, Michael (1999), "On Gilles Deleuze on Jean-Luc Godard: An Interrogation of 'la méthode du ENTRE'", *Australian Journal of French Studies* 36(1): 110–24.

Witt, Michael (2000), "Montage, My Beautiful Care, or Histories of the Cinematograph", in *The Cinema Alone: Essays on the Work of Jean-Luc Godard 1985–2000*, ed. Williams and Temple, Amsterdam: Amsterdam University Press, pp. 33–50.

Witt, Michael (2004), "Shapeshifter: Godard as Multimedia Installation Artist", *New Left Review* 29: 73–89.

Witt, Michael (2007 [2004]), "Altered Motion and Corporeal Resistance in *France/tour/détour/deux/enfants*", in *For Ever Godard*, ed. M. Temple, J. S. Williams, and M. Witt, London: Black Dog Publishing, pp. 200–13.

Witt, Michael (2013), *Jean-Luc Godard: Cinema Historian*, Bloomington: Indiana University Press.

Witt, Michael (2014), "On and Under Communication", in *A Companion to Jean-Luc Godard*, ed. Conley and Kline, Hoboken: John Wiley & Sons, pp. 318–50.

Witt, Michael (2018), "Professor Michael Witt. Inaugural Lecture. University of Roehampton", at <https://www.youtube.com/watch?v=QqB3L72oPYs&t=1999s>

Wollen, Peter (2013 [1969]), *Signs and Meaning in the Cinema*, Basingstoke: Palgrave Macmillan.

Žižek, Slavoj (2008 [1989]), *The Sublime Object of Ideology*, London: Verso.

Index

Note: n indicates a note; *italics* indicate figures

Adorno, Theodor, 44n, 47n, 48n, 154n
Alter, Nora, 69, 183, 192
Aristotle, 38–9, 70–1
art
  art-philosophy distinctions, xi–xiii, 10, 25–6, 44n, 56–7, 164
  Deleuze's conception of, xi, 16n, 23–5, 36, 57, 102, 104
  pedagogy of, 31, 164
artistic research, 3, 164, 169, 170, 172, 183
Astruc, Alexandre, x–xi, 15, 21n, 43, 52n
audiovisual media
  audiovisual media as open formal means, not a genre of use, 13, 37, 175–6
  cineceptual theory and, xiii, 4, 11, 164, 189–90, 194
  Deleuzian concept creation and, x–xii, 2–3
  the formal renewal/development of philosophy and, x, xi, xiii, 2–3, 41
  philosophical thought and, x, xi, 191–2
  quoting or referencing of cinecepts, 190–1
  thinking in and through, 14–15
Aumont, Jacques, 80n, 159n

Badiou, Alain, 85, 105n, 106n
Bal, Mieke, 5
Baross, Zsuzsa, 18n, 166
Barthes, Roland, 50n, 51 n, 171, 184, 185n
Bellour, Raymond, 22n, 42–3, 169, 191
Berg, Thomas van den, 170, 173–4, 179, 180–1, 183
Bergala, Alain, 78n
Bergson, Henri, 26, 27, 59, 85, 88, 95, 96, 99
black/dark background, 1, 4, 8, 63–5, 72–5, 95, 114–21, 125, 128, 130, 143, 145, 147, 149, 151, 188n
Blümlinger, Christa, 183
Bogue, Ronald, 43n, 50n
Bordwell, David, 189
Brenez, Nicole, 72, 140, 167n
Buchanan, Ian, 18n, 50n

Carroll, Noël, 14, 195n
cinecepts
  audiovisual media and, xiii, 4, 8, 11, 164, 189–90, 194
  as compounds of moving images/ sounds/voice/texts/graphics/ montage, 2, 5, 41, 164, 166, 190
  and/as concepts, x, xi–xii, xiii–xiv, 2, 8, 10, 11, 23, 190
  Deleuze's concept of concepts and, xiii–xiv, 3–4, 11–13, 23, 26–33, 37, 161, 163, 165
  explanation of the word choice, 15n
  formal renewal of montage, 9, 154
  the formal renewal of philosophy and, xii–xiii, 42
  as formal structure, 51n
  as potentials, xi, 3, 11–12, 26, 30–2, 76, 104–5
  preliminary conditions, 38–40
  problem plane/space, 8, 9
  quoting or referencing of, 190–1
  the written word and, xii, xiii, xiv, 5, 14–15, 36–7, 40, 41–2, 164
  see also embryonic cinecepts
cinema
  audiovisuality of, 38
  Deleuze's conception of, xi, 13–14, 23, 24
  film as philosophy, xi, xii, 1–2, 3, 5, 6, 16n, 19n, 19n, 22n
  film language, x–xi, 37, 40, 51n, 53
  see also film
clarity, 12–13, 154, 178–84
Comment ça va
  communication and biological reproduction, 138–9
  the new in, 137–9
  problem space, 113
  superimpositions in, 162

concept creation
  Deleuze's conception of, x, xi, xii, 11–12, 24–6
  as a function of problems, 95
  philosophy and, x, xi, xiv, 23, 24, 26
  on the plane of immanence, 8, 25, 32, 33, 35, 44n
concepts
  classification/categorization, reorganization, and recutting as parts of concept creation, 3, 38–9, 70–1, 162
  as co-creation, 32, 104–5
  the concepts-problems relation, xi, 8, 9, 13, 17, 24, 25, 26, 31, 32, 33, 35, 39, 41, 70, 71, 95, 104, 184, 185
  conceptual personae and, 25, 35–6, 44n
  conditions for, 25, 35
  Deleuze's concept of concepts, xiii–xiv, 3–4, 11–13, 23, 26–33, 37, 154, 161, 163, 165
  as determinations of problems, 154, 165–6
  as distinct from Ideas, xiii–xiv, 33, 34
  in Eisenstein's thought, 33, 34
  intensive components, zones of neighborhood, surveying point, 30, 31, 42, 105, 128–9, 137, 144–5, 148, 150, 153
  logic of multiplicity, 3, 26, 27, 30–1, 32, 33, 37, 57
  material form of, 35–6
  as meaning-creating, 31
  the new and, 104–5
  pedagogy of, 10, 31, 39, 164, 185
  as philosophical determinations, xi, xiv, 8, 13, 24, 29, 31–3, 37, 40, 71, 104, 184, 185
  the prevailing idea of cinema as non- or preconceptual, x, xii, xvn.7, 2, 5, 17n, 23, 24–5, 33, 34

concepts (*cont.*)
  representational concepts, 26, 33–4, 35
  scholarly conduct/rigor, 31–2
  term, 33–4
  words/language of, 36, 37
conceptual art, xiii, 2, 16n
Cox-Stanton, Tracy, 175, 176, 183, 184
Cramer, Michael, 123
Cuny, Alain, 193, 194

Daney, Serge, 10, 22n, 24, 39, 63, 80 n, 81n, 82n, 114, 115
Debord, Guy, 65, 66, 69
Deleuze, Gilles
  analysis of AND, 68–70
  concept of concepts, xiii–xiv, 3–4, 11–13, 23, 26–33, 37, 154, 161, 163, 165
  concept of difference, 26–30, 38, 57, 85–91, 97, 100, 103, 105, 163
  conception of art, xi, 16n, 23–5, 36, 57, 102, 104
  conception of the new, 3, 84–5
  definition of philosophy, x, xi, xiv, 5, 11, 23, 26–33, 35–6, 38–9, 104–5
  on the film/cinema-philosophy relation, x–xiv, 13–14, 23–5, 33, 37
  the formal renewal of philosophy, xi, xii–xiii, 2–3, 8
  on Godard, 6, 7–8, 34–5, 38, 42, 59, 68–72, 123, 129, 161
  the logic of Ideas/Problems/ multiplicities, 3, 27–33, 35, 37–9, 40, 57, 68–71, 85–8, 93, 100, 103–4
  three phases, 93–4
  on the voice articulating concepts, 192
Deleuze's cinema books
  cinema as preconceptual, xii, 2, 5, 17n, 24, 33, 34
  cinematic thinking, 24

crystal-images, 99, 100, 101–2
daily state of banality, 93, 98
Deleuze on Godard, 3, 6, 7–8, 34, 35, 38, 39–40, 42, 54, 59, 68–9, 70–1, 72, 99, 123, 129
the movement-image and the time-image as different regimes of thought, 96–8, 109n
the new (as rare) and, 3–4, 76, 84, 85, 88, 93–102
ontology of movement-images, 95–8
sensory-motor re/action, 88, 97
time-images, 24, 40, 70, 95, 96, 98–102
the virtual as a realm of potential, 100–2
Derrida, Jacques, 19n, 62, 81, 114, 184
Didi-Huberman, Georges, 40–1
difference
  actualization, 29, 30, 86, 88, 89, 100, 102–5
  Aristotelian categorization and, 38–9
  Deleuze's concept of difference, 26–30, 38, 57, 85–91, 97, 100, 103, 105, 163
  Deleuze's critique of Hegel, 27–9
  dialectics, 27–8, 29–30, 50n, 65–6, 68–9, 71, 163
  Different/ciation, 30, 86, 103
  frontiére term, 80n, 158n
  the logic of Ideas/Problems/ multiplicities, 3, 27–33, 35, 37–9, 40, 57, 68–71, 85–8, 93, 100, 103–4
  subterranean mechanisms, 28–30
  see also Deleuze, Gilles
Difference and Repetition
  Deleuze's concept of difference, 26–30, 38, 57, 85–91, 97, 100, 103, 105, 163
  on Hegel, 26–8

the logic of Ideas/Problems/
multiplicities, 3, 27–33, 35, 37–9,
40, 57, 68–71, 85–8, 93, 100, 103–4
the new as rare, 84, 89–92
production of the new, 3, 84, 87
relation to the cinema books, 3, 84–5,
95
syntheses of time, 87–90, 99–100,
145
the trivial vs the exceptional, 93
documentary, 12, 68, 180, 183, 193
Dosse, François, 52n., 197
Drabinski, John E., 5, 6, 7, 16n, 40,
80n, 113, 119, 155n
Dubois, Philippe, 78n, 115
Duras, Marguerite, 38
Dziga Vertov Group, 10, 66, 67

Eisenstein, Sergei, 2, 4, 33, 34, 69, 80n
Elsaesser, Thomas, 5
embryonic cinecepts
in *France tour détour*, 76, 113, 139–54
the problem plane/space and, 8, 9
in *Six fois deux*, 76, 113, 123–37
in the Sonimage works (Godard-
Miéville), 4–5, 8, 9, 10, 13, 113,
123–37, 141–54
term, 4, 5, 113, 154
Emmelhainz, Irmgard, 66, 67, 69, 156n,
157n

Farocki, Harun, 15, 43, 76n, 79n, 83n,
115, 118, 120, 186n
film
Deleuzian concept creation and, x–
xii, 2–3, 37
filmic structures, 37, 38
film-philosophy relation, xi–xii, 1–2,
8, 16n.3
film-video distinction, 14
the formal renewal of philosophy
and, xiii, 2–3

as a media form, xii, xiii–xiv, 13,
14–15, 37
see also cinema
Fisher, Mark, 104
France/tour/détour/deux/enfants
content structure, 140–1
conversations with the children,
139–40, 141
dark justice piercing through the
postcard embryonic cinecept,
149–51
embryonic cinecepts, 76, 113,
139–54
evolution and death embryonic
cinecept, 151–3
logic of organization, 76
montage in, 141, 143, 147
preconceptual cinematic thinking,
1–2
the pregnancy scene embryonic
cinecept, 141–6
production of the new, 1, 145–6
typewriting and birth of the letter A
embryonic cinecept, 146–9, *147*

Galibert-Laîne, Chloé, 175
Gibbs, John, 175, 176, 183
Godard, Jean-Luc
Aristotelian categorization, 38–9,
70–1
aural images, 42
cinecepts and the works of, 5–6
the conjunction *and*, 68–9, 72–3
in Deleuze's thought, 3, 6, 7–8, 34–5,
39–40, 42, 54, 68–9, 71–2, 99, 123,
129
Dziga Vertov Group, 10, 66, 67
as a film philosopher, 3, 5–8, 34–5,
43, 53, 54
idea of *rapprochement*, 9, 161–4
montage and a new logic of
organization, 53–83

Godard, Jean-Luc (*cont.*)
  the more poetical than philosophical, 9–10, 12–13, 21n, 40–1, 122–4, 151, 154, 163–6
  the musical in the works of, 9–10
  pedagogy of, 10, 39, 114, 164
  scholarship on, 6–7
  theorems at the edge of problems, 39, 70–2
  thinking with his hands, 15, 55
  the written word and, 40–1, 164, 177
  see also Sonimage works (Godard-Miéville)
Gorin, Jean-Pierre, 66, 79n, 79n, 79n
Grant, Catherine, 170, 171, 172, 173
Guattari, Félix, 7, 20n, 20n, 30, 31, 48n, 57, 76, 91, 94, 105, 116, 131, 147, 160n, 196–8

Hagener, Malte, 5
Hegel, Georg Wilhelm Friedrich, 3, 26, 27–9
Herzogenrath, Bernd, 16n.3
Histoire(s) du cinéma
  as containing no embryonic cinecepts, 9, 21n
  logic of organization, 166
  the poetic and, 9, 41, 164, 165–6, 167n, 177
  as resource for cineceptual form, 4, 9, 41, 154, 166
  the written word and, 40–1
Huillet, Danièle, 38, 101

Ici et ailleurs
  the conjunction *and*, 68, 69–70, 72–3
  Dziga Vertov Group work, 66, 67
  English translation, 76n
  form as deconstruction, 72, 74–5
  montage in, 68, 69, 74–5, *75*, 115
  in relation to the Sonimage films, 76
  self-critique and, 66–7

  towards a new logic of articulation/organization, 38–9, 67, 69–70, 72–6
Ideas
  as distinct from concepts, xiii–xiv, 33, 34
  the logic of Ideas/Problems/multiplicities, 3, 27–33, 35, 37–9, 40, 57, 68–71, 85–8, 93, 100, 102–4
images
  crystal-images, 99, 101–2
  image/text relation, 164–5, 177, 189
  image/voice, 165, 177–8
  Image/word relation, xiii–xiv, 14–15, 40, 41–2, 51n, 164–5, 175–8, 189–91
  the image as the problem, 72
  meaning-creation and, 51n
  movement-images, 24, 26, 33, 38, 95–8
  sound images, 38, 42
  time-image novelty, 96–8, 101–2
  time-images, 24, 33, 40, 70, 95, 98–102
  see also montage
Irigaray, Lucy, 76, 157n

Jacob, François, 151–3
journalism/journalistic, 12, 170, 179, 180, 183

Kant, Immanuel, 11, 35, 44n, 49n
Keathley, Christian, 170, 171, 177, 184
Keating, Patrick, 187n
Kiss, Miklós, 170, 173–4, 178, 179, 180–2, 183, 185
Kracauer, Siegfried, xvn
Kristeva, Julia, 76, 157n

Lahey Dronsfield, Jonathan, 40, 50n, 164, 177

language
   cinecepts and the written word, xii, xiii, xiv, 5, 14–15, 36–7, 40, 41–2, 164
   film language, x–xi, xvn, 37, 40, 51n, 53–4
   image/text relation, 164–5, 177, 189
   image/word differences in video essays, 4, 169, 176–8
Le gai savoir
   connections with *2 or 3 Things*, 63–4
   dark stage/black screens/black ground, 59–60, 62, 64–5
   female emancipation, 60–1
   found images, 65–6
   Godard's whispering voice, 58, 62, 65
   language-image-sound relationships, 60–1
   montage in, 58, 59–61
   reduction in, 58–60
   as a study, 58, 60, 61–5, 76
Leutrat, Jean-Louis, 95, 177
Livingstone, Paisley, 195n
logic of multiplicity
   cineceptual theory and, 69–70
   concepts and, 3, 26, 27, 30–1, 32, 33, 37, 57
   in *Ici et ailleur* and in *Six fois deux*, 68–9
   Ideas/Problems/multiplicities, 3, 27–33, 35, 37–9, 40, 57, 68–71, 85–8, 93, 100, 103–4
   the new and, 85–93
logic of organization
   classification, reorganization, and recutting as key parts of, 38–9, 70–1, 162
   Godard's Aristotelian categorization, 38–9, 70–1
   in *Histoire(s) du cinéma*, 166
   in *Ici et ailleurs*, 38–9, 67, 72–6

   in *Numéro deux*, 75–6, 115
   in *2 or 3 Things I Know About Her*, 53–8
Loshitzky, Yosefa, 7, 156n

MacCabe, Colin, 12, 77n, 79n, 113, 115, 118, 119, 123, 155n, 157n, 159n, 159n
Malraux, André, 164
Martin, Jean-Clet, 45n
Massumi, Brian, 91
Miéville, Anne-Marie
   analytic/pedagogic balance, 10
   key creative role in Sonimage, 10, 21n, 67, 76, 79n, 80n
   see also Sonimage works (Godard-Miéville)
Mittell, Jason, 169–70, 171, 173, 174–5, 176, 184
montage
   articulation of cinecepts and, 9, 154
   category formation and, 71
   different logics of montage and organization/articulation, 54–7, 65–6, 67–8, 69–72, 74–5
   in *France tour détour*, 141, 143, 147
   in *Ici et ailleurs*, 68, 69, 74–5, *75*, 115
   in *Le gai savoir*, 58, 59–61
   in *Numéro deux*, 115
   in political films, 67–9
   rapprochement and, 154, 161–2, 164–5
   in the Sonimage works (Godard-Miéville), xi, 4, 60, 61, 69
Morgan, Daniel, 19n, 20n, 74–5, 77n, 79n, 154n, 163, 167n, 168n
Morrey, Douglas, 19n, 54, 63, 67, 69, 76n, 77n, 78n, 78n, 79n, 118, 155, 155n, 161, 166, 168n
Mulhall, Stephen, xvn, 195n
Mulvey, Laura, 12, 115, 118, 119, 169

new, the
    blockage and, 3, 65, 76, 86, 99, 100, 102, 104–5, 112, 113, 118–21, 138, 147
    in *Comment ça va*, 137–9
    concepts and, 104–5
    conditions for, 85–6
    as continuous becoming in Smith's thought, 85, 86–7, 95
    Deleuze's cinema books and, 3–4, 84, 94–102
    everything as new in Williams's thought, 85, 87, 90–2, 95, 100, 103
    the logic of the Great Event and, 92–3
    the new as rare, 84, 85, 89–92, 95, 101
    new image of filmic thought, 98–9
    a new reading of Deleuze's conception of, 3–4, 84–105
    periodization of Deleuze's thought on, 94
    Shannon's information theory and, 138, 162
    in the Sonimage works, 113
    the three syntheses of time and, 87–90, 97, 99–101, 103
    the trivial vs the exceptional/remarkable, 84, 87, 88, 92–3
Nichols, Bill, 12, 180
Nietzsche, Friedrich, 15, 25, 76n, 90, 92, 113, 114–15, 141
Noys, Benjamin, 47n
Numéro deux
    argumentative clarity, 12
    blockage of the new, 112–13, 118, 119, 121
    dark/black meta-background, 114, 115, 116, 117–18, 120–2
    epilogue, 120–2
    film-video relation, 14
    Godard's preface, 115–16
    images and sounds, 115
    logic of organization, 75–6, 115
    the memory landscape, 119–21
    montage in, 115
    problem space, 113–22
    production and reproduction, 115–16, 117–19
    Sandrine's introduction, 116–18

Ong, Walter, J., 22n.28, 191

Palestinian Revolution, 66
Pantenburg, Volker, 6, 18n
Pasolini, Pier Paolo, xvn, 51n
philosophy
    art-philosophy distinctions, xi–xiii, 10, 25–6, 44n, 56–7, 164
    audiovisual media and, x, xi, xiii, 4, 8, 11, 164, 189–90, 191–2, 194
    conceptual personae, xiii, 2–3, 11, 25, 26, 30, 35, 36, 44n
    Deleuze's general definition of, x, xi, 3, 5, 16n, 23, 24, 26
    film as philosophy, xi, xii, 1–2, 3, 5
    the formal renewal/development of philosophy and, x, xi, xii–xiii, 2–3, 8, 34, 35, 41, 42, 192
    the plane of immanence, 25, 32, 33, 35, 44n
    rigor and clarity, 12–13
Pinker, Steven, 178–9, 180, 182
Pisters, Patricia, 108n
problem spaces
    in *Comment ça va*, 113
    embryonic cinecepts and, 8, 9
    in *Numéro deux*, 113–22
    in the Sonimage works, 3, 4, 8–9, 76, 84, 113, 114, 115, 122, 137–8, 139, 141, 145, 146, 154
purpose and aim as scholarly traits, 32, 172, 181, 183, 185

Queneau, Raymond, 162

Rajchman, John, 57, 93–4
Rancière, Jacques, 20n, 51n
rapprochement
   Godard's idea of, 9, 161–4
   as a method of montage, 154, 161–2, 164–5
representational concepts, 26, 33–4, 35, 98
research problem as a scholarly trait, 32, 172, 179–81, 183
Reverdy, Pierre, 162–4
Rodowick, D. N., 5, 7, 14, 16n, 37, 50n
Roffe, Jon, 110n
Rushton, Richard, 108n, 110n

Sauvagnargues, Anne, 45n, 46n, 107n
Shannon, Claude, 138, 162
Siegel, Amie, 118
Silverman, Kaja, 76n, 79n, 83n, 115, 118, 120
Six fois deux
   borders as revolutionary spaces, 123–9
   embryonic cinecepts, 76, 113, 123–37
   formal inventiveness, 122–3
   logic of multiplicity, 68–70
   logic of organization, 76
   the river between mother and baby, 129–37
Smith, Daniel W., 26, 85, 86–7, 95, 197
Somers, Hall, Henry, 45n
Sonimage works (Godard-Miéville)
   analytic/pedagogic balance, 10, 12
   the black/dark background, 1, 8, 63, 72–5, 114–21, 124, 128, 131, 142, 145, 146, 147, 149, 151, 188n
   Dziga Vertov Group work, compared to, 66, 67

embryonic cinecepts, 3, 4–5, 8, 9, 10, 14, 43, 75–6, 84, 113, 115, 122, 124–37, 138–9, 141–54
   as film philosophy, 6–8
   logic of montage/organization/articulation, xi, 4, 9, 53, 54, 60, 61, 67–72, 74–5
   the problem of the new in, 3, 4, 76, 84, 113, 118, 119–21, 123, 137–9, 141, 145–6, 153
   problem spaces, 4, 8–9, 76, 84, 112–14, 115–22, 137–8, 139, 141, 145, 147, 154
   scholarship on, 6
   themes of pregnancy and birth, 1, 112–15, 117–19, 141, 143–9, 153
   themes of reproduction/production, 60–1, 76, 112–13, 114–15, 116, 118, 119, 120–1, 124, 138–9, 145, 147–9, 151–3
   see also France/tour/détour/deux/enfants; *Ici et ailleurs*; *Le gai savoir*; *2 or 3 Things I Know About Her*
Sontag, Susan, 53
spectators/viewers, xii, xiv, xvn, 16n., 18n, 18n, 19n, 108n, 166, 167n, 175, 183
Sterritt, David, 6
Steyerl, Hito, 67–8, 72, 192–3
Straub, Jean-Marie, 38, 101

thesis as a scholarly trait, 174, 179–81, 183
Thom, René, 138, 157n
Thorgeirsdottir, Sigridur, 114–15
2 or 3 Things I Know About Her
   the coffee cup scene, 63–4, *64*
   connections with *Le gai savoir*, 63–4
   Godard's whispering voice, 54, 58, 63, 64–5
   logic of ideas and form, 53–8

video
    Deleuzian concept creation and, x–xii, xiii, 2–3, 12, 37
    film-video relation, 14
    the formal renewal of philosophy and, 2–3
    the formal renewal/development of philosophy and, x, xi, xiii, 41
    as a media form, xiii, 14–15, 37
    as tool in Godard's work, 10, 14, 78n
video essays
    artistic research, 4, 70, 169, 171, 172–3, 179–80, 183, 184
    cineceptual theory and, 4, 169, 175–6
    cineceptual videography, 184–5
    clarity, 4, 169, 174, 178–9, 180–2
    definition, 169–70
    essay films and, 183, 192–3
    the essayistic, 4, 154, 183–4
    explanatory modes, 170–1, 177, 183
    image/word differences, 4, 169, 176–8
    medium specificity, 4, 169, 175–6
    Method/Process vs. Finished Work, 174–5
    new knowledge and, 171–3
    peer reviews, 173
    poetical modes, 170–1, 177, 183
    scholarly forms of, 4, 169–70, 173–4, 178, 179–80, 181–2
voice
    Godard's whispering, 54, 58, 62–3, 65
    the human voice and audiovisual media, 192
    image/voice, 42, 74, 165, 177–8
    as means for nuance and rigor, 4, 193–4
    as means for seduction and deception, 4, 193–4

Wartenberg, Thomas E., 195n
White, Jerry, 6, 10, 14, 21n, 67, 69, 79n, 115, 119, 121, 123, 141
Widder, Nathan, 91, 106n
Williams, James, 85, 87, 90–2, 95, 100, 103
Witt, Michael, 6, 7–8, 9–10, 15, 16n, 20n, 20n, 67, 78n, 79n, 122–3, 129, 137–8, 139–40, 151, 162, 163–6, 194
Wollen, Peter, 34, 50n, 51n

YouTube
    cineceptual potential, 192
    philosophy channels, 4, 191–2

Žižek, Slavoj, 49n